GARDEN ROUTE
WALKS

Colin Paterson-Jones

GARDEN ROUTE
WALKS

STRUIK

AUTHOR'S ACKNOWLEDGEMENTS

I should like to thank: Dave Osborne, Ivan Donian, Mike Brett, Rory Allardice, Peter Cattell and Rhett Hiseman of the Cape Provincial Administration's Department of Nature and Environmental Conservation, and Dave Reynell, Theo Stehle, Armin Seydack and Dag Willems of the Department of Water Affairs and Forestry as well as Piet Peens of the National Parks Board for all the information and advice they gave so willingly (I am indebted to Dave Reynell particularly for information about the Knysna elephants); Piet Lourens for his useful reference maps; those, including my mother, sister and brother-in-law, who made free with their hospitality while I was working and walking in the southern Cape; Di Stafford who with customary facility typed the text from my abominable script; Angela Whittingham, project editor, for her gentle guidance; and Pam Eloff who drew the maps. My special thanks go to Mike Viviers and Jan Vlok, good friends, who made free with their hospitality, unrivalled expertise, time and energy. I am indebted to my wife, Dee, for her unfailing support, critical encouragement, professional advice and care during a period of great stress for her.

PUBLISHER'S NOTE

While every effort has been made to ensure that the text and maps are accurate and the routes described are safe, neither the author nor the publisher nor the cartographer will accept responsibility for any damages resulting from the use of this book.

FRONT COVER: Nature's Valley beach; inset, left: Hikers in the Groeneweide Forest; centre: The Tsitsikamma Mountains and Salt River kloof behind the De Vasselot reserve; right: The flowers of a Wild pomegranate tree at Nature's Valley.
BACK COVER: A party sets off on the first leg of the Otter Trail.
P. 1:The drawn-out trill of the Dabchick is an integral part of the Lakes environment.
PP. 2/3: The Tsitsikamma Mountains stretch eastwards from the plateau in the De Vasselot reserve.
PP. 10/11: Swartvlei leads into Sedgefield lagoon; the bluff ends in Gericke Point.

Struik Publishers
(a member of The Struik Group)
80 McKenzie Street
Cape Town
8001
Reg. No.: 63/00203/07

First published: 1992

Text © Colin Paterson-Jones
Photographs © Colin Paterson-Jones with the exception of the following:
p. 27: Zelda Wahl; p. 89, bottom left: courtesy Percy Fitzpatrick Institute of Ornithology (Bambine Rauch); centre: Duncan Butchart; bottom right: Peter Barichievy; p. 113: W R Branch; pp. 117, 125 and 127: courtesy Knysna Museum; p. 129: D Reynell; p. 148 (bottom): Zelda Wahl; p. 173 and 174: Duncan Butchart.
Maps © Pam Eloff

Project editor: Angela Whittingham
Copy editor: Jan Schaafsma
Cover design: Tamsyn Ivey
Design and DTP make-up: Tamsyn Ivey

Reproduction by: Unifoto (Pty) Ltd, Cape Town
Printed and bound by: Kyodo Printing Co (Singapore) Pte Ltd
ISBN 1-86825-227-2

CONTENTS

GARDEN ROUTE WEST

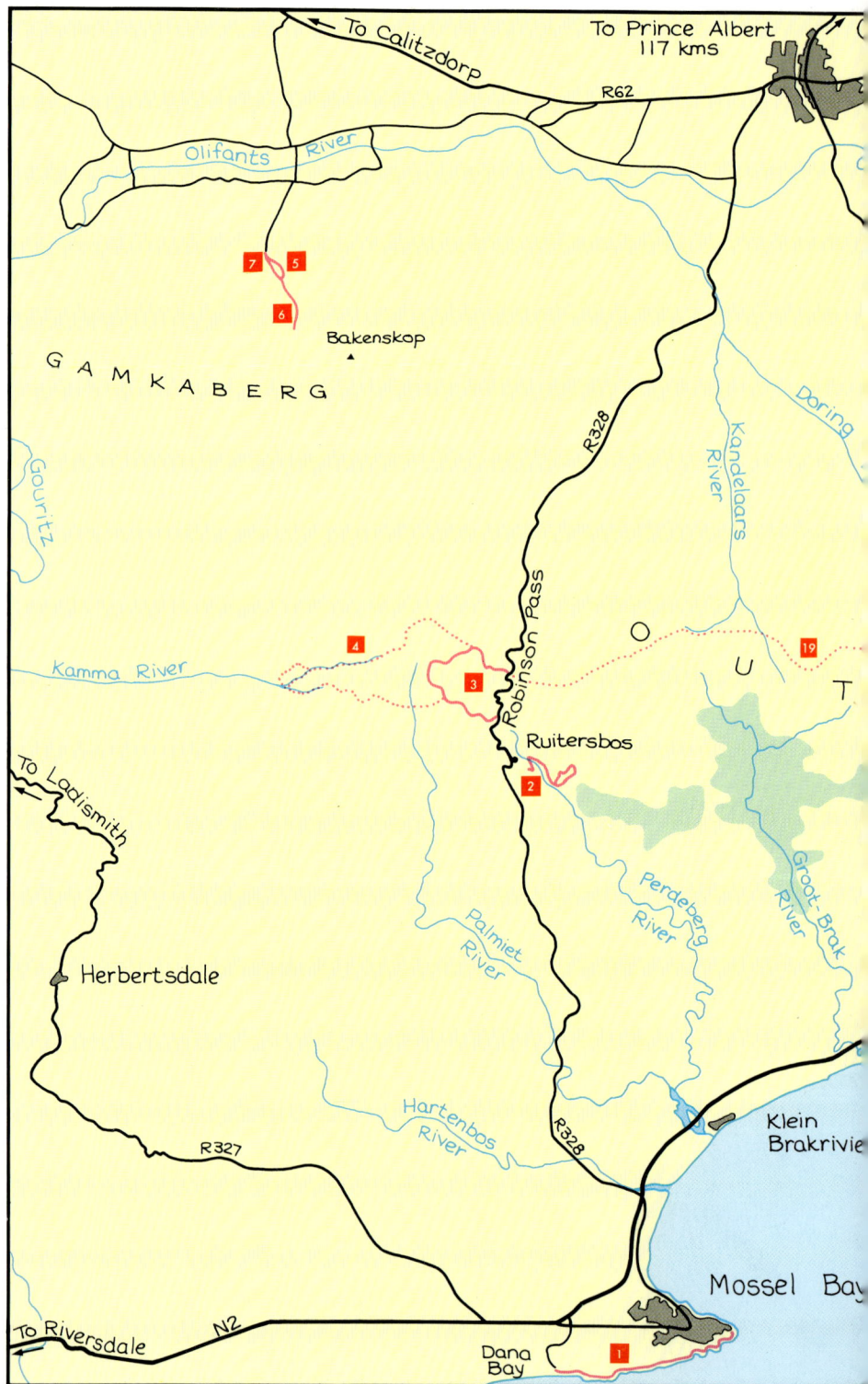

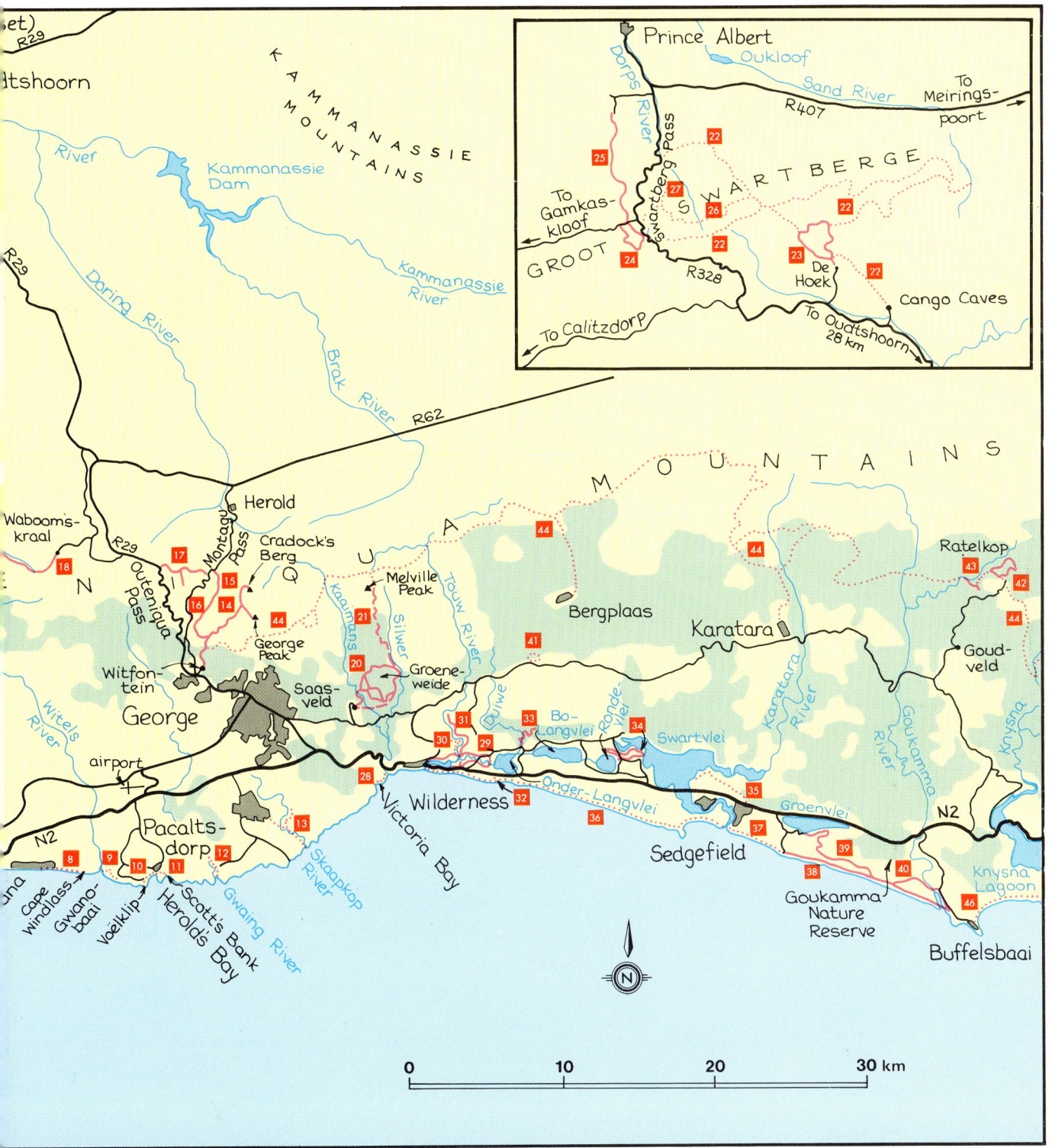

Prince Albert

Oukloof

Sand River

To Meirings-poort

R407

Dorps River

Swartberg Pass

SWARTBERGE

25

27

26

22

22

22

22

23

De Hoek

24

GROOT

R328

To Gamkas-kloof

To Calitzdorp

To Oudtshoorn 28 km

Cango Caves

(et)

R29

dtshoorn

KAMMANASSIE MOUNTAINS

River

Kammanassie Dam

Kammanassie River

Brak River

R62

Doring River

R29

Waboom's-kraal

Herold

18

17

Montagu Pass

Cradock's Berg

15

16

14

George Peak

44

Outeniqua Pass

N

Q

Melville Peak

Kaaimans

Silwer River

Touw River

44

44

Bergplaas

Karatara

Ratelkop

43

42

44

Goud-veld

21

Witfontein

George

20

Saasveld

Groene-weide

41

Bo-Langvlei

Ronde Vlei

34

Swartvlei

Karatara River

Goukamma River

Knysna

airport

31

33

Duiwe

30

29

Wilderness

32

Victoria Bay

Onder-Langvlei

35

Groenvlei

N2

28

36

Sedgefield

37

13

Pacalts-dorp

Witels River

N2

8

9

10

11

12

Skaapkop River

39

38

40

Knysna Lagoon

Goukamma Nature Reserve

46

Cape windlass

Gwano-baai

Voëlklip

Scott's Bank

Herold's Bay

Gwaing River

Buffelsbaai

N

0   10   20   30 km

GARDEN ROUTE EAST

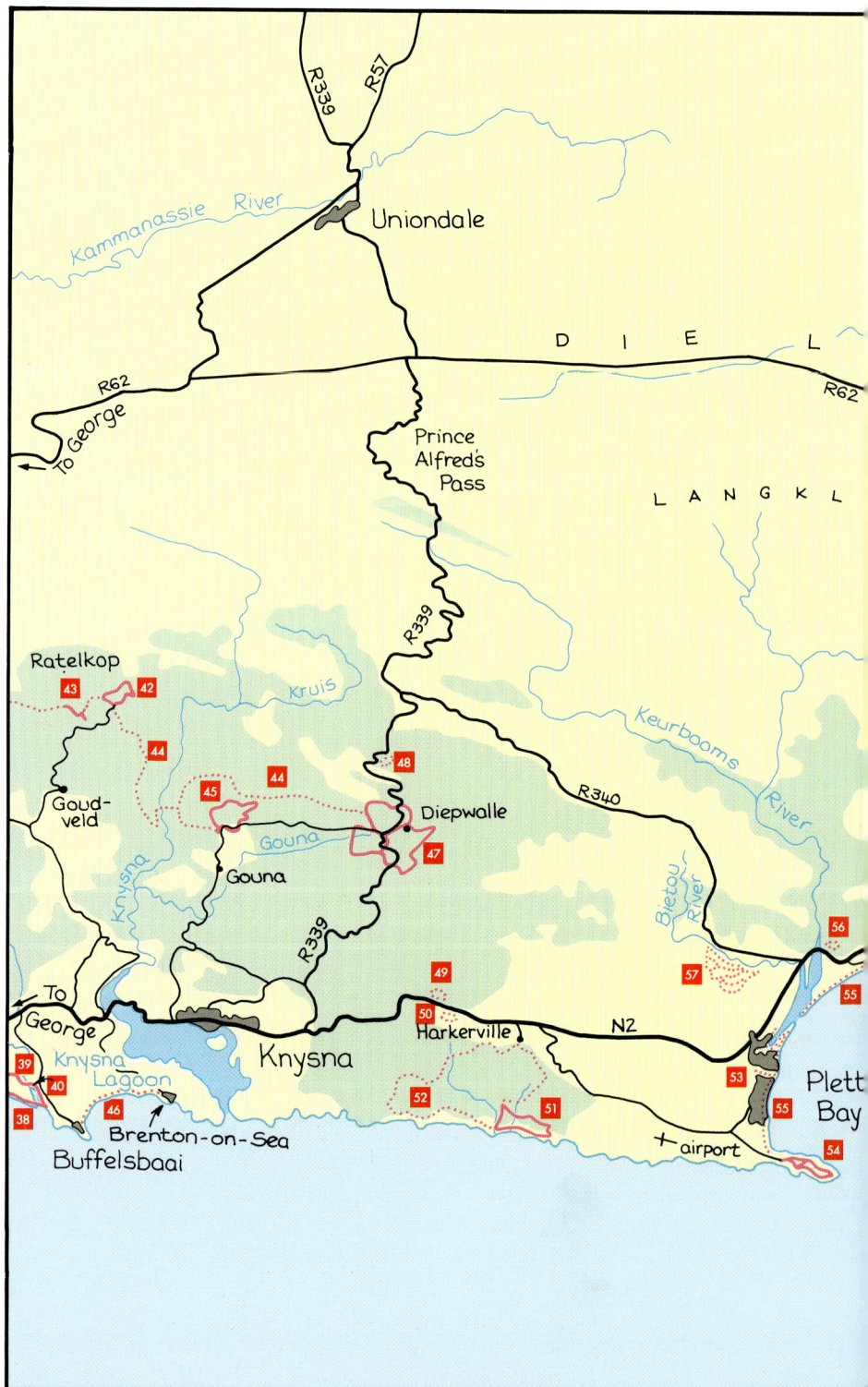

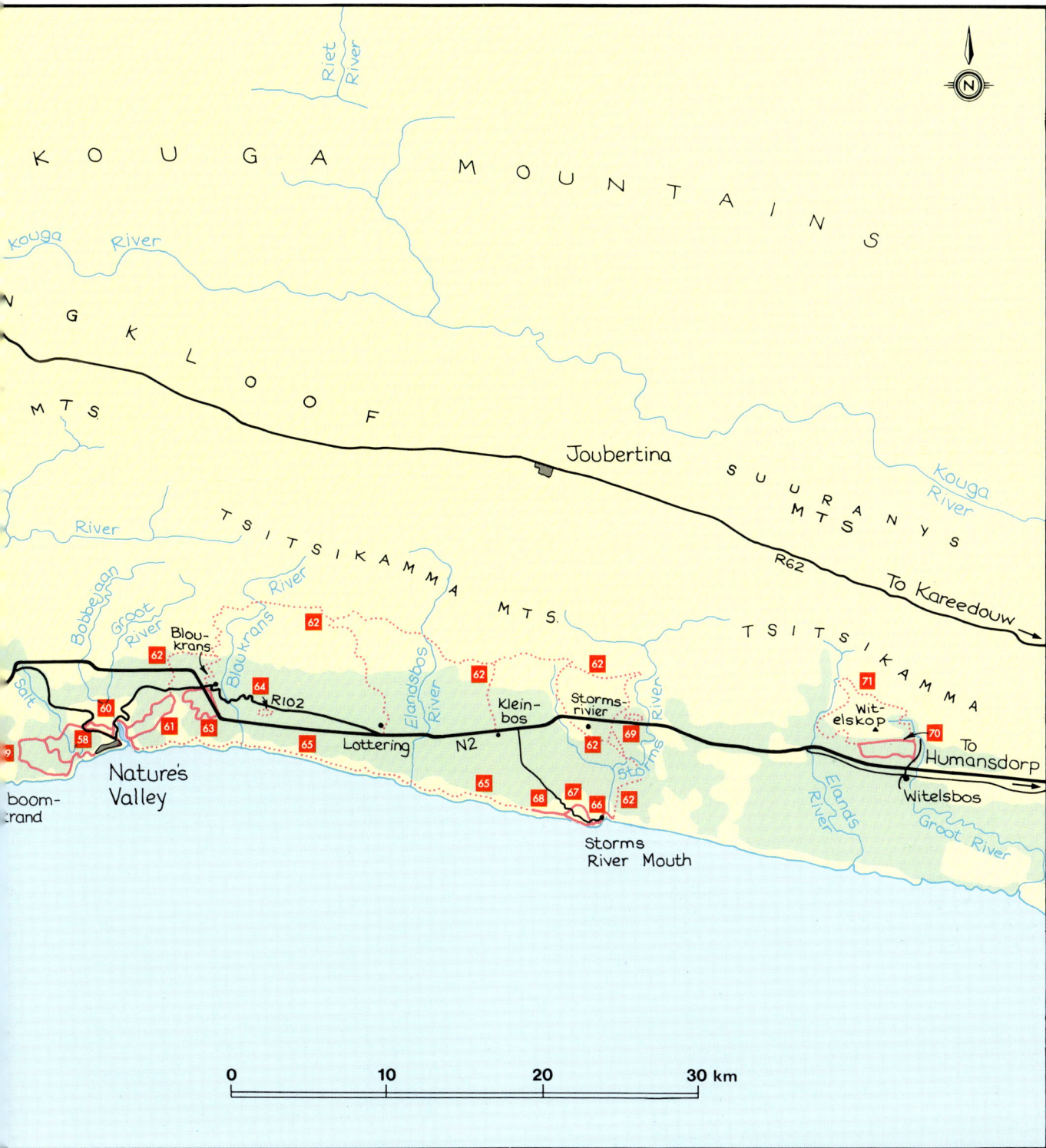

KOUGA MOUNTAINS

Riet River

Kouga River

NGKLOOF MTS.

River

Joubertina

SUURANYS MTS

R62

To Kareedouw

River

TSITSIKAMMA MTS.

TSITSIKAMMA

Bobbejaan

Groot River

Bloukrans

62

Bloukrans River

Elandsbos River

62

62

Kleinbos

Storms-rivier

62

71

Witelskop

Salt

60

64

R102

58

61

63

65

Lottering

N2

69

62

70

To Humansdorp

Witelsbos

9

65

68

67

66

62

Storms River

Elands River

Groot River

Nature's Valley

boom-crand

Storms River Mouth

0   10   20   30 km

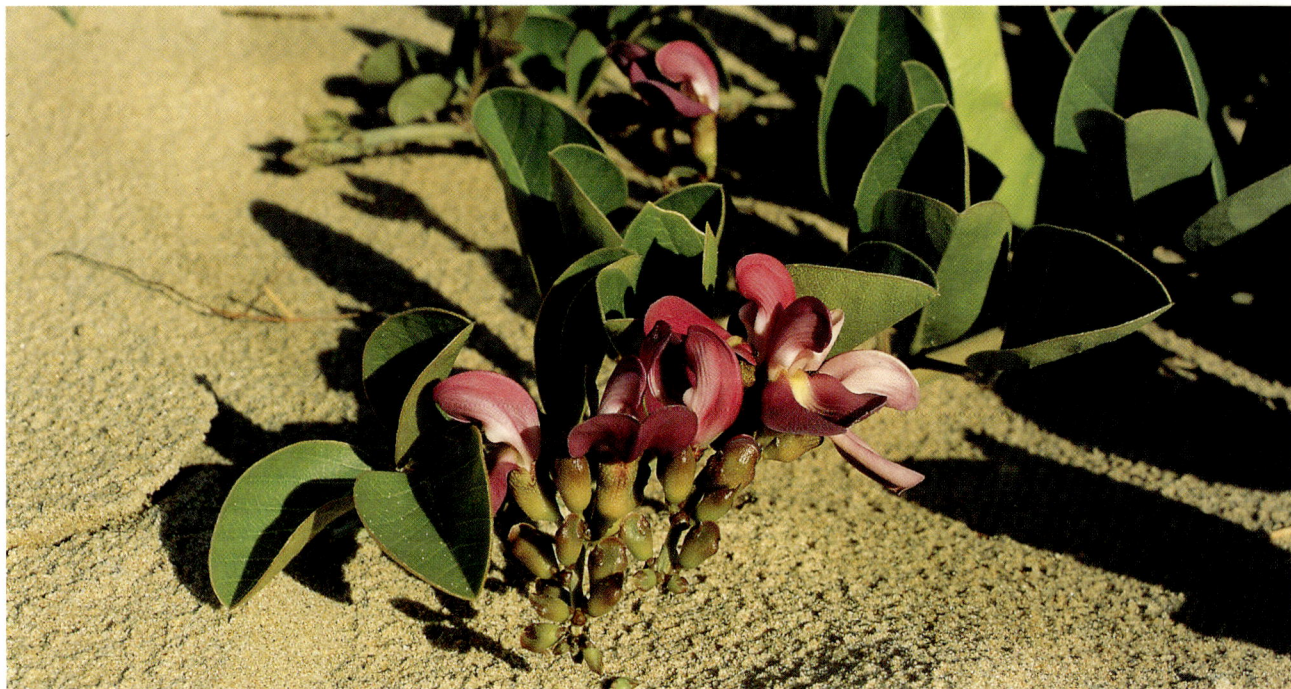

ABOUT THIS BOOK

The term `Garden Route' has been interpreted broadly, in this book, to include not only the coastal belt from Mossel Bay in the west to Witelsbos beyond the Storms River in the east, but also the inland tourist area of the Little Karoo and the Swartberg mountain range.

The Garden Route has been divided into 11 geographical subregions, each of which is the subject of a separate chapter. In the introduction to each chapter, day-walks accessible to the public in that subregion are briefly discussed. All the routes are traced in consecutive order, from west to east, on one of the two regional maps at the front of the book. The focus of each chapter, however, is a selection of the *best* walks within that subregion, for which detailed descriptions are given. Each of these is accompanied by a detailed map and a brief summary giving the length of the route, the controlling authority, permits required, other maps and information available, how to reach the start and end points, where to begin walking, the best times to undertake the walk, and any precautions that need to be taken. In addition, an estimate is given of the time required (excluding stops) to complete the route; these estimates are consistent

within the book and apply to a reasonably fit person. An indication is given of the exertion each route demands; the routes described as requiring very high exertion should not be attempted by anyone who does not walk (or take some other form of exercise) regularly.

All the walks described are day-walks on recognized routes open to the general public; some of these are new. Walks on private property, such as in privately owned reserves or the grounds of a hotel, are not included. Likewise, very short walks, such as those laid out at some of the forest picnic sites, have not been described in detail - not because they are not beautiful, but because they can be done on the spur of the moment. For those whose appetites for longer routes are whetted by the day-walks described, there is a summary on page 170 of established and new two-day and longer hiking trails in the Garden Route region.

ABOVE: *A branch of* Canavalia rosea *on the seasand at Nature's Valley; this species grows next to the high water mark.*
RIGHT: *The soft, friable nature of dune sandstone is evident in these eroded rocks.*

INTRODUCTION

The scenic beauty of the Garden Route attracts hundreds of thousands of visitors every year. Most of these are South African holiday-makers but increasing numbers of tourists from elsewhere make this region their destination after visits to the more traditional venues of the Kruger National Park and Cape Town. They come not only to relax on the easily accessible beaches but to enjoy the splendour of the Cango Caves near Oudtshoorn and the novelty of the ostrich farms of the Little Karoo. Although the holiday season on the Garden Route is all year round, thanks to its mild climate, summer is most popular with South African families, for practical reasons.

The region is extraordinarily diverse; it is the combination of mountains, valleys, coast, lakes and rivers which makes it uniquely lovely. Associated with each of these different features is a range of habitats which contain distinct types of plant and animal life. The contrast, for example, between the dense indigenous forests that cover much of the wet, lower southern slopes of the Outeniqua and Tsitsikamma mountains and the sparse succulent vegetation of the arid Little Karoo, not far away, could hardly be more extreme. The birds which live in the fynbos on the Swartberg are quite distinct from the water fowl which inhabit the Knysna lakes.

Man has changed the face of this region appreciably, particularly during the last two centuries, but not so much that its essential loveliness has been effaced. There are still large areas in a more-or-less natural state - the majority of them actively conserved - where the visitor can gain a fair impression of what the region looked like before it was settled. Walking is the best (and in some cases the only) way of experiencing and enjoying the beauty and variety of these areas. They are the main focus of this book.

TOPOGRAPHY AND GEOLOGY

The southern Cape is dominated by two long, parallel ranges of high mountains - the Outeniquas (which merge with the Tsitsikamma Mountains in the east) and the Swartberg range 50 km to the north. The Outeniquas are simply an extension of the Langeberg, the western end of which stretches to Montagu in the south-western Cape. Between the Outeniqua/Tsitsikamma range and the Indian Ocean lies a more-or-less flat ledge of land of varying width - the coastal plateau. The surface of the plateau is deeply cut by the steep-sided courses of many rivers which rise in the mountains behind. In some places the plateau drops precipitously into the sea, while in others it is separated from the ocean by stable, vegetated sand dunes. In the Lakes area near Wilderness, the dunes contain a series of estuaries and fresh-water lakes.

Between the western Outeniqua Mountains and the Swartberg lies the Little Karoo, a dry, wide valley. The eastern end of the Little Karoo is bounded by the Kamanassie Mountains, part of a broken line of mountains which lies between the Swartberg and Outeniqua ranges, and which includes Gamkaberg. These topographical features of the

Mountain Group, which characteristically appears as hard quartzites and sandstones; second, the Bokkeveld Group (of shales alternating with sandstones); and, third, the Witteberg Group (typically quartzites). These three rock types form the so-called Cape Supergroup.

It is generally accepted that, at this time, Africa was part of a super-continent named Gondwana, which also comprised what is now Madagascar, India, South America, Australia and Antarctica. The southern Cape was part of a huge, rather featureless plain. About 290 million years ago pressures which had built up in the land mass around the south-western and southern Cape resulted in buckling, shearing and uplifting along fold lines to form the Cape fold mountains. In the west, the fold lines ran roughly north-south, but in the south they ran due east-west, producing the two parallel ranges of mountains there (Swartberg/Witteberg and Langeberg/Outeniqua/Tsitsikamma), as well as a third, broken ridge between them which includes Gamkaberg. Although these mountains have been modified by further faulting and erosion since they were formed, they determined the present landscape. Rocks of the Cape Supergroup and soils derived from them are predominant. The more erosion-resistant Table Mountain and Witteberg sandstones and quartzites form the body and ridges of the mountains, with softer Bokkeveld shales in the intervening valleys and on large parts of the present southern coastal plateau.

About 140 million years ago Gondwana started to break up. South America began to break away from what is now the African continent some 120 million years ago, the Atlantic Ocean became wider, and Africa was left with more or less its present outline. In the southern Cape the rift appeared well south of the current coastline at the edge of the Agulhas Bank; this is now submerged, leaving a narrow ledge between the Outeniqua Mountains and the sea.

Although the formation of the Cape fold mountains and the break-up of Gondwana gave the southern Cape its basic shape, the landscape was subsequently modified somewhat by inundation, faulting and erosion, processes which resulted from the disintegration of Gondwana and which deposited new rock formations in places, for example the Enon conglomerates in the Little Karoo and recent marine sediments on the coastal plateau. Erosion also carved the river courses which are such a characteristic feature of the coastal plateau. The dunes along the Garden Route's coast are of more recent formation, associated with fluctuations in the sea-level which accompanied expansion and retraction of the polar ice-caps.

southern Cape are a result of geological processes which took place over an enormous period of time. All of the rocks of the southern Cape except granite are sedimentary. They were formed when land masses subsided and were inundated, allowing the gradual deposition of sands and silts eroded from rocks elsewhere in the water body, and/or the remains of marine organisms. In time, this material accumulated and compacted.

The most ancient rocks known in this area are up to 950 million years old; some of these are exposed on the northern edge of the Little Karoo and on the coastal plateau. Between 600 and 500 million years ago these ancient rocks were 'intruded' in places by magma which formed granite; an example of one of these granite bodies is beneath George. Between 440 and 350 million years ago, during periods of subsidence and inundation by the sea, three distinct types of rock were laid down by sedimentation: first, the Table

CLIMATE

The climate of the Garden Route is as varied as its geographical features, and owes much of its variation to these. Rain falls throughout the year, but along the coast the winter months are slightly drier. From the coastline, which receives an annual average of some 700 mm, the rainfall increases over the coastal plateau (1 000 mm) to as much as 1 400 mm on the high southern slopes and peaks of the Outeniqua and Tsitsikamma mountains. On the northern slopes of these mountains the rainfall drops off rapidly towards the Little Karoo, which is in the rain shadow of the Outeniquas and is arid. The top of Gamkaberg in the middle of the Little Karoo receives 500 mm of rain annually, while the Nature Conservation station at the bottom of the mountain receives only half this. Moving further inland, at the Ou Tol on top of the Swartberg Pass the annual average rainfall is just over 600 mm; the peaks of the Swartberg range receive slightly more. The southern slopes are wetter than the northern but on both sides of the Swartberg the rainfall drops off rapidly with decreasing altitude.

On the coastal side of the Outeniqua and Tsitsikamma mountains temperatures are moderate; the minimum and maximum average daily temperatures for the coldest (July) and hottest (January) months in George are 8,1 and 18,6°C, and 14,7 and 24,5°C respectively. Inland the variation is much greater; the figures for the Ou Tol near the top of the Swartberg Pass are -7,2 and 16,3°C, and 3,6 and 29,2°C respectively. (Walkers take note!) Strong winds are not uncommon in the area. The predominant winds are from the south-west (associated with the approach of cold fronts), backing to southerly or south-easterly as the fronts pass to the east. In winter hot, dry berg winds occasionally blow. At such times, the risk of fire on the mountains is highest. Snow falls two or three times a year on the coastal mountains but seldom lasts more than a few days. Snow is more frequent on the peaks of the Swartberg, where it can lie for up to two weeks. One of the constants of the weather along the Garden Route is its rapid changeability. Walkers must be alert to any weather changes and, particularly on the mountains, to cloud which can descend in minutes.

LEFT: *Graphic evidence of geological tilting and folding on the north face of the Swartberg Pass.*
RIGHT: *The peaks of the Outeniquas are often under cloud; the fynbos on their southern slopes is adapted to high moisture levels.*

HISTORY

When the early Portuguese explorers and traders sailed past this coast after Bartolomeu Dias's historic voyage in 1488, they remarked on the number of fires they saw on the land. Many fires were started by the Khoi-khoi, who burnt the veld to improve the grazing for their herds and to stimulate the growth of edible bulbous plants. Numerous place names in the southern Cape recall the tribes which used to occupy the area, such as the Outeniqua and the Attaqua. Bushman paintings on Gamkaberg and in the Swartberg and the Tsitsikamma Mountains show that they, too, once lived in this region. Excavations in coastal caves such as the one at Storms River Mouth, Guanogat on Robberg and the St Blaize Cave at Mossel Bay indicate that Strandlopers also lived along this coast. Because of their small numbers and

migratory lifestyle, none of these peoples had any permanent effect on the areas they occupied.

Soon after the establishment of the Dutch East India Company's (DEIC) settlement at the Cape in 1652, the Dutch settlers began to reconnoitre the land to the east. Their motives were hunting, exploration, and barter with the Khoi-khoi tribes for sheep and cattle to sustain the settlement. In 1689 Ensign Isaac Schrijver led an expedition across the Outeniqua Mountains into the Little Karoo via Attaquaskloof west of the present Robinson Pass; this was the first recorded crossing of the Outeniquas by Europeans. Attaquaskloof was a pass well known to the local Khoi-khoi. Gradually, areas further east were farmed: the Mossel Bay area was settled in the 1730s, the George area in the 1740s, and the Little Karoo in the 1750s.

Along the coast, the Kaaimans River gorge and the dense forests were a major hurdle to journeys further east, but some pioneers did reach and use pockets of land near Knysna and Plettenberg Bay. The famous botanist Carl Thunberg, who travelled to the area in 1771, reported that there were few European farmers between the Kaaimans River and Knysna, and no wagon tracks or roads. Thunberg was guided through the forests by the local Khoi-khoi and reported having to crawl through the undergrowth in places. In 1788, ships started to use Plettenberg Bay as a harbour, a development which gave farmers in the surrounding area access to markets for their produce. Towards the end of the 18th century, a drift across the Kaaimans River came into use; although it was notoriously difficult to cross, it did make travel to the east by ox-wagon possible.

From the environmental viewpoint, the cardinal difference between the nomadic Khoi-khoi and the farming settlers was that the latter radically altered the land they occupied, thus changing the face of the countryside. European settlement also had a profound effect on the forests. At first, the fine timber available was used only for the needs of settlers in the area, but within two decades it became exploited to satisfy the rapidly increasing demand for timber at the Cape. It was Thunberg who reported to the DEIC seemingly inexhaustible potential timber supply in the southern Cape forests; in 1776 a woodcutters' post was

Beside the historic milkwood tree in the Bartolomeu Dias Museum complex is a whimsical reminder of the tree's use five centuries ago.

THE BARTOLOMEU DIAS MUSEUM

The replica of Dias's caravel is the central exhibit at Mossel Bay's Maritime Museum.

The Bartolomeu Dias Museum complex occupies a site of cardinal importance in South Africa's history, as it overlooks the bay where Dias made his historic landing in 1488. The spring from which this early explorer and the sailors who came after him took fresh water still flows just to the west of the Post Office tree - a Milkwood (*Sideroxylon inerme*) which is, reputedly, the same tree on which these first visitors took to leaving messages for other ships. A replica of the *padrão* or stone cross planted by Dias to signal Portugal's claim to this area has been raised on the site of the original, nearby.

The Maritime Museum occupies a large stone building, erected in 1901, which once housed a mill and now provides galleries for exhibits depicting the early exploration of South Africa's coast and the maritime trade routes between Europe and the East which developed as a result. Pride of place is given to the replica of Dias's caravel which sailed from Lisbon on 8 November 1987 in a re-enactment of his historical journey five centuries before and arrived in Mossel Bay on 3 February 1988.

The Shell Museum is accommodated in another attractive stone building, erected in 1902 as an annexe to the mill. The Local History Museum's quarters are the town's first municipal building, built in 1858 and now a National Monument, and a larger building, erected in 1879 as municipal offices. The Information Centre is a replica of the granary which once stood on the same site. It contains a photographic exhibition of the southern Cape's mountain passes; the history of these passes is one of the museum's research projects.

established where the town of George now stands. In 1788, the first cargo of timber was shipped to Cape Town from Plettenberg Bay. The rape of the forests which would continue for over a century had begun.

Settlement of the southern Cape increased steadily and five years after the second British occupation of the Cape in 1806, the colonial government proclaimed the town of George, thereby satisfying a need that the Dutch East India Company had already acknowledged.

In 1825 the governor, Lord Charles Somerset, founded the village of Knysna. A port developed here which thrived until the railway line reached the town just over a century later. (There is more about Knysna's fascinating history on page 111.) In 1867 work started on the Passes Road, designed by Thomas Bain, which linked George and Knysna and opened the intervening area to further settlement.

The Montagu Pass, which provided the first easy route over the Outeniqua Mountains to the Little Karoo, was opened in 1847. Also in this year, the first erven were sold in the new town of Oudtshoorn; eight years later it became a magistracy, the commercial centre of an already well-settled farming community in the Little Karoo.

In all this time, the coastline between George and Plettenberg Bay had remained largely unaffected. With the construction of the new road between these towns (part of the network of National Roads) after World War II, this changed. Now, at last, access to much of the coast was without impediment and increasing numbers of people settled in the coastal towns. More importantly, this new N2 highway opened up the area to holiday-makers and tourists.

*Plants of the Sea pumpkin (*Arctotheca populifolia*) on the beach at Nature's Valley; this species is adapted to growing in unstable sand in highly saline conditions.*

THE COAST

The Garden Route has an enormously varied coastline. In places the coastal plateau drops abruptly to the sea to provide the spectacular scenery along the cliffs west of Mossel Bay, between Kranshoek (west of Knysna) and Plettenberg Bay, and along most of the seaboard of the Tsitsikamma Coastal National Park. Elsewhere dunes have formed between the land and the ocean; below them and fringing the bays are many long stretches of sandy beaches, the delight of holiday-makers.

Two large bays, well known to the early Portuguese explorers, give the coast its distinctive shape. They are Mossel Bay in the west and Plettenberg Bay in the east. The southern extremities of both these bays - Mossel Bay's cliffs and the uniquely beautiful Robberg peninsula - are rocky.

The formations clearly visible in both places include marine sediments which were laid down relatively recently over older rocks such as Table Mountain sandstone. One of these layers on Robberg contains fossil remains, examples of which are on display at the Information Centre there.

South of George, between Knysna and Plettenberg Bay and east of Keurboomstrand, the edge of the coastal plateau is not separated from the shore by dunes. The vegetation on the steep sea-facing slopes is the same as that on the plateau behind - forest or fynbos, depending on their soils and underlying rock. Many rivers flow into the sea along these parts of the coast. The meeting places between fresh water and the ocean are some of the loveliest spots on the Garden Route. Some of the rivers, such as the Storms and the Bloukrans, flow straight into the sea through rocky defiles, while others, like the Groot River, have formed estuaries. The reason for the difference lies in the nature of the local rock - soft rock such as shale erodes easily and widely.

On the stretch of coast between Wilderness and Knysna the edge of the coastal plateau is separated from the sea by a series of dunes covered in vegetation. The highest vegetated dune in South Africa (201 m) overlooks Groenvlei. These sand-dunes are the most recent geological formations in the Garden Route; before they were formed, this region was a large bay. During the last two to three million years the polar ice-caps have expanded and contracted. In the glacial periods large quantities of the oceans were locked into the polar ice-caps and sea levels dropped; as the earth warmed up in the periods in between, sea levels rose again. The world is presently in a relatively warm period, a so-called interglacial. During the periods of high sea level, sand ridges were formed underwater next to the coast by the action of waves and currents; trapped in the sand were shells of marine organisms. When the sea level dropped, sand was blown from newer ridges onto older ridges which were closer to the land and which had become partially stabilized by vegetation and by the gradual cementing together of the sand by the action of fresh water on the remains of shells. In this way a series of stable dunes built up parallel to the edge of the coastal plateau. The oldest of these stands north of Ruigtevlei and Swartvlei; the youngest exposed dunes lie directly behind the beaches. The scouring effect of wind and water on the dunes is dramatically and beautifully shown on the sandstone cliffs along the beach in the

Goukamma Nature Reserve and, in particular, between Plat-bank and the mouth of Swartvlei to the west. Beneath the sea, the ridges extend south, forming a series of reefs renowned for their sea life.

The dunes are covered with dune fynbos and (one of their characteristic features) the Milkwood (*Sideroxylon inerme*) forests which occupy the wetter sites. Both types of vegetation are adapted to the calcareous sands which make up the dunes. Dune fynbos is of recent origin and does not contain the wealth of different species which is a hallmark of older fynbos communities, and contains few species of the protea, erica and restio families which generally characterize fynbos. Instead, dune fynbos is dominated by shrubs such as Blombos (*Metalasia muricata*), Bietou (*Chrysanthemoides monilifera*), Waxberry (*Myrica cordifolia*), the aromatic *Agathosma apiculata*, and *Passerina vulgaris* - a small shrub with ericoid leaves and insignificant flowers. *Leucadendron salignum*, the most widespread of the leucadendrons, is the predominant proteaceous species here. Below the shrubs grows a variety of herbs such as *Geranium incanum*, bulbous plants such as *Freesia alba*, *Gladiolus rogersii* (the Riversdale Bluebell) and *Gladiolus cunonius*, and terrestrial orchids such as the green-and-white flowered *Bonatea speciosa*, the yellow *Eulophia speciosa* and the rare *Satyrium princeps*, with its carmine-flowered spikes.

The Milkwood forests are really a type of scrub forest in which Milkwoods predominate and, in places, form almost single-species stands of large trees. Fringing these forests is shrubby growth which contains forest precursor species such as Kershout (*Pterocelastrus tricuspidatus*) and Bastard saffronwood (*Cassine peragua*). Both species have leaves whose waxy, leathery surfaces give them protection against salt spray.

The plants which grow on the edge of the shore are highly specialized, adapted to cope with the extreme saline conditions there. Plants such as the Sea pumpkin (*Arctotheca populifolia*), *Canavalia rosea* (a sprawling plant with purple flowers) and certain grasses which grow in the sand next to the high-water mark play a vital role in the development of sand dunes where conditions for their formation are favourable. These plants act as sand traps and are able to grow out of and over the sand as it builds up around them. One of the best places to see vegetated dunes in the making is at the mouth of the Groot River near Nature's Valley,

Low cloud and mist frequently soften the colours of the lakeside vegetation at Rondevlei.

where several incipient dunes no more than 2-3 m high are already being colonized by dune fynbos species such as *Passerina vulgaris* and Blombos.

The beach itself carries a very specialized fauna. The intertidal zone (between the high- and low-water marks) is a difficult environment for its inhabitants: at low tide, the sand is dried out by the sun; at high tide, it is submerged then drained by waves. The organisms which live in the intertidal zone, such as sand mussels (*Donax* spp.) and Plough snails (*Bullia* spp.) are uniquely adapted, capable of burying themselves rapidly in the sand as the waves retreat. The snails are scavengers, often seen in large numbers making a feast of a stranded jellyfish; sand mussels are filter-feeders which extract plankton from the water.

Kelp Gulls scavenge the shore, which is also the habitat of

the African Black Oystercatcher, Whitefronted Plover and Cape and Whitebreasted cormorants. Although you will see ample evidence of its occupation of the dunes behind the beach, you are unlikely to see the Cape dune molerat, the largest known completely subterranean rodent in the world. (Adult males reach 33 cm in length.) However, you may be fortunate enough to glimpse a Cape clawless otter; this surprisingly large animal forages for its prey - mainly crabs and octopuses - in rock pools along the coast or in river mouths.

Lakes and lagoons

The string of lakes or `vleis' which lie next to the coast east of Wilderness make this one of the loveliest parts of the Garden Route. The backdrop of the Outeniqua Mountains enhances the beauty of the setting and it is no coincidence

that this area has become extremely popular with holiday-makers and is increasingly favoured as a retirement centre.

The Lakes owe their present form firstly to the formation of the dunes which contain them and secondly to the sea level which, in terms of the fluctuations that have accompanied the expansion and retreat of the polar ice-caps, is currently neither very high nor very low. The largest is Swartvlei, which is periodically open to the sea and represents the flooding of what was a river valley in drier times. Groenvlei was once connected to Swartvlei, but has been isolated by the movement of sand on the dunes and is now essentially a freshwater lake fed by seepage from the surrounding dunes. Rondevlei lies close to, but is not connected with Swartvlei; instead, it joins up with Langvlei. Rondevlei is the result of the flooding of a depression caused by wind

Redknobbed Coots and their reflections glide across Groenvlei.

erosion during a dry period, while Langvlei was a natural low-lying area between dunes before it, too, became inundated by the present sea level. Neither Rondevlei nor Langvlei is fed directly by rivers, although Langvlei is connected, via Eilandvlei ('Island Lake'), which is fed by the Duiwe River, to the Serpentine. Downstream, the Serpentine is joined by the Touw River. The formation of successive ridges of dunes has caused a sideways diversion of the Touw and Duiwe rivers' original outlets to the sea, so that their flow ends up in the Wilderness Lagoon.

Wetlands are recognized as amongst the most threatened habitats all over the world. In September 1984, the International Year of the Wetlands was declared to focus attention on their conservation. The Lakes of the Garden Route are a unique collection of wetlands whose preservation is threatened by afforestation, agriculture and settlement on the surrounding land. Uncontrolled recreational activity on the surfaces of these water-bodies can also upset the sensitive ecosystem of which they are part. There is a delicate balance between the micro-organisms, fish and other life which live in the water, the plants which grow in the water and on the surrounding land, and animals and birds which are dependent on these for their food. This natural balance is easily disturbed, for example by erosion overloading the water with silt, destruction of the fringing vegetation, and leaching of fertilizers from surrounding cultivated lands to cause an excess of nutrients in the water. Because these areas are so attractive, a balance has to be maintained between their use for settlement and recreation, and their conservation as a healthy, functioning ecosystem.

Estuaries are of special interest and importance since they provide an interface between fresh water and the sea. The lifecycles of many fish are dependent on their access to estuaries. Eight species of South African fish, including the Knysna seahorse, which is found only in Knysna Lagoon, are reliant on estuaries for the duration of their lifecycles; 22 species, amongst them the well-known angling fish, Spotted grunter, White steenbras and Cape stumpnose, depend on healthy estuaries for their survival because this is the only habitat in which their juveniles can develop. Many other fish species, some of which are commercially or recreationally important, utilize estuaries in the course of their lifespans. Many of the plants and other life forms of the estuaries are uniquely adapted to varying levels of salinity. Their destruction by man's activities interrupts a complicated web of interaction and interdependence which can have profound effects on the fishing industry all along the coast.

Because the Lakes area contains such a variety of habitats, it has a wealth of bird life. Rondevlei is a bird sanctuary now incorporated into the Wilderness National Park. Groenvlei - part of the Goukamma Nature Reserve - is similarly recognized. Some 60 species of birds associated with the dunes, forests, fynbos and scrub have been recorded at Groenvlei, including forest birds such as the Knysna Lourie and Blackheaded Oriole. There are 47 species associated with the lake itself, including residents such as the Dabchick and Redknobbed Coot. Among the birds associated with the fringing vegetation are kingfishers, cormorants and herons. The Goukamma Nature Reserve is also home to a wide variety of animals, although these are less evident than the birds. They include the Cape clawless otter, large-spotted genet, ratel (honey badger), bushpig, vervet monkey, caracal, blue duiker, bontebok and bushbuck.

It is fortunate that, despite the threat to the southern Cape coast and its lakes and lagoons posed by the increasing numbers of people settling and holidaying there, large areas representative of the diversity of landscape and habitat are conserved. These include the recently expanded Tsitsikamma Coastal National Park, the Wilderness National Park, the Goukamma and Robberg Nature Reserves and stretches of coast under the management of the Department of Water Affairs and Forestry. All of these provide exceptional opportunities for walkers to enjoy natural habitats.

THE COASTAL PLATEAU

Between the southern Cape coastline and the steep southern slopes of the Outeniqua and Tsitsikamma mountains lies a more-or-less flat area of land. This coastal plateau in fact comprises two terraces. The lower plateau, which rises steeply from the coast to a height of 150 m, is 5-15 km in width and slopes gently to the foot of the second terrace. The higher plateau rises to altitudes of 200-600 m; in the west it merges with the lower slopes of the Outeniqua Mountains, but further east it is up to 20 km wide. East of Plettenberg Bay the higher plateau narrows again and in places is indistinguishable from the foothills of the Tsitsikamma Mountains. The many rivers which run their short course to the sea from the higher slopes of the mountains have carved deep and steep-sided kloofs into the plateau, witness to the high rainfall in the catchment area, both recently and at certain times in the past.

Like the mountains themselves, the upper plateau is made up of Table Mountain sandstone with conglomerate and shale strata of the same formation. Most of the lower plateau is composed of Table Mountain sandstone and Bokkeveld shales with other rock types - granite and pre-Cape and more recent shales and conglomerates - in places. The soils derived from these rocks are thin, acid and (except for some weathered shales) deficient in nutrients. Generally speaking, this is why the area is not particularly suited to farming, despite its lush appearance.

Before settlement of the area, the coastal plateau was covered with two distinct vegetation types, namely fynbos and a broad, uninterrupted belt of Afromontane forest. In general, the fynbos occupied areas with highly acidic, extremely leached topsoils derived from Table Mountain sandstone,

The coastal plateau rises steeply from the seashore beyond the mouth of Crook's River near Kranshoek.

while the forests grew on shale-derived soils. This is a broad generalization, since the interface between forest and fynbos fluctuated as a result of other factors such as fire and climatic changes. The coastal plateau was, for obvious reasons, the area most influenced by the eastern expansion of settlement from the Cape and today large parts of it are urbanized, under cultivation or planted to exotic trees. Between the Kaaimans and Keurbooms rivers only a narrow belt of natural forest still exists - merely a fraction of what once grew here. Large tracts were so depleted by felling that they were cleared for agriculture before the forests were declared inalienable in 1888. Subsequently, much of the land covered with fynbos was put under plantations of pines and eucalyptus by the State and private growers.

In broad terms, the fynbos of the coastal plateau is indistinguishable from the montane fynbos on the southern slopes of the mountains behind. It is a particularly tall-growing, dense type, not particularly rich in species in comparison with other fynbos types. Large areas are covered with stands of *Leucadendron eucalyptifolium*, a plant that can grow into a tree 5 m tall if left unburnt for long enough.

Forests

The natural forests of the southern Cape coastal belt are unique. In spite of the intense felling and clearing which took place from the second half of the 18th to the early part of this century, and the ravages of a fire which burnt both forest and fynbos between Swellendam and Uitenhage in 1869, they still cover some 65 000 ha, of which some 46 000 ha are State Forest. This is by far the largest contiguous area of natural forest in South Africa.

They owe their existence to the combination of high, year-round rainfall and mild temperatures found along this coast. A few thousand years ago, when southern Africa had a warmer, wetter climate, large parts of the sub-continent were forested and tropical forests extended from Central Africa to the north-eastern Transvaal, Natal and the southern and south-western Cape. As the climate became drier and cooler, remnants of these forests found refuge in areas which had sufficient rainfall and moderate temperatures.

During the process of the forests' southwards expansion then northward retreat, the species composition of the forests changed; the southern Cape forests have affinities with the forests in the mountains of East Africa, but do not contain many of the species that occur there. Some genera are represented by species which have evolved from tropical ancestors under the pressures of a changing environment.

Two of these, the Stinkwood (*Ocotea bullata*) and the Kershout (*Pterocelastrus tricuspidatus*), have been exceptionally successful and adaptable, and today occupy both hot and dry sites in scrub forest and cool, moist sites in high forest. The high forest of the southern Cape (which is most similar to tropical forest) is found only on the wetter sites. Together with the trees common to or evolved from the tropical forests, there are species which are remnants of more ancient forests of the area: the two Yellowwoods, the Outeniqua yellowwood (*Podocarpus falcatus*) and the Real yellowwood (*P. latifolius*), are two prominent examples. Fossil trees near Knysna show that these species grew here several million years ago. The southern Cape forests are not uniform. The height of the canopy and the types of tree which predominate in a particular area depend on the rainfall, the aspect and the soil type and depth. They can be subdivided as follows:

● Dry scrub forest grows on warm sites with low rainfall and shallow soils which lose moisture quickly. This forest type is found in many places along the coast on the edge of the lower plateau. It comprises a dense understorey of shrubs and stunted trees such as the aromatic *Buddleja saligna*, the Spike-thorn (*Maytenus heterophylla*), the Bastard saffronwood (*Cassine peragua*), the Num-num (*Carissa bispinosa*), the Kershout and the Milkwood, overtopped by trees which include White stinkwood (*Celtis africana*), a few Outeniqua yellowwoods and that glory of summer when it flowers, the Cape chestnut (*Calodendrum capense*).

● A totally different scrub forest (wet scrub forest) is found on wet sites with especially shallow soils. It is characterized by an abundance of ferns on the forest floor and a shrubby understorey which includes the Cape stock-rose (*Sparmannia africana*) and the Tree fern (*Cyathea capensis*); the trees found here grow to 6-10 m and include Rooiels (*Cunonia capensis*), Stinkwood, Witels (*Platylophus trifoliatus*), Real yellowwood, Cape beech (*Rapanea melanophoeos*) and, on the forest edge, Keurboom (*Virgilia divaricata*).

High forests, whose canopies are between 15 and 20 m above the ground and which have individual trees extending well above this, are also classified according to the moisture regime where they grow:

● Wet high forest is found on shallow, permanently wet soils where year-round rainfall is high. The dominant trees are Rooiels (*Cunonia capensis*), Real yellowwood (*Podocarpus*

This scene near the start of the Terblans Trail typifies the beauty of the Garden Route's forests.

latifolius) and Stinkwood; Tree ferns are also characteristic.

● Moist high forest is found where there are deep loam soils kept moist by sufficient rainfall; this forest type produces the giant Kalanders (*Podocarpus falcatus*) which, at up to 40 m high, tower over the canopy. Making up the high canopy here are the Ironwood (*Olea capensis* subsp. *macrocarpa*), White pear (*Apodytes dimidiata*), *Nuxia floribunda*, with its sprays of creamy white flowers in October, Real yellowwood, and Stinkwood. A middle canopy comprises immature trees of all the above, as well as lower-growing species such as Kershout and Assegai (*Curtisia dentata*). The lowest canopy (understorey) is made up of juveniles of all of the above, together with Kamassi (*Gonioma kammassi*) and Onderbos (*Trichocladus crinitus*), better known in some circles as 'witch hazel'.

● A slightly different medium-moist high forest grows in areas of similar rainfall but where soils have better drainage; the dominant species resemble those in moist high forest but also include Hard pear (*Olinia ventosa*) and Kershout. Despite the dense understorey of Onderbos, the regeneration of trees is most prolific in this type of forest.

Most of the natural forest of the southern Cape (46 000 ha) is managed by the Department of Water Affairs and Forestry. The Department harvests marketable timber from 20 per cent of this area, which represents the accessible parts of only medium-moist and moist high forest types, as these are best able to tolerate disturbance and their regeneration is rapid. In a prescribed block, only individual trees (mainly senescent ones) are selected for felling, in a way that the species composition of the block remains balanced. Only trees which can be felled and moved with minimal damage to the canopy and the understorey are chosen. Felled logs are 'slipped', that is, dragged out of the forest along slip-paths by horses (stocky, big-boned, beautiful Percherons) and mules, so that disturbance of the environment is minimized. A block is generally allowed to rest for a full 10 years between harvests.

Of the remaining 80 per cent of natural forest under the Department's control, 55,5 per cent, representing all forest types, is under 'protection management', a practice which aims to maintain the forests as a healthy, functioning ecosystem. For this reason, windfalls and dead trees of commercially valuable species are retrieved from such areas only when it can be done with minimal disruption. In suitable areas, controlled harvesting of the Seven week's fern (*Rumohra adiantiformis*) is carried out.

Some 23 per cent of the forests under the administration of the Department, representing all forest types, is left undisturbed. This area comprises nature reserves, which enjoy the highest conservation status. Forest areas in the Tsitsikamma Coastal National Park are also nature reserves. The reserves are essential because they act as controls in the assessment of the results of research on forest management carried out by the Department and other bodies.

Half a per cent of the forests administered by the Department is set aside for recreation and conservation education, which go hand in hand. The forest trails described in this book run through these areas.

The forests form a highly vulnerable ecosystem. Anyone who has seen the shallow root system of a forest giant, such as an Outeniqua yellowwood, blown over by one of the periodic high winds will realize that the soils are not deep. As they are also poor in mineral substances, the growth of forest trees depends on the decomposition of leaf litter and other plant material on the forest floor by a variety of living things, including fungi, which makes nutrients available to their roots. A disturbance of the environment can therefore have profound effects on this cycle of growth and decay; once interrupted it is not readily re-established.

For walkers, the forests provide a unique environment - a world of dappled light and muted colours. However, it is easy to become bored with the apparent sameness of the forests, which reveals its treasures only to those who make the effort to look and listen. For one thing, forest birds and particularly animals tend to be shy; for another, they are not easily seen in the dim light.

You cannot mistake the loud cackling of a group of Redbilled Woodhoopoes or the harsh grunts or 'kok-kok' call of the Knysna Lourie, but you have to listen carefully for the soft knocking which reveals the presence of the Olive Woodpecker. You will hear the distinctive 'Willy' call of the Sombre Bulbul everywhere, but the bird is aptly named and difficult to spot. So too is the Blackheaded Oriole, resident of the high canopy, although its liquid call is easy enough to recognize. In summer, Paradise Flycatchers flit below the canopy. If you are particularly observant you may see a Narina Trogon on a high perch under the canopy or recognize its hooting call; these are fairly common birds and not particularly shy, but are seldom seen because they can perch quietly and remain motionless. A wealth of birds occupy the understorey. Tiny birds (11-13 cm in length) such as the Cape Batis, Yellowthroated Warbler and Barthroated Apalis glean insects from stems and leaves, and even Lesser Doublecollared Sunbirds busy themselves in the undergrowth.

Pottering about on or near the forest floor are Cape Robins, Chorister Robins (in summer) and Olive Thrushes.

With patience, you will see the birds, but the forest animals are shy and retiring. Exceptions are bushbuck, which sometimes browse in open areas next to the forest in the early morning or late evening, and vervet monkeys and Chacma baboons. The only signs of bushpig are their droppings and the turned earth where they have dug for roots and bulbs; these are strictly nocturnal animals, like the tiny blue duiker, the porcupine and the large-spotted genet. Honey badgers (ratels) are occasionally seen, but very few people have spotted a leopard or caracal.

The chances of coming across the remnant herd of Knysna elephants, even when walking in their range, are extremely remote. (They spend most of their time in the Gouna, Parkes and Diepwalle forest reserves.) Smaller forest mammals include bats, mice, shrews and moles. Of the snakes you may occasionally see in or on the margin of the forests, the most poisonous is the boomslang, but this is a retiring creature which will only strike in defence if cornered and frightened. The Knysna dwarf chameleon poses absolutely no threat to anything other than the insects on which it lives.

A bushbuck doe looks up from feeding on the forest edge in the early morning.

THE MOUNTAINS

The Outeniqua and Tsitsikamma mountains rise steeply from the coastal plateau to a height of up to 1 500 m. The equally steep northern slopes of the Outeniquas drop through a series of lower subsidiary ranges into the valley of the Little Karoo which is bordered in the north by the Swartberg, which here reach a height of 1 950 m. On the north side of this part of the Swartberg range, the peaks slope to a flattish area at an altitude of 1 300-1 500 m; this is dissected by deep kloofs and its edge drops steeply into the Great Karoo. Gamkaberg and Rooiberg in the Little Karoo form a relatively low ridge which is split by the course of the Gamka River.

The southern slopes of the Outeniqua Mountains receive a high rainfall and this is reflected in the type of fynbos (wet fynbos) which covers them, and in the presence of forest in the kloofs; the northern slopes are drier and support a somewhat different fynbos (mesic fynbos). The Little Karoo is in the rain shadow of the Outeniquas; Gamkaberg is dry, with arid fynbos covering the top of the mountain and Spekboomveld on the lower, shale slopes. The low northern slopes of the Swartberg range are made up of shales, which support succulent Karoo vegetation; this gives way higher up to Renosterveld, characterized by the Renosterbos (*Elytropappus rhinocerotis*), which in turn becomes fynbos where the rocks change from shale to the Table Mountain sandstone of the middle and upper slopes. Fynbos also covers the northern slopes of the Swartberg, which are in general drier - the rainfall diminishes rapidly with decreasing altitude to the arid floor of the Great Karoo. On the edge of the Karoo the fynbos changes directly to succulent Karoo veld as Table Mountain sandstone meets the shale.

The fynbos of the southern Cape is atypical in that it grows in an area of year-round rainfall; fynbos is most commonly associated with winter-rainfall climates. As in the case of all fynbos vegetation, fire plays a major role, allowing the regeneration of veld in which the plants are too old to set seed effectively and the flowering of the bulbous plants which are best seen (in some cases seen only) shortly after a fire. Too frequent burning, however, leads to the suppression or loss of some of the shrubby components which need a minimum time to grow and set sufficient seed for their regeneration. Within the broad categories of wet, mesic and arid fynbos are different communities of plants which reflect local conditions of micro-climate, soil and aspect. The plants which grow high up on the peaks of the Swartberg range, for example, are quite different from those growing on the slopes below. The fascination of the fynbos lies in its enormous diversity. The walks described in this book traverse a representative selection of many of these fynbos communities. In addition to the beauty of their plant life, the mountains provide the walker with the most spectacular scenery of the Garden Route.

Several of the birds which live in the fynbos are endemic - these include Orangebreasted Sunbirds, Cape Sugarbirds, Cape Siskins and Cape Rockjumpers, all of which are commonly seen on the mountains. Another endemic, Victorin's Warbler, which spends most of its time in thick stream-side vegetation, is not easy to see but can sometimes be heard.

Many other birds which are not confined to the fynbos are found here, including the Cape Rock Thrush, Cape Francolin, Rock Pigeon, Southern Boubou, Spotted (Karoo) Prinia, Redwinged Starling and Malachite and Lesser Doublecollared sunbirds. In addition to the smaller raptors, Black and Martial eagles are often observed on the more remote mountains such as Gamkaberg and the Swartberg.

Besides dassies and mongooses, the animals most likely to be seen are klipspringer, grysbok, grey rhebok (in the Swartberg) and the ubiquitous Chacma baboons. Dangerous snakes include the puff adder, berg adder and (in the Swartberg) the Cape cobra. None of these poses any great danger to the careful and considerate climber.

The gentle outline of the Outeniqua Mountains leads west from the valley of the Doring River.

CONSERVATION

To the average eye, the coastal belt of the southern Cape generally presents a lush appearance, with its pleasing profusion of trees. To anyone who can distinguish between natural and exotic vegetation, the scene is not necessarily so attractive. In terms of the numbers of aggressively invasive exotic plants, this area is without doubt among the worst affected in the country. Some of the exotic trees which are out of control here are species of Eucalyptus, and Australian acacias such as the black wattle (*Acacia mearnsii*) and the blackwood (*Acacia melanoxylon*). Despite strenuous efforts by the conservation authorities, large tracts of the Outeniqua and Tsitsikamma mountains are infested with pines (*Pinus pinaster*) and an Australian member of the protea family,

Hakea tenuifolia. In contrast, there has been little invasion of the fynbos on the Swartberg, which remains in an almost pristine state.

The accelerated 'development' of the coastal belt threatens its wildlife and, ironically, its aesthetic appeal. It is therefore fortunate that large natural areas are actively conserved by three major organizations: the Cape Provincial Administration's Department of Nature and Environmental Conservation, the State's Department of Water Affairs and Forestry, and the National Parks Board. Despite some differences in their approach, these bodies are by and large effective in preserving the remaining natural areas of the Garden Route - which are the parts of prime interest to hikers.

SAFETY AND RESPONSIBILITY

Hiking is certainly one of the safest pastimes, but mishaps and accidents do occur. Most often these can be avoided if you are properly prepared before you set out and adhere to the following rules:

* Do not walk alone, especially on long and remote routes.
* Use a good map and keep to the route. Do not take (apparent) short cuts. Consider carrying a compass on a forest walk, as it is easy to lose your sense of direction among tall, thickly growing trees.
* Make your route known to someone at home before you set out, and advise them when you expect to be back; be realistic about the time you need to complete the route.
* Always (and I mean always) carry warm water- and windproof clothing; wear comfortable walking shoes or hiking boots with thick soles; they should be worn-in, not brand new. A hat will protect your head and face from sunburn and is strongly recommended. A `space-blanket' can save a life and should be part of every hiker's kit.
* Know your level of fitness and allow for off-days.
* *Always carry liquid*; preferably take some food.
* Beware of changes in the weather and what they might mean. A sudden rainstorm can turn a small stream into a raging torrent. Weather changes can be rapid and dramatic on the mountains, particularly the Swartberg.

* Getting lost in the forest can be frightening, especially in the dark. If you feel you are no longer on the route, carefully think back to where you may have left it, and retrace your steps while marking your way.
* If you become really lost anywhere, find shelter, keep warm and *stay where you are* until you can see without any doubt where to go, or until someone finds you. *Don't panic.*

The remaining natural areas on the Garden Route are unique and precious: help to conserve them. *Do not:*
* Pick flowers or collect momentos; these acts are offences in protected areas and carry stiff fines on conviction.
* Light a fire anywhere but in designated places.
* Discard rubbish of any kind, especially burning cigarette butts; take your litter home with you for disposal.
* Write graffiti of any kind anywhere.
* Take short cuts; on steep slopes these cause erosion.

IN AN EMERGENCY

The first people to contact should be the nearest police; they are the first link in an effective and established chain of organizations equipped to deal with emergencies; others in the chain include the Metro Rescue Service, the National Sea Rescue Institute and the Mountain Club of South Africa.

CHAPTER ONE

MOSSEL BAY

Driving into Mossel Bay from the west, you are greeted by a scene which is tacitly regarded as the start of the Garden Route: a broad sweep of sandy beach embracing a sheltered stretch of the Indian Ocean, bounded in the north by the edge of the coastal plateau and backed by the purple silhouette of the Outeniqua Mountains. This beautiful bay has great historical significance for South Africa, for it was here that explorers from Europe first made contact with the natives of the south coast of southern Africa. The meeting on 3 February 1488 was not friendly. When the Portuguese landed to fill their water-barrels from a fresh-water stream, their attempts to communicate with the Khoi-khoi herdsmen who had watched their ships anchor in the bay were met by a volley of stones. In retaliation a Khoi-khoi was killed, and Bartolomeu Dias sailed away from the bay without making any further contact.

Nine years later Vasco da Gama was more successful. He established the trade with the Khoi-khoi which ensured vital supplies of fresh food for the seafarers. The bay became a regular port of call for Portuguese ships rounding the Cape during their long voyages on the trade route between Europe and the East. Messages from one ship to another were left in objects such as sea-boots fixed to a Milkwood tree (*Sideroxylon inerme*) which grew next to the spring where the sailors replenished their water supplies. The spring and post office tree are still there today, and both are National Monuments. Around this historic spot are the buildings of the Bartolomeu Dias Museum.

In time, Mossel Bay developed into one of South Africa's

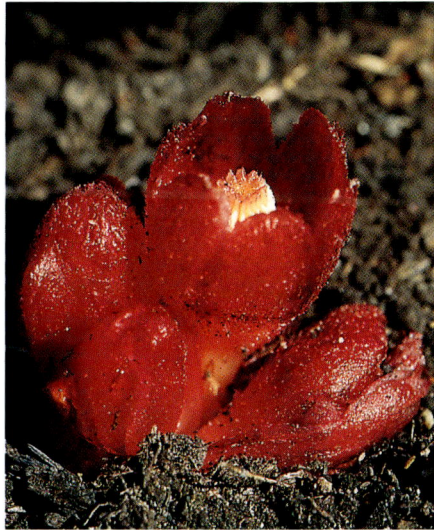

The parasitic Aardroos grows on the roots of other plants in sandy areas.

major ports. It handled the agricultural output of the surrounding area, including huge quantities of ostrich feathers produced near Oudtshoorn in the years around the turn of the century, when this industry experienced a boom. Although the importance of the harbour declined after World War I, the port subsequently acquired South Africa's first submarine pipeline. The pipeline is used to transfer petroleum products from tankers to the storage tanks in the industrial area of Voorbaai. The construction of the enormous Mossgas plant to the west of Mossel Bay, which is designed to produce synthetic fuel from natural gas piped from offshore wells, has had a profound effect on the town, temporarily swelling its population considerably. Despite the impact of industrial activity on its environment, Mossel Bay and its surroundings provide several opportunities for walking.

There are walks on the long expanse of sand to the north of the town, to as far as Cape Windlass. This stretch of beach is accessible from several holiday resorts and small towns along the old road between Mossel Bay and George. Off the coast about 2 km east of Glentana are the remains of a floating dock which was wrecked in a gale in 1902; a walk to the wreck or beyond, to Cape Windlass, must be done at low tide, as the rocky headlands cut off the beach when the tides are high. It is, however, the coastal stretch between Cape St Blaize, where the lighthouse stands above the commercial part of Mossel Bay, and Dana Bay to the west which provides the most spectacular walk in this area, and the St Blaize Trail is the one I have chosen to describe.

Mossel Bay enjoys an equable and sunny climate. On average it experiences only three or four cloudy days per month - significantly fewer than George and Knysna, which are closer to the mountains.

The elevated cliffs west of the lighthouse on Cape St Blaize make a scenically spectacular start to the St Blaize Trail.

St Blaize Trail

An easy but long hike above the rugged cliffs between Mossel Bay and Dana Bay, offering dramatic views of the coast.

Time: 5 hours (one way).

Distance: 13,5 km (one way).

Exertion: Light.

Controlling authority: Mossel Bay Municipality.

Permits: Not required.

Maps and information: A map with interesting information on the reverse is obtainable from the Information Bureau at the Bartolomeu Dias Museum.

Start: The St Blaize cave under the lighthouse.

End: The houses on the coast alongside the path at Dana Bay.

How to get to Dana Bay: From Mossel Bay, drive west along Marsh Street and turn left onto the R102 in the direction of the N2 to Cape Town. Just before the junction with the N2, turn left to Dana Bay. Follow this road to Dana Bay. Keep left until you reach the houses which line the end of the trail, and park here.

How to get to start: In Mossel Bay, drive east along Marsh Street, circle the campsite and park under the Cape St Blaize lighthouse.

Trail marker: White bird in flight.

Best times to walk: Spring if you want to see flowers, but magnificent at any time.

Precautions: Walking this trail in high winds could be dangerous and should be avoided. Although the path is always safe and wide, there are sheer drops at certain places. If you visit the caves or coastal rocks, beware of high waves.

Features: Rugged coastal scenery, caves, rock formations and varied vegetation.

This trail takes its name from Cape St Blaize, the promontory on which stands the lighthouse overlooking the commercial part of Mossel Bay. The trail was completed as recently as 1987 and was a co-operative project between the municipality of Mossel Bay and the St Blaize Wildlife Society of the Point High School.

Bartolomeu Dias was the first European explorer to make a landfall on the coast of southern Africa east of the Cape when he put in to Mossel Bay. He named the bay *Baia dos Vaqueiros* (Bay of the Cowherds) after the Khoi-khoi and their herds of cattle which he saw along the shore. Nine years later Vasco da Gama made a landing there and, on his maps, called the bay *Aguade de São Bras* (Watering place of Saint Bras) since the day on which Dias had landed was this saint's day. 'St Blaize' is a corruption of 'São Bras'.

Directly below the lighthouse is a large cave. A Dutch captain, Cornelis de Houtman, visited the bay in 1595 and gave it its modern name, 'Mossel Bay', after the piles of mussel shells he found in the cave. According to legend Khoi-khoi inhabited this cave, and excavations in 1888 and 1932 revealed the presence of artefacts dated to the Middle Stone Age.

It is a sad commentary on the respect the general public has for this historic spot that the St Blaize cave and its surroundings are now covered with graffiti, littered with broken beer bottles and other trash and permeated with the smell of human excrement. The cave marks the start of the St Blaize Trail, and so repelled was I by its state that I was initially reluctant to include the walk in this book. If the cave is still in such a mess when you visit it, don't be deterred - just beyond it lies 13,5 km of wonderfully scenic coastline with a fascinating variety of plant life and rock formations.

If you intend to walk all the way to Dana Bay, you will need transport at the other end. (See directions to Dana Bay in the box above.)

Although the path itself is perfectly safe, this is not a walk on which young children should be allowed free rein, as there are very high, sheer falls close to the path at many places. Sufferers of vertigo should also take note! The trail is well marked with signs at regular intervals. There is only

This form of the Leeubekkie, Nemesia versicolor, *grows in the sand of the dunes along the southern Cape coast .*

one place where there could be any confusion over the route: just beyond Tunnel Caves there are several side paths; keep to the top of the cliffs here and, in fact, all along the trail, except beyond Pinnacle Point where the path drops almost to sea level.

Nowhere on the route are there any strenuous climbs, apart from the short haul from the parking area at Cape St Blaize, past the cave, to the level of the lighthouse.

The appearance of the coastline is the result of a turbulent geological past. The consequent variety of rock and soil types which the trail traverses is reflected in the plant cover. Unfortunately, thickets of rooikrans (*Acacia cyclops*), an extremely invasive Australian plant, have all but overwhelmed the indigenous vegetation in some places, but in others the veld is more or less natural and in reasonable condition. In spring, the diversity of veld flowers here makes a colourful sight.

Just beyond the lighthouse the path crosses a short section of shale, where the distinctive plant life includes the beautiful shrub *Anisodontea scabrosa*, with its masses of small, deep pink hibiscus-like flowers. The clay soils give way to sand which is covered with a monotony of rooikrans, but the lack of interesting vegetation here is more than compensated for by the views of the cliffs ahead, the turbulent sea below and the distant silhouette of the Cape St Blaize lighthouse back along the path. Beyond this stretch, the rooikrans yields to a veld-type which could be described as Strandveld, where leached sands overlay calcrete or limestone. Here grow *Aloe ferox*, Skilpadbos (*Zygophyllum morgsana*), Needle bush (*Azima tetracantha*) - take care not to prick yourself on its thorns, which can really hurt, the Boerboon (*Schotia afra*),

Sarcostemma viminale (a leafless climber), and Milkwoods (*Sideroxylon inerme*) stunted by the wind, amongst a host of shrubby plants. In more open patches grows *Acmadenia heterophylla*, a low, dense shrub with highly aromatic needle-shaped leaves and covered with deep cerise flowers in spring; this species is typical of sandy pockets in limestone outcrops.

Above the Tunnel Caves, a path from Mossel Bay's golf course crosses the trail and drops down a gully to the left of

The breeding colours of one the commonest lizards, the Southern rock agama, are gorgeous to the eyes of the female of the species.

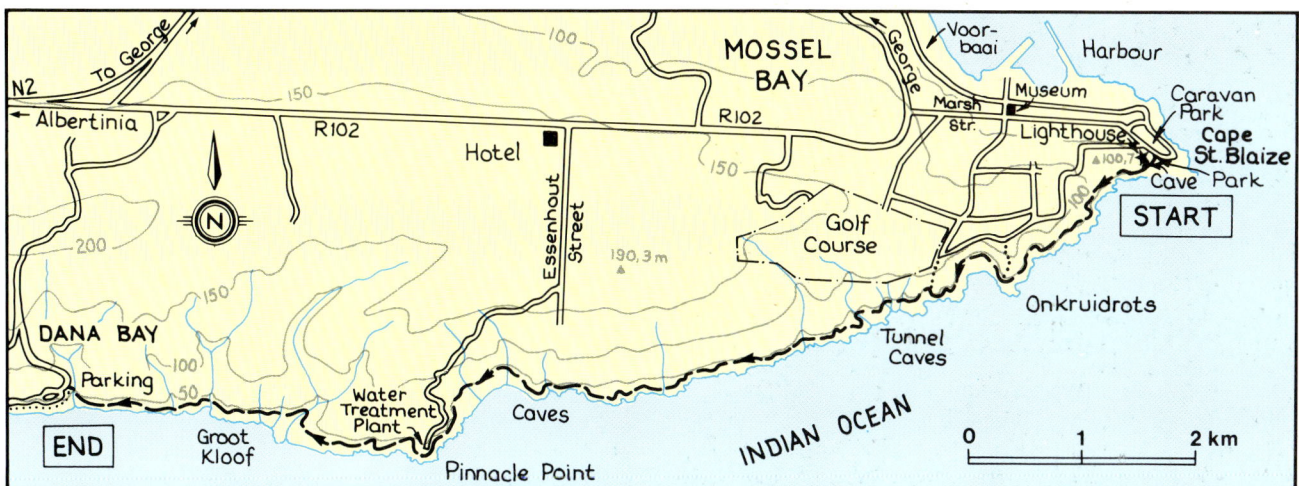

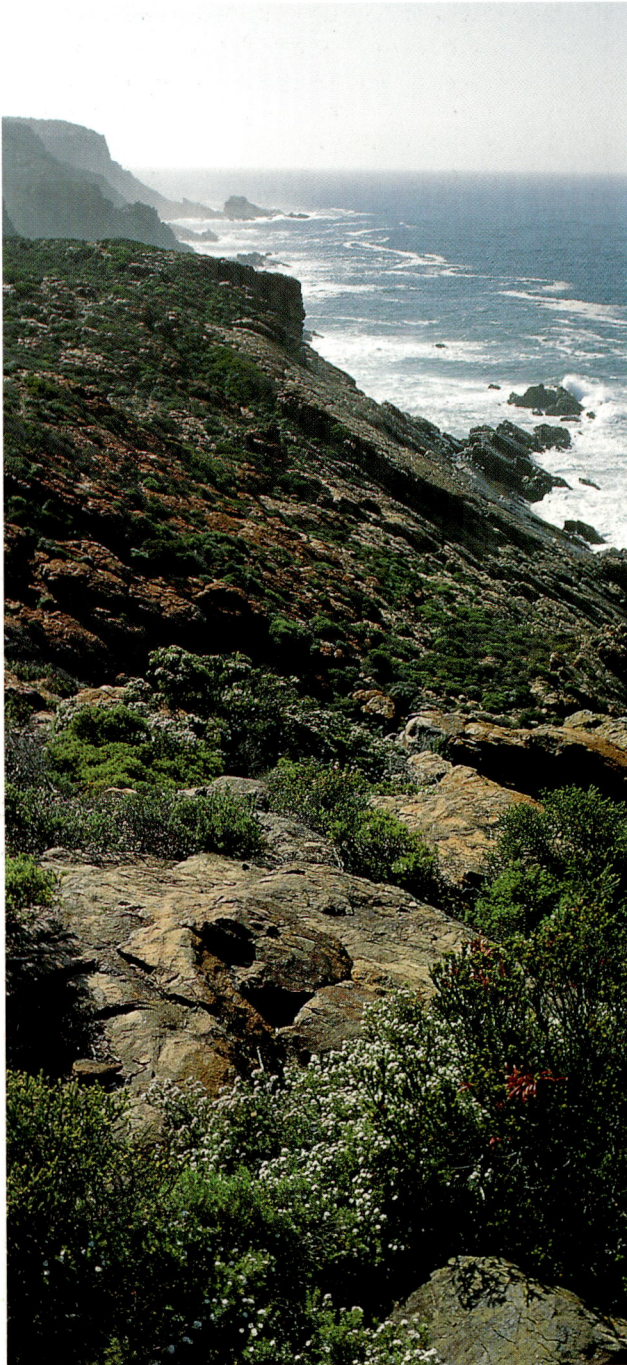

the trail to the sea and the caves themselves. A sign warns that visiting these caves can be dangerous because of freak high waves, infrequent though they might be. Next to the path, just before you reach this crossroads, there are several bushes of *Protea lanceolata*, a species endemic to the coastal strip between Cape Infanta and Great Brak River. Beyond the crossroads the path zigzags up on to the cliff-top where, in spring, flowers of *Freesia alba* give off their strong, sweet scent. Further on are some odd chunks of a conglomerate rock, probably of recent geological origin (Enon conglomerate). In early summer the flowers of *Bobartia* (probably *aphylla*), form sheets of yellow in the sandy patches. The reed-like stems of bobartias resemble those of some restios.

ABOVE: *Fynbos on the rocks near the Tunnel Caves.*
RIGHT: *The orange-coloured cliffs that rise above the Indian Ocean at Onkruidrots are warmed by the early morning sun.*

Before you reach Pinnacle Point - easily identified by the two buildings on its skyline - a large bay with sandy beaches comes into view. These are accessible via several paths near the buildings (a water treatment plant) on the point itself. As it is possible to get to Pinnacle Point by a road and track from the R102 out of Mossel Bay, it can serve as an early exit from the trail. From the eastern side of Pinnacle Point, Dana Bay and the long line of dunes beyond come into view. In fact, just past the Point the trail traverses the start of the dunes and the vegetation changes. Here are plants characteristic of dune vegetation: the Candelabra flower (*Brunsvigia orientalis*); *Struthiola argentea*, a member of the Thymelaceae which has sprays of tiny yellow flowers;

Salvia africana-lutea, a grey-leaved bush with unusual brown flowers; *Felicia bergiana*, a perennial daisy with flowers of intense blue and, in dampish places among low tufts of restio, *Gladiolus cunonius*, whose deep-red, narrow and elongated flowers are bird-pollinated.

The bird life ranges from coastal birds to those associated with the shrubby vegetation. We disturbed a grysbok along the way and took care not to annoy a puff adder sunning itself next to the path some way further on. All the way from Pinnacle Point to Dana Bay the spoor of some small cat or genet were clearly visible in the sand on the path.

The houses of Dana Bay alongside the path signal the end of this magnificent trail.

CHAPTER TWO

ROBINSON PASS

The Robinson Pass forms part of the route which connects Hartenbos, just north of Mossel Bay, with Oudtshoorn. Opened in 1869 and named after Mr R. Robinson, then Commissioner of Roads, the pass was built by the famous Thomas Bain over the Outeniqua Mountains which separate the coastal plateau from the Little Karoo to the north. The Robinson Pass does not carry a heavy volume of traffic today, but it had a brief moment of glory in the 1930s when the National Roads Board unveiled a plan to start the N1 National Road in George (rather than Cape Town), lead it over the pass to Oudtshoorn and thence through the Great Karoo to Johannesburg and Beit Bridge. This was to create a `spine' from which other National Roads would branch off. The plan came to nought, however, and eventually the Outeniqua Pass was built, to provide a direct route between George and Oudtshoorn.

A few kilometres to the west of the Robinson Pass lies Attaquaskloof, named after the Attaqua, the Khoi-khoi tribe which once lived in the area. The first Europeans to cross the Outeniquas did so via Attaquaskloof in 1689, with the help of Khoi-khoi guides. The purpose of the expedition, which was led by Isaac Schrijver, was to establish trade with the Inkwa tribe of the Khoi-khoi in the Eastern Cape. This kloof, once an elephant path, probably became the route most often used by hunters and farmers in their explorations eastward. The next recorded crossing of the Attaquaskloof Pass was by Ensign Beutler in 1752, on his journey from the Cape to the Kei River. By this time, there were farms on the southern slopes of these mountains. Among the distinguished

A male Cape Sugarbird perches on Protea neriifolia.

Two common proteaceous plants of the fynbos on the Outeniquas, Protea eximia *and* Leucadendron uliginosum.

travellers who toiled up the slopes of the Attaquaskloof Pass were Thunberg (1772 and 1773) and Sparrman (1775 and 1776), the famous botanists, followed by Van Plettenberg (1778), Patterson (1777 and 1779) and Gordon (1786). The pass only declined in importance after the construction of the Cradock and Montagu passes behind George in the 19th Century.

The higher parts of the Robinson Pass are scenically very beautiful, and offer distant views of mountains and the sea; the summit of the pass is at an altitude of 838 m. The surrounding mountains are made up of Table Mountain sandstone and, except for the areas under cultivation and the large tracts of pine plantations, the upper southern slopes are covered with the wet and medium-wet fynbos and forest patches typical of this part of the Outeniquas. In this area two very attractive hikes have been laid out, both of which are described in this chapter: the Ruitersbos Forest Walk, in the Ruitersbos State Forest to the east of the pass, and the Koumashoek Circuit, on the other side of the pass and higher up. The latter uses a short cut to bridge the outward and return legs of the new two-day (alternatively three-day) Attaquaskloof Hiking Trail (*see* page 000) which joins the Robinson Pass with its historical predecessor, the Attaquaskloof Pass.

The southern slopes of the Outeniquas receive a relatively high rainfall, and cloud is a factor which should be considered when planning a hike here. These mountains form an effective trap for clouds brought in by south-westerly and southerly winds. On the north side of Robinson Pass the rainfall drops off rapidly towards the Little Karoo. In fact, less than 30 km away, due north from the top of Robinson Pass, lies Gamkaberg, an arid mountain in the rain shadow of the Outeniquas.

RUITERSBOS FOREST WALK

Two interconnecting loops which run through natural forest and plantation alongside the Perdeberg River and its subsidiary streams.

Time: 3 1/2 - 4 hours.

Distance: 10,3 km. (A shorter walk of 4,8 km takes in the first loop only.)

Exertion: Light.

Controlling authority: Ruitersbos State Forest Station.

Permits: Available from the reception desk at Eight Bells Mountain Inn or the office at Ruitersbos State Forest Station. Register at the start of the walk.

To walk on Protea Hill you need permission from the management of the Inn.

Maps and information: A sketch map and information are available from both the Inn and the forest station.

How to get there: Take the turn-off to Oudtshoorn at Hartenbos on the N2 (near Mossel Bay), drive 32 km, then turn right onto the dirt road, signposted 'Ruitersbos Hiking Trail', just before the Ruitersbos Forest Station. Follow this road east for 1,7 km, past forestry labourers' cottages and Protea Hill, and park next to the plantation. Alternatively, from the turn-off at Hartenbos, drive 28,5 km to the Eight Bells Mountain Inn.

Start/end: At the parking area next to the pine plantation (or the Inn, for a longer walk).

Trail markers: White shoe-prints. Green signs identify specific points by letter and give the distance to the next point.

Best times to walk: Delightful at any time.

Precautions: Avoid very wet weather, when crossing the Perdeberg River is difficult.

Features: River and natural riverine forest; ferns and stream-side vegetation.

The start of the walk can be approached either from the Eight Bells Mountain Inn or from the gravel road just before the Ruitersbos Forest Station on Robinson Pass. From either direction, it is worth making a small detour to walk up onto Protea Hill. From this vantage point, there are distant views of the Outeniqua Mountains and the kloof through which the trail runs. The surrounding fynbos and open vista provide the perfect counterpoint to the limited perspective you have once you are enveloped by the trees and riverine vegetation down in the kloof below.

BELOW LEFT: *Between the high peaks of the Outeniqua range and the farms in its southern foothills lies the Perdeberg River Valley.*

Apart from some short sections through pine plantations, the path generally follows the course of the Perdeberg River and two small side-streams. It is the beauty of these watercourses and the stream-side vegetation that provide the trail's main attraction; the forest (Stinkhoutbos) for which it is named is confined to the kloofs through which the rivers pass. For anyone interested in ferns, this trail is a must, as there is a lush abundance of these plants - including Tree ferns (*Cyathea capensis*) - particularly at the beginning of the walk downstream.

The route is clearly and comprehensively marked. From the parking place (B) next to the pine plantation, the trail follows a forestry track for 200 m down to the next point (C).

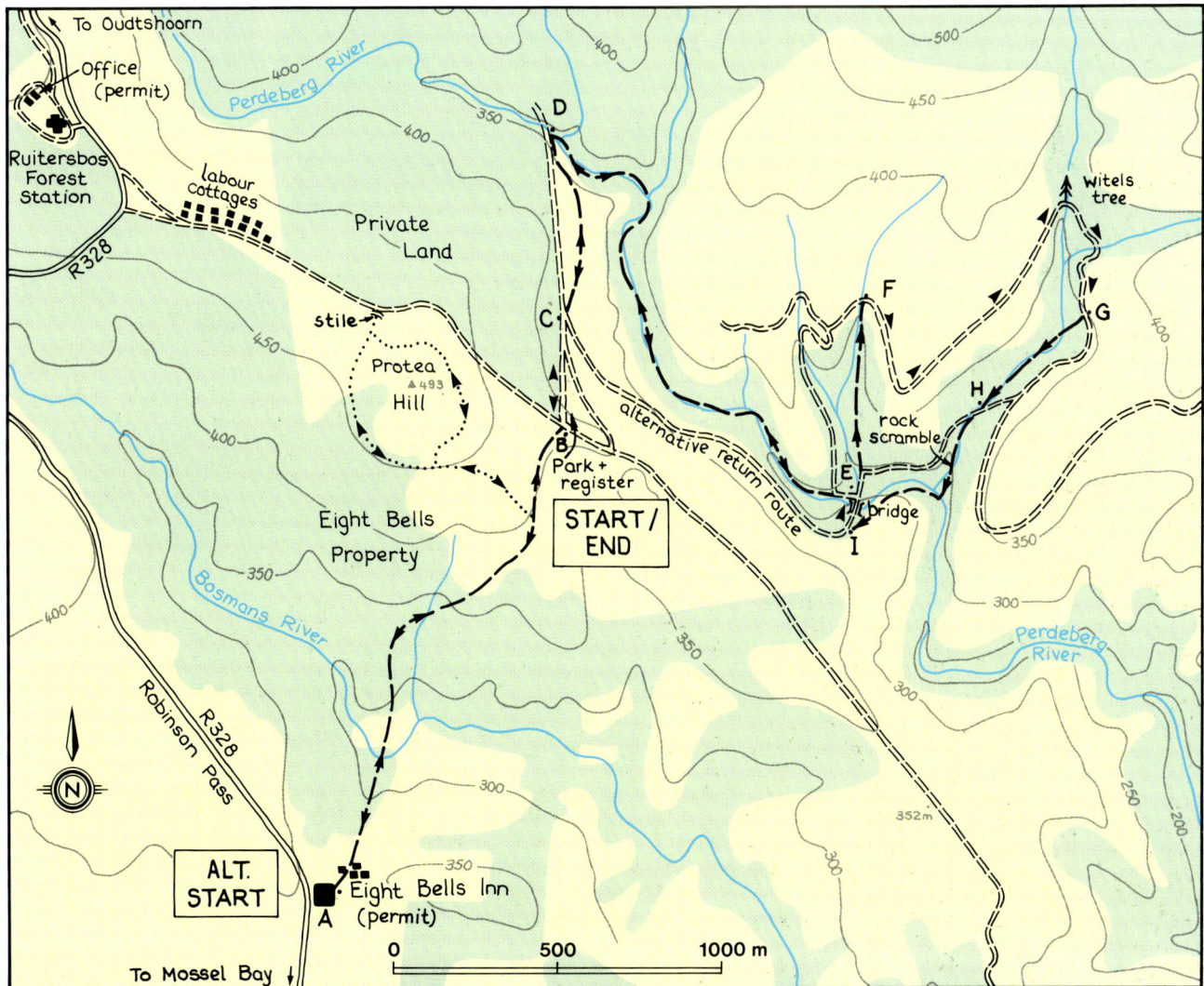

Here it descends and runs sometimes in, sometimes next to the plantation. Finally, the path passes through a stand of Outeniqua gonna (*Passerina falcifolia*) and Keurboom (*Virgilia divaricata*), which marks the edge of the riverine forest, to reach point D on the Perdeberg River.

This is the start of what I consider the loveliest part of this walk. The path first leads across the river and then closely follows it downstream, crossing and recrossing it a total of nine times. On the way it passes mainly through forest containing many Stinkwoods (*Ocotea bullata*), but occasionally through the lighter shade of copses of Keurboom and Outeniqua gonna. The combination of water, mossy rocks, ferns and trees is enchanting. After a final crossing to the left bank of the river, the path leaves the water, emerges into pine plantation and follows a track down to a forestry road. If you have elected to do the short walk, turn right here and follow the road through the plantation, past point I, back to point C and the parking place.

To complete the full trail, turn left to point E and climb up through the forest beside a small stream bed. When you reach a track (point F) turn right. At first the track runs through pine trees, then it crosses a stream in a clearing, from where there is a rewarding glimpse of mountain peaks behind the fynbos-covered slopes above. A magnificent, very old Witels (*Platylophus trifoliatus*) grows next to the stream, and this is a perfect place for a breather. At point G just along the track, the path drops down a steamlet through Keurboom and Witels and crosses the stream four times on small log bridges in its short descent to a forestry track at point H. At a signboard a few metres to the right, the path leaves the track, descends, crosses another bridge and continues down the kloof. The stream drops more steeply now and a bit of rock scrambling is necessary before the path crosses the stream and climbs steeply up the opposite bank to the plantation. The path skirts the pines for a few hundred metres, then meets the forestry road at point I.

From this point you can return through the pine plantation by turning left along the track, but I thoroughly recommend turning right. This takes you back across the bridge to point E, where you can return to the start along the Perdeberg River to point D and thence to the parking place via point C. This gives you the opportunity to experience the beauty of this stretch once more, without too much extra walking.

The essence of the Ruitersbos Forest Walk - foliage, ferns, mossy rocks and sunlit stream.

FERNS

One of the delights of walking in the forests or along the streams of the Garden Route is the profusion of ferns. It is the delicacy and intricacy of their form and the subtlety of their colouring which provide their attraction.

Ferns are very ancient plants: fossil records show that ancestors of the present-day ferns and fern-like plants existed on earth 400 million years ago, and that in southern Africa they were most abundant 160 to 100 million years ago. Unlike seed-bearing plants, ferns do not flower. Instead of seeds they produce spores; when these germinate, they develop into small growths with male and female parts. Only when fertilization between these parts occurs does a new plant emerge. Ferns are also related to mosses but, unlike mosses, are vascular plants: they have a system for the transport of water and nutrients in their leaves and stems.

The most common habitats of ferns are shady, moist or wet areas, but some species - such as *Todea barbara*, which flourishes on the open south-facing slopes of the Outeniqua Mountains - have adapted to harsher conditions. There are even those that occur in arid areas.

The fronds of Seven-week's ferns are highly prized by florists for their long-lasting qualities, and these ferns are periodically harvested in certain Knysna forests by private companies under contract to the Department of Water Affairs and Forestry. Most of the crop is exported to Europe.

BELOW: *Seven-week's fern and* Blechnum tabulare.

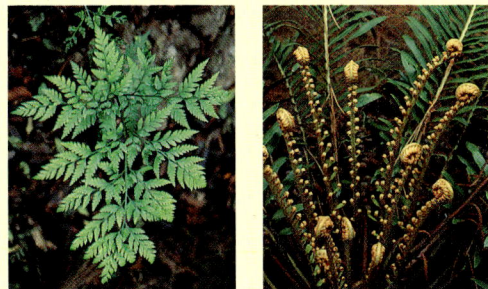

KOUMASHOEK CIRCUIT

A long, strenuous trail with steep climbs through unspoilt, exceptionally beautiful fynbos in the mountains west of the Robinson Pass.

Time: 6 hours from the start to the top of the Pass. It takes another $1/2$ hour to complete the circuit by returning to the start down the Pass.

Distance: 14,7 km and, if you do not have transport waiting, an extra 3 km back to the start.

Exertion: Very high.

Controlling authority: Cape Provincial Administration: Department of Nature and Environmental Conservation - Outeniquas office in George.

Permits: Self-issue at start.

Maps and information: Sketch map on permit; information from controlling authority.

How to get there: Take the turn-off to Oudtshoorn on the N2 at Hartenbos (near Mossel Bay). Drive 35,9 km past the Eight Bells Hotel and Ruitersbos Forest Station to a picnic site on the left of the Robinson Pass. If you wish, leave a second car at the top of the pass, where the trail meets the road, 3 km further on.

Start: A stile next to a green gate opposite the picnic table.

Trail markers: Klipspringer motif.

End: The top of the Robinson Pass or back at the start.

Best times to walk: Clear weather at any time of year.

Precautions: This trail is strenuous; you must take water; be prepared for mist.

Features: Magnificent fynbos and mountain scenery.

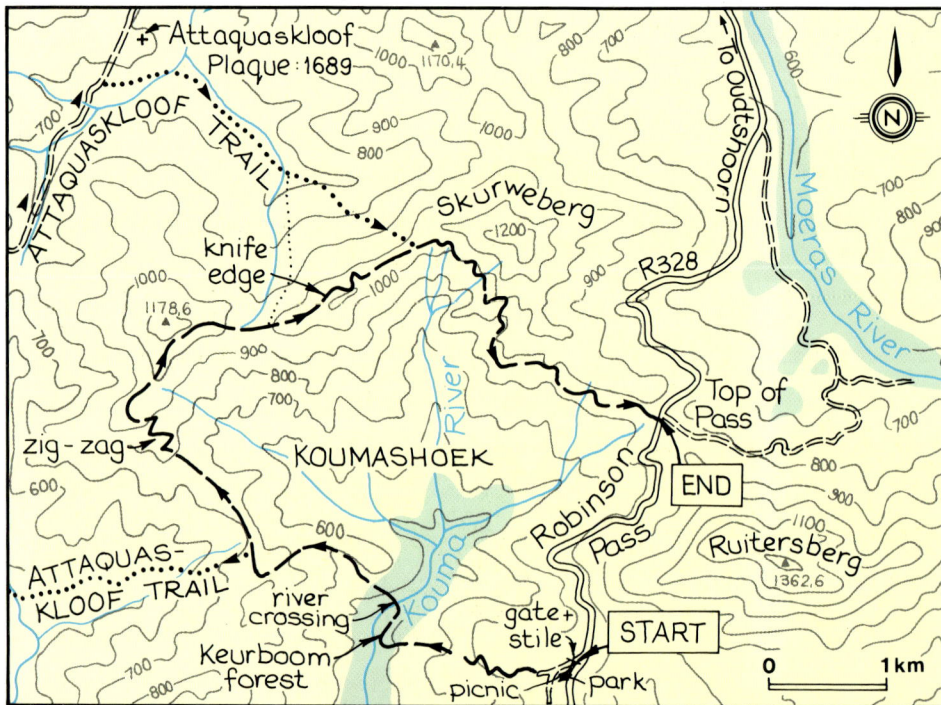

RIGHT: *A rustling next to the path is seldom a snake but more likely a lizard or striped mouse.*

BELOW OPPOSITE: *An outcrop of Table Mountain sandstone stands stark against the muted colours of the fynbos, in an afternoon mist.*

The Koumashoek Circuit is a new one-day walk which takes advantage of the recent establishment of the two-day Attaquaskloof Hiking Trail (*see* page 170) in the mountains on the western side of the Robinson Pass. The first part of the circuit follows the final section of the return leg of the Hiking Trail, and the last part the first section of the Trail, the two being linked by a new path which follows a convenient ridge. This is a strenuous walk, one I rate almost as taxing as the 1 300-m ascent of Cradock's Berg (*see* page 49); in fact, the cumulative height climbed on this circuit is not far short of that. There is some sustained climbing up steep slopes, particularly on the middle part of the route - and no reliable water source on this section, as there are on the outward and return legs. You must, therefore, take sufficient liquid with you. If you do not arrange to have transport waiting at the top of the Robinson Pass, you will have a 3-km walk back along the road to the start, but the going is easy and virtually level all the way.

The scenery along the Koumashoek Circuit is nothing short of sensational. The Koumashoek Valley, which the route encircles, is an unspoilt, virtually untouched part of the Outeniqua Mountains and is very lovely indeed. In addition, from the height you reach on the second half of the circuit you are rewarded with extensive views south to the coast, west to Attaquaskloof and north to the distant line of the Swartberg beyond the foothills of the Outeniquas bordering the Little Karoo. Except for a small patch of Keurboom (*Virgilia divaricata*) surrounding the Kouma River on the outward leg of the circuit, the entire route traverses fynbos. On the open slopes the fynbos is dominated by proteaceous shrubs, but on the steep, wet, south-facing slopes of Skurweberg (the highest peak in this area) crossed by the final leg of the route, Mountain cypress (*Widdringtonia cupressoides*), restios and the large fern *Todea barbara* are the prominent species.

I walked this trail when it had only just been laid out; it was October and the veld was ablaze with colour. A few metres from the stile and gate which mark the start of the walk were flowering plants of *Gladiolus rogersii* var. *vlokii*, one of the exceptionally lovely so-called bluebells, which grows only in this area. Right beside it, *Erica viridiflora* flaunted its deep-green flowers. Down the ridge, stands of a *Leucadendron uliginosum* ssp *uliginosum* were flowering silver-yellow against the green of the surrounding hillsides.

The path zigzags down the steep south slopes of the ridge. A troop of baboons silhouetted on the crest above us watched as we made our way to the trees which line the Kouma River. Keurboom often surround patches of forest in

these mountains, but here they form an almost single-species stand. We crossed the river accompanied by the call of the Piet-my-vrou (Redchested Cuckoo). Because the canopy of the Keurboom is open and it is relatively light in the trees, I was able, for the first time in my life, to see one of these birds whose call is such an integral part of summer in the Cape. The river is the last source of drinking water before the long, sustained climb which follows, and you should fill all water bottles here.

The path clings to the bank of the river for a short distance before climbing the side of a small valley and around its head to a spur; just below this the Attaquaskloof Trail branches to the left. The Koumashoek Circuit path drops slightly to a nek and then begins to climb - at first gently, then increasingly steeply - up the ridge ahead, zigzagging to the top of a rocky knoll from which there are extensive views west to Attaquaskloof and east back into the Koumashoek Valley. The path continues to climb, then swings across the southern slopes of the mountain about 100 m below its peak and drops along the eastern ridge to a nek; from this section there is a panorama of the mountains and coastal flats to the south.

On the nek a path branches to the left; ignore this and start to climb up the rocky ridge ahead. On top, the way leads along a knife-edge through the rocks. There are wonderful views here: to the north of the distant Swartberg range over the subsidiary ranges of the Outeniquas, and south, through the Koumashoek Valley, to the coast. From the knife-edge, the path drops slightly to another small nek, where it meets the Attaquaskloof Trail. Turn right on the Trail, which climbs again up a ridge, swinging away from the northern slopes of the Skurweberg, then zigzags up and over a rocky promontory. From here there is a short, more gentle climb onto the mountain's steep southern slopes. Numerous small streams run down these wet slopes, but water is not always easily accessible.

The last part of the walk is easy going, as the path drops steadily, and in one place steeply, as it crosses the peaty slopes of Skurweberg. The last 2 km or so to the top of the Robinson Pass are virtually on the level. The views from this part of the circuit into the Koumashoek Valley and westwards are exceptionally lovely and a fitting climax to this scenically exciting, if demanding, walk.

From the path on the south slopes of Skurweberg, you can see all of the Koumashoek Valley and beyond, to the Attaquaskloof Mountains.

CHAPTER THREE

GAMKA MOUNTAIN NATURE RESERVE

The Gamka Mountain Nature Reserve was proclaimed in 1974 for the conservation of the Cape mountain zebra. It occupies 9 428 ha and covers the greater part of Gamkaberg, which is just one in a discontinuous line of mountains lying between and parallel to the Swartberg and Outeniqua ranges. There is a large plateau on the mountain top, covered in dry mountain fynbos. This is the preferred habitat of the Cape mountain zebra. Gamkaberg's western boundary is formed by the Gamka River, which flows past Gamkaskloof (Die Hel) in the Swartberg.

Gamkaberg is essentially a Table Mountain sandstone formation, but overlaying the sandstone on the lower slopes and base of the mountain are shales of the Bokkeveld series, which

A Redfaced Mousebird strikes a characteristically upright pose.

form the substrate for a community of plants quite distinct from the fynbos growing further up, and known as 'succulent mountain veld'. Two of the most dominant and prominent species in this plant community are the Spekboom (*Portulacaria afra*) and the Sosatiebos (*Crassula rupestris*). Whereas the top of the mountain normally receives some 500 mm of rainfall, spread throughout the year, the lower slopes are considerably drier, as is evident from their plant cover. High temperatures are common during summer; overnight frost is frequent in winter. On some of the higher shale slopes where the rainfall is sufficient there is a certain amount of Renosterveld, characterized by the Renosterbos (*Elytropappus rhinocerotis*), which gives way to fynbos at the transition from shale to sandstone. The 'succulent Karoo veld' which covers the floor of the Little Karoo extends a short distance into the reserve from its boundary.

Beyond these Bokkeveld shale slopes on the first leg of the Pied Barbet Trail lies the entrance to Tierkloof.

The flat top of the Gamkaberg is cut by several deep kloofs, of which Tierkloof is one. Along the course of its most often dry stream-bed grows riverine vegetation with a surprisingly large variety of small trees as well as the Botterboom (*Tylecodon paniculatus*), instantly recognizable by its pale, fat stems. As Tierkloof opens out, the stream-bed vegetation changes and *Acacia karoo* becomes dominant.

Apart from the mountain zebra, there are grey rhebok, klipspringer, duiker, grysbok and steenbok in the reserve. Leopard and caracal have been sighted very occasionally. You are most likely to hear the baboons before you see them, often on the steep cliff faces above the entrance to Tierkloof. The glory of the reserve's fauna, however, is its bird life, which is prolific, particularly in the areas traversed by the trails. To date, some 110 species of birds have been recorded in the reserve. Apart from the Pied Barbets and Speckled and Redfaced Mousebirds which give two of the trails their names, you can expect to see Karoo Robins, Bokmakieries, Cape Bulbuls, Malachite and Lesser Doublecollared Sunbirds, Southern Boubous and Cardinal Woodpeckers. A resident pair of Black Eagles and two pairs of Booted Eagles currently breed in the reserve.

From the Information Centre, there is a series of very short interleading circuits - the Spekboom, Gwarri and Botterboom walks; these are really just strolls in the adjoining vegetation. The Pied Barbet Trail and its short cut, the Mousebird Trail, run on the shale slopes to the start of Tierkloof and back along the riverbed. The Tierkloof Trail follows the twisting course of the kloof deep into the mountain to an overhang cave and beyond, if you have the energy and time. The major trails are well worth walking and I have described both in this chapter.

PIED BARBET TRAIL

A gentle, short walk through Spekboom veld and along a dry riverbed amongst Acacia karoo *trees where birds are plentiful.*

Time: 1 1/2 - 2 hours.
Distance: 4 km.
Exertion: Very light.
Controlling authority: Cape Provincial Administration: Department of Nature and Environmental Conservation - Gamka Mountain Nature Reserve.
Permits: Self-issue at Information Centre, where you should register.

Maps and information: A sketch map with useful information and an interpretive guide to the trail is available at the Information Centre.
How to get there: From the centre of Oudtshoorn, take the Calitzdorp road and drive 9 km to the Warmbad turn-off on the left. Continue for 18,5 km along this concrete road to the clearly signposted turn-off left to the

Gamka Mountain Nature Reserve. The gate to the reserve is 5,9 km from the turn-off, on a gravel road through a crossroads. Drive 400 m into the reserve and park next to the Information Centre.
Start/end: The Information Centre.
Trail markers: Where necessary, arrows, or signs carrying letters which correlate with those of

the interpretive list on the information sheet.
Best times to walk: Winter and spring for the flowers; any time for the birds; early morning and late evening to see buck and other animals.
Precautions: Avoid walking at midday in summer.
Features: Prolific bird and animal life, fossil traces and arid vegetation.

The Pied Barbet Trail is the longest of the short trails in the Gamka Mountain Nature Reserve - a circuit about 4 km long, with its furthest point at the entrance to Tierkloof. You could complete it in an hour but you would miss the wealth of interest that the trail offers, so it is wiser to allow two. Along the way various points are marked by small boards, each carrying a letter; these letters correspond with a short interpretive list on the self-issue permit which you collect at the Information Centre before setting out. A short cut across the valley between the outward and return legs of the trail provides a circuit called the Mousebird Trail which reduces walking time by about 30 minutes.

The immediate impression given by this valley is of aridity - the annual average rainfall here is only 300 mm. When you begin to walk through it, the richness of the bird life in the *Acacia karoo* thickets which grow in the valley bottom makes an equally strong impression. The birds advertise their presence by their song. The most obvious species are Karoo Robins and Fiscal Flycatchers, but you can also see Mousebirds (Speckled, Redfaced and Whitebacked), Pied Barbets and many other species, some of which I mentioned in the introduction to this chapter. You are also likely to catch a glimpse of a common duiker as it disappears into the bush when disturbed by your approach.

The outward leg of the trail soon leaves the acacias along the dry river bed and climbs partway up the north-facing shale slopes. These slopes support a very different plant life, dominated by succulents with Spekboom (*Portulacaria afra*)

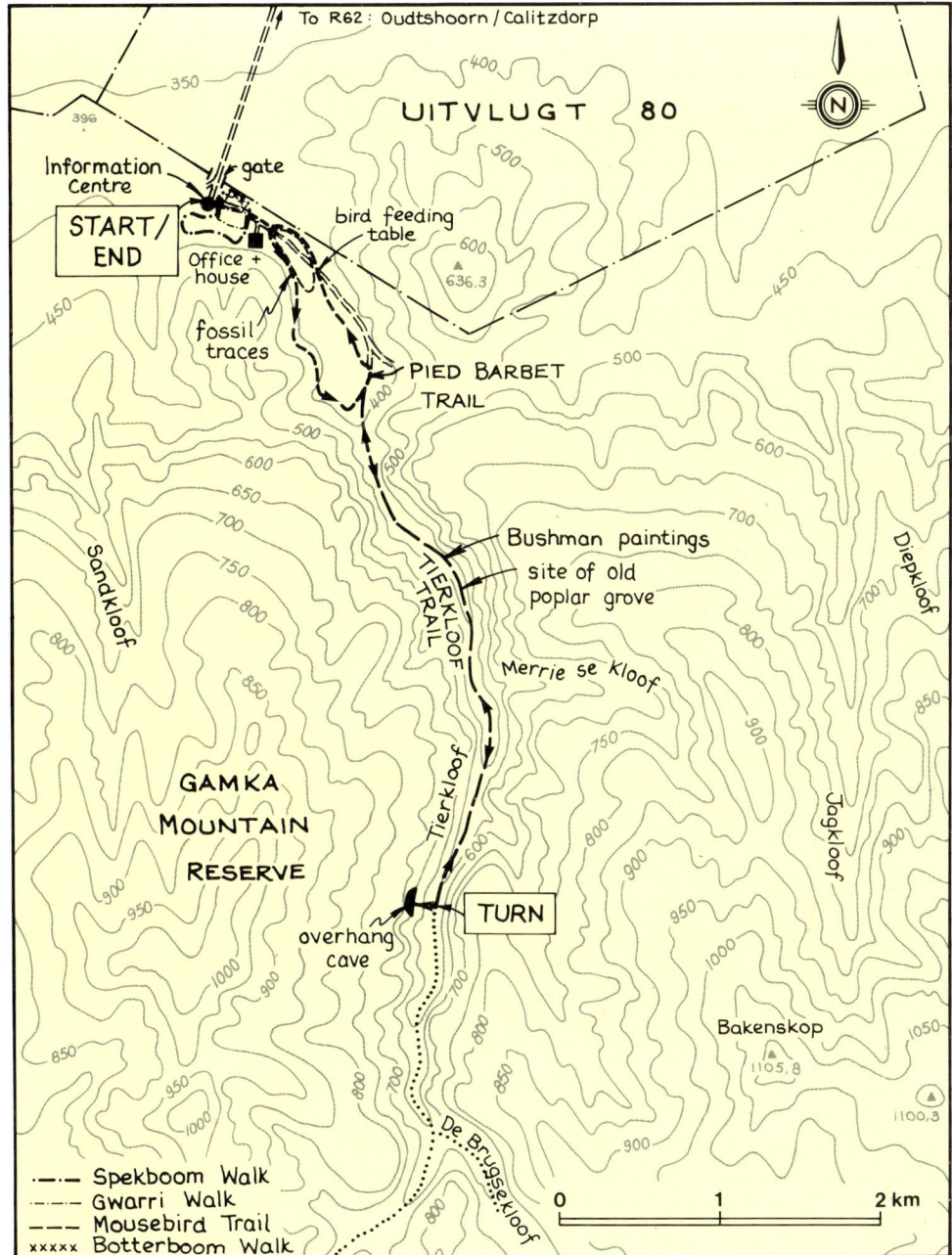

To R62: Oudtshoorn/Calitzdorp

UITVLUGT 80

Information Centre

gate

START/ END

bird feeding table

Office + house

fossil traces

PIED BARBET TRAIL

Sandkloof

Bushman paintings
site of old poplar grove

TIERKLOOF TRAIL

Merrie se kloof

Diepkloof

GAMKA MOUNTAIN RESERVE

Tierkloof

Jagkloof

TURN

overhang cave

Bakenskop
1105,8

1100,3

De Brugsekloof

–··– Spekboom Walk
–·– Gwarri Walk
––– Mousebird Trail
xxxxx Botterboom Walk

0   1   2 km

ABOVE LEFT: *Holes in the trunks of Acacia karoo trees are the preferred nest sites of local Pied Barbets. Several clutches of eggs may be laid in one season.*

LEFT: *Traces of fossils, such as these shells of bivalves, show clearly in the rocks along the first leg of the Pied Barbet Trail.*

and Sosatiebos (*Crassula rupestris*) common. As you climb, keep a look-out for a band of darker-looking rock across the path (at point B). In this rock are clear fossil traces - the impressions of shells, bivalves, and stems of small, palm-like plants. The remains of the organisms which gave rise to these fossils were trapped in the sediment when this area was under water 150 million years ago. This sediment formed the Bokkeveld shales, the rocks which make up these lower slopes. Higher up are weathered cliffs of Table Mountain sandstone. On these near-vertical slopes, klip-springer can often be seen moving with their characteristic easy grace.

The trail drops back to the dry river course near the entrance to Tierkloof, where it meets a track. To the right is the Tierkloof trail; keep left here, and a short way down the track, turn left onto the path back. The return leg passes through *Acacia karoo* thickets and gives you the opportunity to study and enjoy the birds. At point G, look out for the bird feeding-table just off the path, where you can relax on the bench provided and, if you have brought some suitable titbits, entice birds to feed. If you walk this trail in late winter or spring after rain, you are likely to find tiny daisies, nemesias, diascias and other flowers providing bright points of colour among the white stones and the bleached thorns of fallen acacia branches.

*A Botterboom (*Tylecodon paniculatus*) and an* Acacia karoo *tree typify the return leg of the Pied Barbet Trail.*

MIMETES CHRYSANTHUS

Since the earliest days of European exploration of the Cape, the extraordinary diversity of the plants in the fynbos has fascinated and delighted professional botanists and laymen alike. Despite centuries of intense study, new species of plants are still being discovered in this botanical treasure-house. By 1987, however, no-one would have suspected that there was an as yet undiscovered species of *Mimetes*, a genus of the Proteaceae which has been exhaustively researched and which contains some of the most beautiful and showy plants in the fynbos.

Yet, on 7 September of that year, Willie Julies, a game guard patrolling on foot in the Gamka Mountain Nature Reserve, made a note of a shrub which was unfamiliar to him. The next day the officer in charge of the reserve, Rory Allardice, collected a small sample for identification. Jan Vlok, then at the Saasveld herbarium, sent it to John Rourke at the Compton Herbarium at Kirstenbosch, who immediately confirmed that the plant was a new and unique species of *Mimetes*. Not only is this plant new to science, it is also an exceptionally lovely species, which promises to be easy to propagate and cultivate.

The discovery of *Mimetes chrysanthus* was one of the most exciting botanical events of the century.

Mimetes chrysanthus *flowers in the heat of March.*

TIERKLOOF TRAIL

A fairly lengthy walk, on the level, through riverine vegetation bordering a dry riverbed at the base of the rugged sandstone cliffs of Tierkloof; it returns on the same route.

Time: 5 - 5 1/2 hours, plus 2 hours for viewing.
Distance: 14-15 km.
Exertion: Light.
Controlling authority: Cape Provincial Administration: Department of Nature and Environmental Conservation - Gamka Mountain Nature Reserve.
Permits: Self-issue at the Information Centre; register here.

Maps and information: No other map available; information from the office at the reserve.
How to get there: From the centre of Oudtshoorn, drive 9 km on the Calitzdorp road to the turn-off to Warmbad on the left. Continue for 18,5 km along this concrete road to the signposted turn-off left to the Gamka Mountain Nature Reserve.

The gate is 5,9 km from the turn-off, on a gravel road through a crossroads. Park next to the Information Centre 400 m beyond the gate.
Start/end: The Information Centre.
Trail markers: None in Tierkloof; keep to the path along the riverbed.
Best times to walk: Any season, but the kloof can be hot at mid-

day in summer. The cliffs are at their most beautiful early and late in the day.
Precautions: You must take water; the going is rough along the river bed, and you will need to wear suitable shoes or hiking boots.
Features: Dramatic kloof scenery, Bushman paintings, prolific bird life, buck and other animals.

'Tier' or 'tijger' (meaning 'tiger') was the name given by the early Dutch farmers to the leopard. These animals must once have been more numerous and obvious here for this beautiful kloof to have taken their name. Leopard are only very occasionally seen in the Cape mountains these days, although the ranger in charge of the Gamka Mountain Nature Reserve, Rory Allardice, has seen one in the reserve (not in this kloof); spoor are not uncommon.

Tierkloof is essentially the result of ancient erosion by water which carved its twisting course deep into Gamka Mountain. It is clear that the climate then was very different from today's: the stones which line the dry river bed in the kloof are angular - not rounded pebbles, which is evidence that for a very long time little water has flowed down the kloof. Tierkloof must have been somewhat wetter earlier this century, however, because the broad path which leads up the first roughly 3 km of the kloof from the turning point of the Pied Barbet Trail was cut by farmers in the neighbourhood in order to reach a permanent spring. A grove of poplars once grew here (they have been cut down by the conservation authorities) and every ten days or so the farmers' families would gather there for a communal washday.

The start of the Tierkloof Trail (*see* map, page 49) can be reached from either the outward or return legs of the Pied Barbet Trail. At a deliberate, undistracted pace, this takes 30-40 minutes' walking. In summer this first section can be hot and it is best tackled early in the day. It is much cooler in the kloof, more especially since the riverine scrub screens

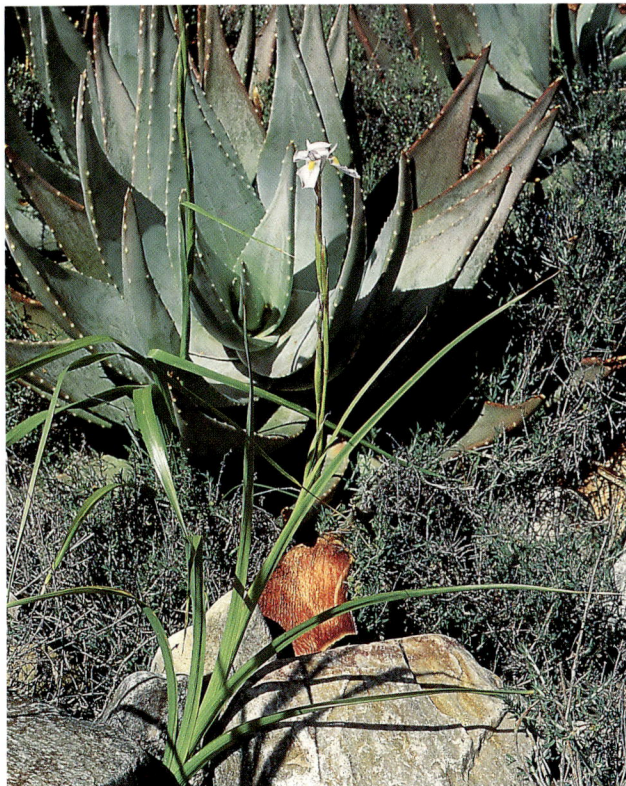

Delicate flowers on the slender stems of the Bloutulp (Moraea polystachya) contrast with the fleshy leaves of Aloe comptonii.

the sun most of the way up.

One of the loveliest features of Tierkloof is the sound of birdsong echoing off the steep, orange sandstone cliffs which enclose it. The clear, characteristic melodies of the Southern Boubous and the Bokmakieries calling to other birds (or echoes!) accompany you up the kloof. There are many other birds to be seen, including Rock Martins wheeling next to the cliffs. On an inaccessible ledge high up on a west-facing cliff just before the spot where the poplar grove once grew is the nest of a pair of Black Eagles; the site is easy to spot by the white streaks of droppings on the rocks just below the nest. The eagles themselves can often be seen riding the thermals above the cliffs or perched on the rocks near the nest.

When I walked the trail for the first time, there were baboons on the top of the cliffs shouting across to another troop on the other side. This was during a period of severe drought which had apparently not left these adaptable animals unscathed. The aloes (*Aloe comptonii*) which grow on the cliff faces should have been flowering, but the buds had been broken off many of them and eaten by the baboons. Even leaves had been torn off and bitten into. Aloe leaves are particularly bitter and unpalatable, and the baboons must have been desperate to resort to this fare. Lower down the cliffside was a group of three klipspringers looking sleek and healthy despite the condition of the veld.

It is about 40 minutes' walk (3 km) from the entrance to Tierkloof to the site of the old spring, which is marked by the trunks of the felled poplars. Some 50 m before this spot the path runs next to a stone face. Under a small overhang are some Bushman paintings - figures and animals in monochrome orange. If you find these, do not wet them to bring out the colour (they are rather faint) or tamper with them in any other way: simply wonder at this earliest evidence of human occupation of the kloof.

Prominent among the riverine scrub on this section of the trail are the fat succulent stems carrying bright green fleshy leaves of the Botterboom (*Tylecodon paniculatus*) in amongst the stones alongside the trail. There are a surprising number of tree species in the kloof including the Wild olive (*Olea europaea* ssp. *africana*), Cabbage tree (*Cussonia spicata*), Sagewood (*Buddleja salviifolia*), Witolienhout (*B. salignum*), Star apple (*Diospyros lycioides*), Karee (*Rhus undulata*) and trees which also grow in the coastal scrub forests to the south - Wild peach (*Kiggelaria africana*) and Kershout (*Pterocelastrus tricuspidatus*). A feature of the lower-growing vegetation is the large number of pelargonium species (*Pelargonium*

heracleifolium, P. fruticosum, P. citronellum, P. glutinosum, P. exstipulatum and others). Most of these have aromatic leaves which, when crushed, produce scents which some people find attractive.

From the site of the old poplar grove the path continues up the kloof, often in a tunnel of dense vegetation. At one point the path emerges on a sandy area below a huge, sheer rock-face - an amphitheatre facing east - before plunging into the scrub again. A further hour's walk (approximately 3 km), brings you to a split in the path. To the left it crosses the dry riverbed. To the right is a short, steep climb on loose stones up to an overhang cave which provides an ideal resting place and a suitable turning point. The Reserve's management plans to instal some rudimentary bunks and a water and wood supply here, so that hikers can spend the night before returning down the kloof.

ABOVE: *In spring,* Oxalis obtusa *flowers below the acacias.*
OPPOSITE LEFT: *A short way into Tierkloof these massive rock bastions frame the distant ridge of Gamkaberg.*

If you wish, you can continue further up Tierkloof. About another 3 km further on ($^3/_4$-1 hour's walk) another kloof - De Brugsekloof - joins Tierkloof from the east. Beyond this, Tierkloof opens out into a sandy area where four kloofs meet. Here is the margin of the arid fynbos; Waboom (*Protea nitida*) and *Leucadendron salignum* are prominent amongst restios, grasses and some ericas.

It takes 2-3 hours to walk at a steady pace from the Information Centre to the overhang cave, and about 2 hours back, but I would recommend that you allow at least another 2 hours to enjoy the environment, which makes this outing a full day's walk.

CHAPTER FOUR

GEORGE

Besides being the largest town on the Garden Route, with a sizable resident population and a small industrial area, George is an important transport centre. It has an airport served by regular flights by SAA and other airlines and is both the meeting point of the major roads to the southern Cape coast from the north and west and the spot at which the railway line from Cape Town branches to Knysna and Oudtshoorn.

Under the administration of the Dutch East India Company, the area where George now stands - and that to the east - was administered by the landdros of Swellendam. In the late 18th century the area became increasingly settled, mainly by people involved in the exploitation of the forests to supply the demand for timber in Cape Town. After the second British occupation of the Cape the new governor, the Earl of Caledon, recommended that a new magisterial district be created in Outeniqualand. This was proclaimed in 1811 and the first magistrate, Adrianus van Kervel, set out the new town of George, named after the reigning king of England, George III.

In the early days, travel to George from the west was relatively easy, but travel further north or east was a nightmare. The coastal plateau on which the town stands is backed by the high Outeniqua Mountains, which presented a formidable barrier. To the east the plateau is deeply scored by many ravines - the steep-sided courses cut by several short rivers which rise in the Outeniquas and run directly down to the Indian Ocean. Along the coast itself is a succession of sandy vleis. To travel east, ox-wagons had to cross the kloofs, a particularly hazardous undertaking which cost

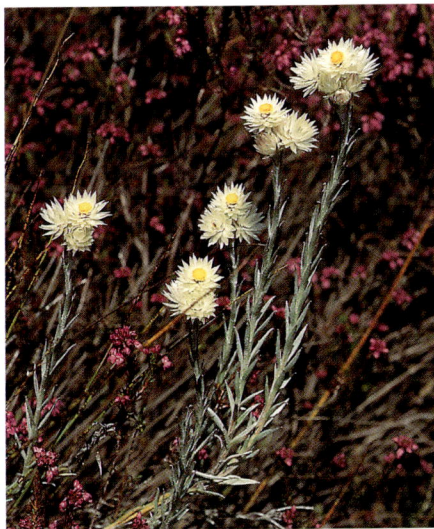

From the nek where the paths to Cradock Peak and George Peak part, the Outeniqua Mountains extend into the distance.

An Everlasting and an Erica cubica *flower next to the path on Cradock Pass.*

the lives of several drivers and spans of oxen. It required the efforts of a span of 32 oxen, for example, to drag a wagon through the kloof of the Kaaimans River, which has precipitous banks and periodical strong flow.

The newly established town had to wait some 50 years before Thomas Bain was given the job of planning a proper road between it and Knysna. The result, the Passes Road, is still very much in use today. Along this road, a few kilometres from George, is Saasveld, home of the Forestry Training College. Saasveld is on the edge of one of the remaining substantial areas of natural forest, the Groeneweide Forest, in which there is a network of lovely trails described here. The Training College is also the start of a very long walk through the Groeneweide Forest, past Groenkop to the top of Melville Peak. This Melville Peak Mountain Trail, which is 26 km long (there and back) and takes 11 hours, is only for the fit.

The first route north over the Outeniqua Mountains from George itself was the Cradock Pass, laid out and constructed by Van Kervel soon after the establishment of the town. The Montagu Pass was built some 30 years later and the Outeniqua Pass was completed in 1951. At first, Italian prisoners of war provided the labour for its construction; they were replaced by South African labour at the end of the war.

It is the very ruggedness of the terrain in the mountains behind George, once such an obstacle to travel to the north, that provides the scenic splendour of this area. The routes built to overcome the mountainous barrier now give access to some of the finest walks around George - the old Cradock Pass itself, the new walk between the Montagu and Outeniqua passes, and the walk along the Doring River Valley, which is reached from the northern side of the Outeniqua Pass. All of these are described in this chapter. The Doring

River Trail follows the first part of a new two-day hiking trail (*see* page 170) which links the Outeniqua and Robinson passes through the Doring River Wilderness Area. This trail also joins up with the new Attaquaskloof Hiking Trail (again, *see* page 170).

The walk to the peak of Cradock's Berg (also detailed in this chapter) takes you to the highest point in this part of the Outeniquas, a lofty 1 579 m above sea level. The first leg of the renowned Outeniqua Hiking Trail climbs the south slopes of these mountains from the Witfontein Forest Station to the Tierkop hut behind Saasveld. On the Montagu Pass is the very short (1 km), newly laid-out Keur River Bridge Nature Trail.

Because of their acid soil and the high rainfall they receive, the southern slopes of the Outeniqua Mountains behind George are covered with wet fynbos, with patches of natural forest in the kloofs. This vegetation contains a wealth of beautiful plants, including many showy ericas, proteas, pincushions (*Leucospermum* spp.), leucadendrons, legumes and everlastings. The lower slopes are covered with the pine plantations of the Witfontein State Forest. It was at Witfontein that the first nursery in the Outeniqua area for the propagation of exotic trees was established. Since 1896 this nursery, which is soon to be closed, has supplied saplings to the plantations which have taken the place of the indigenous forests as the source of most timber. The northern side of this mountain range is drier and is covered with mesic (moist) fynbos.

Between George and the sea, past the industrial area, lies the town of Pacaltsdorp. In 1813, two years after the establishment of George, the London Missionary Society founded a mission station here for the Khoi-khoi who had settled in the area. The Reverend Charles Pacalt was the station's first missionary. Meetings were held under a tree which still grows next to a recently built information centre. From Pacaltsdorp there is a 5-km (3-hour) walk to the mouth of the Skaapkop River. From the road past Pacaltsdorp there is a turn-off to the Gwaing River mouth, from where there is a 3-km walk upriver and a 1-km walk to a viewpoint. The coastal plateau south of George has generally been taken over by agriculture, but there are several short walks which can be made from various points on the coast:

* from Herold's Bay there are two short (2-km) walks to viewpoints at Voëlklip and Scotts Bank respectively;

* from Rooikransies there is a walk to Ghwanobaai (4 km);

* from Victoria Bay you can walk to the mouth of the Kaaimans River (3 km along the railway line).

A feature of the weather in George is its changeability and unpredictability. Locals tend to scoff at Weather Bureau forecasts which, in my own experience, can be totally wrong for days on end! Therefore, when walking on the mountains, particularly on the higher routes, be prepared for fairly dramatic changes in the weather, and take the necessary precautions before setting out.

Chacma baboons are frequently encountered in the mountains - often heard before they are seen. A troop is led by a dominant male, portrayed here.

CRADOCK'S BERG AND GEORGE PEAK TRAIL

The views from many points on this long, steep and strenuous walk up Cradock's Berg and/or George Peak and back have to be seen to be believed.

Time: Cradock Peak 7 $^1/_2$-8 hrs; George Peak 6 $^1/_2$ hours; both peaks 8 $^1/_2$-9 hours.

Distance: Cradock Peak 19 km; George Peak 17,2 km; both peaks 21,1 km.

Exertion: Very high.

Controlling authority: Cape Provincial Administration: Department of Nature and Environmental Conservation - Outeniquas office in George.

Permits: Self-issue permit and register at start.

Maps and information: Sketch map on reverse of permit; information at CPA office.

How to get there: From its intersection with York Street in George, drive 3,7 km west along C.J. Langenhoven Road in the direction of Oudtshoorn. Turn right to the Witfontein State Forest Station; 200 m on, turn right and park.

Start: Next to the register at the car park.

Trail markers: Yellow wedges marked on rocks and, in the plantation, on tree trunks.

Best times to walk: Clear weather in any season.

Precautions: Warm and windproof clothing essential; water available at one place only; parts of the path are slippery.

Features: Spectacular scenery and wet mountain fynbos.

The walk from Witfontein to Cradock Peak and George Peak is not a stroll in anybody's terms; from the start you climb a total of 1 330 m to Cradock Peak - a considerable height. Once you reach the slopes of George Peak below the railway line, you must be prepared for a stiff climb for most of the way. The reward for all the exertion is the spectacular view once you reach the nek on the ridge between the peaks, and again from the beacon on Cradock Peak. At 1 579 m Cradock Peak is the highest in this area and from the beacon on the summit there are unsurpassed vistas in all directions. The outlook from George Peak, which at 1 337 m is scarcely higher than the nek, is not as extensive but is nonetheless magnificent. Because the return route is the same as the outward, you can turn back at any stage if time, energy or the weather becomes limiting.

The first part of the route from the parking area - through the plantations of the Witfontein State Forest, across two streams and up onto the south slopes of George Peak - is identical to that of the walk up Cradock Pass (*see* page 60) and takes one hour. The point where the route to Cradock and George peaks leaves the jeep track and heads up the

ABOVE: Mimetes splendidus *flowers in mid-winter.*

slope is well signposted. A short climb brings you to a point where another jeep track comes to a dead end. From here there is another climb to the railway line. In spring the veld here is alive with colour, the intense blue of *Psoralea sordida* contrasting with the yellows of a variety of daisies.

A sign points the way east along the railway, and some 30-40 m further on another sign directs you up the slope. The path zigzags up a steep south-facing incline covered with dense fynbos growing on a moisture-retentive, peaty soil which is noticeably springy to walk on. Below the path there are two shrubs of *Mimetes splendidus*, the only silver mimetes species on the Langeberge/Outeniquas range. If you spot these treasures, never numerous in any one locality, enjoy them from the path, as any trampling of the soil around the plants destroys their delicate surface roots, and they die. Past a small rocky outcrop, the path continues to climb. Further up, where it swings left on the final zag to the crest of the ridge are some George (or Knysna) lilies (*Cyrtanthus elatus*), but these are unlikely to flower until the March following a veld fire.

The path swings right onto a rocky outcrop on the ridge, from which there are views of the Outeniqua Pass snaking its way up the opposite mountain slope. From this point the route essentially follows the top of the ridge in a series of three steep climbs broken by two short stretches on the level. The vegetation here is less lush than on the southern slopes below. On the second level stretch of path there is a place where you can drink, signposted `water'. Growing nearby are five bushes of a small proteaceous species, *Spatalla barbigera*, which is a rare plant in this area. The third steep climb brings you onto a nek where a sign marks the point where the paths to George Peak and Cradock Peak diverge. The climb to this point should have taken you about $2^1/_2$ hours. The views west from the signboard are splendid, but nothing prepares you for the wonderful vista east along the

Outeniqua Mountains that can be had by walking a few steps over the rise.

It is an easy 1-km (20-minute) walk from here to George Peak. At first the path drops to a lower nek, then it climbs over a low knoll before reaching the short final pull to the beacon. A radio mast has been built on the peak next to the end of the old path (now closed) coming in from the west, up the steep south slopes of George Peak. The town of George is laid out below, and there are distant views of the coast and coastal plateau from beyond Mossel Bay in the west, past the Lakes and Goukamma to the Knysna coast in the east.

It is a more difficult climb from the nek to Cradock Peak, a leg that takes about 1 hour. The path climbs gently up the ridge at first, but then steeply to a small peak at a height of 1 456 m. From here it drops slightly, then climbs abruptly up some knolls to the foot of the rocky ridge which marks the top of Cradock's Berg. At this point, keep to the top of the rocks (the way is clearly marked) and avoid a false path along the north side of the rocks above a long, sheer drop. A bit of easy rock scrambling is required in order to reach the

path leading to the beacon. On the summit are two radio masts and some solar-powered equipment.

From the top of Cradock's Berg, the views are immense; you can see all the features which make up the Garden Route landscape, and the environment for all the other walks in this book. You can also see the enormous changes made by man to this region, side by side with areas as yet largely untouched. Thanks to gravity, the walk back down. passes more quickly than the walk up and you can take time to enjoy the variety of views along the path back to the nek. From there it is a knee-straining $1\frac{1}{2}$-hour walk down to the jeep track and another hour back to the start.

BELOW: *An Outeniqua's endemic,* Mimetes pauci-florus, *is relatively common on the high ridges of Cradock's Berg. It flowers in spring.*

CRADOCK PASS TRAIL

A strenuous hike from Witfontein onto the slopes of George Peak, up and over the historic Cradock Pass to the north side of the Montagu Pass.

Time: 5 hours.

Distance: 12,4 km.

Exertion: High.

Controlling authority: Cape Provincial Administration: Department of Nature and Environmental Conservation - Outeniquas office in George.

Permits: Self-issue at start.

Maps and information: Sketch map on permit; information from controlling authority.

How to get there: From its intersection with York Street in George, drive 3,7 km west along C.J. Langenhoven Road towards Oudtshoorn. Turn right to the Witfontein State Forest; 200 m on, turn right and park.

Start: Next to the register.

Trail marker: Yellow ox-wagon motif.

End: On the north side of the Montagu Pass, 1 km from the top, marked by two prominent green CPA Nature Conservation signboards; you will need transport waiting here. Alternatively, it is 10,9 km (3 hours' walk) from here down the Montagu Pass back to the start.

Best times to walk: The fynbos is most colourful in winter, spring and early summer.

Precautions: Take water. Watch out for cloud high up the pass.

Features: Historical interest, fynbos, and extensive views of the mountains and passes behind George.

The first landdros of George, Adrianus van Kervel, persuaded the governor of the Cape Colony at that time, Sir John Cradock, to make available funds for a new and direct route over the mountains to link George to the Little Karoo and Oudtshoorn. In 1812, a pass was constructed through Cradock Kloof, at a cost of 5 000 rix-dollars, in a mere two months. The Cradock Pass was unpopular from the start, and when you walk this route, you will understand why it sometimes took three days for an ox-wagon to cross the mountains using the pass. Nevertheless, the pass remained the only route from George to the interior until 1847, when the Montagu Pass over the Outeniquas was completed; it is still very much in use today. The railway line linking George and Oudtshoorn, which was built between 1908 and 1913, crosses the mountain over the same nek as the Montagu Pass, but follows a more tortuous route that provides the necessary gentle gradients.

The Post Office chose to revert to Cradock Pass for the routing of a telephone line which, admittedly, does blot the kloof landscape somewhat. However, neither this nor other evidence of man-made things, such as the pylons for a major electricity power line, can detract from the sheer magnificence of the scenery on the walk over Cradock Pass. In addition, the route traverses some prime wet fynbos displaying an abundance of beautiful plants.

This is a fairly strenuous walk: the total climb of some 800 m includes some steep hauls. Those who anticipate having plenty of energy left after climbing Cradock Pass can walk back to the start via the Montagu Pass, a distance of almost 11 km, virtually all downhill. Those who do not

should arrange to have transport waiting at the trail end.

The initial part of the walk (*see* map, page 59) is through pine plantations on forestry tracks. The Outeniqua Hiking Trail and the route up Cradock's Berg and George Peak share some of the same route. At a well-signposted T-junction, the Outeniqua Trail turns right to Tierkop. You must turn left here.

A short way beyond this junction, over a rise, the path leaves the forestry track and drops steeply to a stream. Here, beneath a grove of Keurboom (*Virgilia divaricata*) and Witels (*Platylophus trifoliatus*) intermingled with Tree ferns (*Cyathea capensis*), there is permanent running water. On the opposite bank the path keeps to the trees along the course of the stream for a bit. Then it crosses a side-stream, clears the trees on the other side and zigzags up through open fynbos under power lines, eventually to meet a forestry track. It takes about an hour to reach this point from the start.

At this junction, the path to Cradock's Berg and George Peak branches off, while the Cradock Pass route turns left down the forestry track. Both directions are clearly signposted. In the veld next to the track are the first of many examples encountered on the walk of *Mimetes pauciflorus*, a particularly beautiful member of the Proteaceae which flowers in September and is endemic to the fynbos of the wet southern slopes of the Outeniqua Mountains. The forestry track swings round the slope and soon meets another track coming in from the right. Here you must keep left along the

The grooves worn by the wheels of ox-wagons as they braked down the steep ridge on the north side of Cradock Pass.

power lines and head towards the Ou Tolhuis. The original users of the Montagu Pass had to pay $^{3}/_{4}$ of a penny per wheel for a cart with brakes and three pence per wheel for one without; a penny was charged for each animal drawing a cart. Some way down the track, where King proteas (*Protea cynaroides*) flower deep red in the veld, a signpost `Cradock Pass' shows the way to a path which winds down the slope to the right. Eventually this falls fairly steeply into Tierkloof. There is permanent running water here, too - the last reliable supply on the route.

Across the stream in Tierkloof, the path follows the course of the telephone line up a spur and is joined from the left by a path from the Montagu Pass. You are now on the old Cradock Pass; in certain places the original dry-stone construction is discernible through encroaching vegetation. More easily visible is the first of a series of large stone cairns, demarcating the pass, which were built for the centenary of the Great Trek in 1938.

It is a steady climb all the way up the ridge along the pass, which is more or less dogged by the telephone line. The gradient levels out for the stretch before the railway line. From this point, however, you are faced with a sustained, steep and, in wet weather, slippery climb up Cradock Kloof to the nek which marks the top of the pass at a height of 982 m. As compensation for the exertion, there are increasingly grand views of the mountains. Along one section of the path you can see the Montagu Pass, the Outeniqua Pass and the railway line all at the same time. In spring, the veld along the south side of the pass is lit up by the brilliant-yellow flowers of *Cyclopia subternata*, the source of bush tea (also known as *gewone bossiestee* or *bergtee*).

The Cradock Pass Trail used to share the pass with the first leg of the Outeniqua Trail but, because this was considered too strenuous a start, the hiking trail has been rerouted. (Don't let the old white shoeprint markers confuse you.) Further proof of this is the signboard just before the nek showing a path which was the old Outeniqua Hiking Trail route to Tierkloof. From here there is a wonderful panorama extending from the Outeniqua Mountains in the east, to the north, where farms lie in the valley below.

If anything, the incline of the north side of the pass is steeper than the slope you have just climbed. That ox-wagons found this a difficult section is recorded by the grooves, clearly visible in the rocks, caused by the sliding of braked wagon wheels. The gradient eases as the pass rounds the mountain and follows the slope of a low ridge to the gravel road that leads from the top of the Montagu Pass down to Herold. You deserve to feel proud of yourself when you reach this point after five hours of determined walking!

There is a constantly changing view of Cradock's Berg from the lower section of Cradock Pass.

PASS-TO-PASS TRAIL

A short route, with steep climbs, which links the Montagu and Outeniqua passes and provides spectacular views of the mountains and the town of George.

Time: 3 hours.

Distance: 7,3 km, including a 2,6-km detour to Losberg.

Exertion: Moderate.

Controlling authority: Cape Provincial Administration: Department of Nature and Environmental Conservation - Outeniquas office in George.

Permits: Self-issue at start.

Maps and information: Sketch map on reverse of permit; information from George office of the controlling authority.

How to get there: From its intersection with York Street in George, take C.J. Langenhoven Road and drive 7,1 km in the direction of Oudtshoorn to the signposted turn-off to the Montagu Pass; drive 7,5 km to the top of the Montagu Pass.

Start: The old quarry on the west side of the top of Montagu Pass.

Trail markers: George lily motif.

End: The top of the Outeniqua Pass, 14,9 km from York Street, George; you will need transport waiting.

Best times to walk: Beautiful in any season, but the fynbos is alive with colour in spring and early summer.

Precautions: Parts of the trail are steep, and slippery when wet.

Features: Rich fynbos, extensive mountain scenery and views of George.

The male Orangebreasted Sunbird (shown here) is aggresive towards other males; the species is a fynbos endemic.

There is a satisfying sense of symmetry about this newly laid-out short trail which links the Montagu and Outeniqua passes. The path runs on the south slopes of the high peaks which lie between the passes (*see* map, page 59). From the top of the Montagu Pass the path drops into a valley where a patch of forest surrounds a stream, then rises up the other side to the ridge which runs north-south and links Losberg and a subsidiary peaklet to the main chain of mountains. On the other side of the ridge the process is repeated: the vegetation changes in an identical pattern as you descend into a valley, with its own tract of forest, and climb the other side to the top of the Outeniqua Pass.

Unless you plan to turn around at the end and walk back to the start, which is quite feasible, you will need to have transport waiting. The trail can be walked in either direction, but I walked it from east to west and will describe it that way. The authorities plan to rehabilitate the quarry at the start and put up some information boards there.

The path begins by running past the southern edge of the quarry over a low rise beyond which Losberg comes into view. From the crest, the path descends, at first gently and then increasingly steeply, passing through a stand of the silver-leaved *L. uliginosum* subsp. *uliginosum*, an elegant plant which is particularly beautiful when it flowers in October. On the northern slopes of the Outeniqua Mountains are found populations of the other subspecies (*L. uliginosum* subsp. *glabratum*), which lacks the hairs on the leaves which give the typical subspecies its silver appearance. These two subspecies illustrate how separate populations of plants with a common ancestor can develop, through long-term environmental change, into distinct subspecies and even species. In the rocky areas on the ridge there are examples of the low, compact *Erica seriphiifolia*, bearing bright pink flowers which contrast strikingly with the silver-yellows of the surrounding leucadendrons.

At the base of the slope is a patch of natural forest, characteristically fringed with Keurboom (*Virgilia divaricata*) alongside which the path swings right into very tall vegetation (*Leucadendron eucalyptifolium* and *Penaea cneorum*) on the banks of a stream. The path drops very steeply down the peaty bank to this beautiful little watercourse, which is lined with Tree ferns (*Cyathea capensis*). After climbing a spur, the path reaches the same height as the start, then, keeping to the contour, swings left along the ridge between Losberg and the slopes above. On the level crest of the ridge you will come to a branch in the path. The left-hand fork leads further along the ridge, then up the rocky slopes of a knoll, down over a nek and up onto Losberg. This 1,3-km detour is worth the effort: from the knoll there are views north of the mountains; from Losberg, the scene, to the south, is of George. When this path comes to a dead end you must return to the branch.

The main path immediately begins a steep descent towards a second patch of natural forest, finally zigzagging towards the stream in the bottom of the valley. It was on this section that I heard the calls of Victorin's Warblers and spotted one of these elusive birds. Victorin's Warbler is a fynbos endemic which inhabits dense stream-side vegetation. In the breeding season (early summer) the birds will occasionally emerge for a song and this is the best time to see them.

A ladder is provided for the final descent onto the rocks next to the stream. The watercourse is flanked by a narrow band of forest with a wide fringe of Keurboom, which becomes evident as you start the stiff climb up the other side. No concession has been made for the initial steepness, and the path simply runs straight up the slope. The gradient eases when the path begins to run diagonally up the side of the ridge. Once over the ridge, the path drops a little and makes a broad swing over two small streams hidden beneath the peaty ground. You reach the fenced-off area around a squat construction carrying TV antennae after a final, short zigzag climb. On this last section are some handsome examples of the King protea (*Protea cynaroides*) which flowers in late spring. A concrete road leads from here to the top of the Outeniqua Pass.

ABOVE: *Stormclouds gather on the peaks between the Outeniqua and Montagu passes.*

DORING RIVER TRAIL

An easy walk, ideal for a family outing, through the valley of the Doring River, a Wilderness Area of unspoilt fynbos.

Time: 3 1/2-4 hours.

Distance: 15 km return.

Exertion: Light.

Controlling authority: Cape Provincial Administration: Department of Nature and Environmental Conservation.

Permits: From the Outeniquas office in George of the controlling authority.

Maps and information: From the Outeniquas office in George of the controlling authority.

How to get there: From its intersection with York Street in George, drive the 18,3 km along C.J. Langenhoven Road (or Davidson Road) and over the Outeniqua Pass to the turn-off left to Waboomskraal. Drive 7,7 km along the tarred road in Waboomskraal to a gravel road turn-off on the left (heading west). This gravel road splits 3,3 km further on; take the right-hand fork over the dam wall and park 800 m down the road next to the fence.

Start: The track alongside the fence south-east of the parking place.

Trail markers: Baboon motif.

End: Back at the parking place.

Best times to walk: Winter, spring and early summer for the flowers; mid-summer to autumn for a swim in the river.

Precautions: None.

Features: Rich, beautiful and unique fynbos, mountain scenery, the river and a rock pool for a swim.

Note: A new path is being cut which will provide a circular day-walk in the Doring River Valley - consult the controlling authority for directions.

This walk takes you along the first 7,5 km or so of a new hiking trail, the Doring River Wilderness Trail, in a recently proclaimed wilderness area on the northern slopes of the Outeniqua Mountains west of George. It returns on the same route. Water is available along the route from the Doring River and, except in very dry weather, its side-streams. The walk is along a track all the way and is not strenuous. In fact, it is ideal for young children, the more so because there is a rock pool on the river a short way into the valley which is perfect for a dip if the weather is right.

I could as well have called this the `Leucadendron Walk' because you can see no fewer than seven leucadendron species in the space of a few kilometres, one of them rare and another confined to this valley. This is in addition to a wealth of ericas, proteas, restios and other plants which make up the fynbos mosaic. Typical fynbos birds such as the Orangebreasted Sunbird and Cape Sugarbird are everywhere, and if you are lucky you may, as I did, glimpse a grysbok before it dashes off into the thick plant growth in the way it does when disturbed.

The Waboomskraal Valley, where the walk begins, is a hops-growing area. The characteristic frames which support the plants are evident in the fields alongside the tarred road through the valley.

After parking your car, head down the forestry track which gives access to the wilderness area. The track drops, crosses a stream and then climbs fairly steeply up the slope on the other side before swinging west to a low nek. The wilderness area boundary is just before the nek, marked by

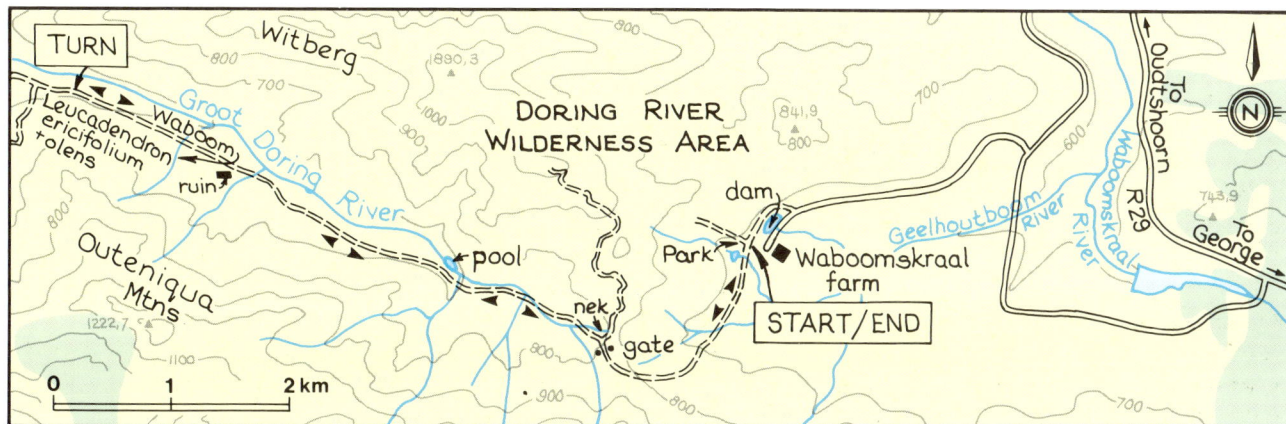

a Cape Provincial Administration signboard which reads 'Doringrivier Wilderness Area'.

Up to this point, the track runs through private land among an uncontrolled tangle of pines, hakea (*Hakea tenuifolia*), black wattle (*Acacia mearnsii*) and blackwood (*Acacia melanoxylon*) - all of them alien plants which have virtually smothered the natural vegetation. The contrast between this first section of the trail and the wilderness area beyond is an obvious and succinct lesson in the importance of controlling the spread of invasive alien plant growth. Over the nek, the first view down the Doring River Valley is framed by a population of a very lovely leucadendron, *Leucadendron uliginosum*. These tall, sparse plants with their silver leaves and silvery-yellow inflorescences in October grow naturally only on the Outeniquas. On the nek the track splits; the right-hand branch leads up the ridge. Take the left-hand branch, which gradually descends into the valley, passing a profusion of ericas, proteas (*Protea eximia, P. neriifolia, P. aurea*), mimetes (*Mimetes cucullatus*), *Berzelia intermedia* (a member of an endemic fynbos family, the Bruniaceae), and restios (*Elegia persistens* and the tall fronds of *Cannomois virgata*) - all characteristic elements of the fynbos plant community. Mixed with these are a large number of a very prominent leucadendron, *Leucadendron eucalyptifolium*, a tall upright plant which, under favourable conditions, can grow into a small tree and is endemic to the Langeberg and Outeniqua ranges. Amongst these are a few plants of *Leucadendron spissifolium*, a smaller shrub which favours damp sites.

About 1,5 km from the nek, the track crosses a side-stream from the kloof which opens out on the left. Some 20-30 m beyond the stream and hidden from the track there is a rock pool in the Doring River which makes a lovely spot to rest. It can be reached after a bit of bundu-bashing from the stream crossing or from the track directly above it.

You could turn around here, but if you would like to see more of the valley and its plants, continue along the track. Next to a side-stream a little further on, growing tall in the fynbos, are some neat shrubs with slender, reddish stems; these are *Leucadendron conicum* plants, another species characteristic of these mountains. It, too, can grow into a tree. Further on, the vegetation changes slightly and the common Tolbos (*Leucadendron salignum*), which is brilliant yellow when it flowers in winter, replaces *L. eucalyptifolium* as the dominant leucadendron. This area may be slightly drier than that higher up the valley.

Along the course of the Doring River to the right is a large stand of Keurboom (*Virgilia divaricata*). Some way beyond a clearing next to the remains of a hut, on the other side of a small stream, look out for a group of Waboom (*Protea nitida*), recognizable by their blue-grey leaves, on the slope to the left of the track. Above these are the first of a population of *Leucadendron ericifolium*, strange-looking plants with tufts of bright green foliage at the base and thin flowering stems waving high in the breeze. When Dr Ion Williams published his revision of the genus *Leucadendron* in 1972, he had been unable to find *L. ericifolium* in the wild and thought it might have become extinct. Since then, several populations have been found on the northern foothills of the Outeniqua and Langeberg ranges.

There is no point in tramping through the veld to see these plants: five minutes' walk further on, more plants grow alongside the track. Here also is *Leucadendron olens*, a low, spindly plant with erica-like leaves closely pressed to the stems. It is no great beauty, but is of major scientific interest. Dr Ion Williams discovered this new species in 1980 while examining the population of *L. ericifolium*. *L. olens* is known only from this one population which stretches for a distance of about 4 km along the valley. When I photographed the species in 1981 for Marie Vogt's book *South Africa's Proteaceae*, the whole area was overrun with hakea, but Nature Conservation officials have since done a magnificent job in eliminating the threat it posed to this rare and interesting *Leucadendron*. *L. olens* is not the only new species of the Proteaceae which has been found in this area. A few kilometres to the west, a remarkable new species of pin-

ABOVE: Leucadendron conicum *grows near streams and can become a small tree. Shown here are the flowerheads of a male tree.*
OPPOSITE LEFT: *On the nek at the head of the Doring River Valley,* Protea eximia *flowers amid rocks of Table Mountain sandstone.*

cushion, *Leucospermum hamatum*, was first discovered in 1978. Despite extensive botanical exploration over centuries, the fynbos continues to yield new and exciting plants.

The way back to the start is the way you came. While the entire route can easily be covered in 3 hours, you will need more than this to enjoy the magnificent surroundings.

A new circular day-walk in the Doring River Valley is being designed. This will leave the track at the nek near the start of the existing walk, and make use of the short track up the ridge to the north. A new path will link the end of this track with that along the Doring River described here. The resulting circuit will provide a second and even more interesting day's walk in this lovely wilderness area.

GROENEWEIDE FOREST TRAILS

A long but fairly easy circuit through natural forest that is particularly appealing on a hot day. Short cuts provide two shorter circuits.

Time: 5 1/2 hours.

Distance: 15 km; optional shorter circuits cover 11 km and 7 km respectively.

Exertion: Light to moderate.

Controlling authority: Witfontein State Forest; this will change when the Witfontein Forest Station closes soon.

Permits: Self-issue at start. Also sign the register.

Maps and information: Black- and-white map (of limited use) at start. Colour map with information sold at Department of Water Affairs and Forestry office in Knysna.

How to get there: Take the Saasveld turn-off 3 km from the intersection of York Street and Courtenay Street in George and follow the Passes road for 5,2 km to Saasveld. Turn in at the gateway, follow the road that runs between the houses and the forest, then take the right hand branch to the main College building; drive to the car park at its eastern end and leave your car here.

Start/end: Signposted at the edge of the forest in front of the College building.

Trail markers: White or yellow shoeprints.

Best times to walk: Any time, but summer is ideal.

Precautions: Keep to the route, as getting lost in the forest is

no picnic!

Features: Beautiful forest, where trees can be identified by their National Tree List number; ferns, two natural swimming pools (one on the Silver River), and forest birds.

The Groeneweide Forest, part of the Witfontein State Forest, is an extensive stretch of natural forest. Here three trails have been laid out to form, in effect (after the first 2 km which are common to all three), a set of nested loops of 15 km, 11 km and 7 km long. The trails mostly follow forestry tracks and paths used by the old woodcutters; they are still used today in the management of the forest.

Although the shorter routes will leave you with a lasting impression of the beauty and peace within this forest, I re-

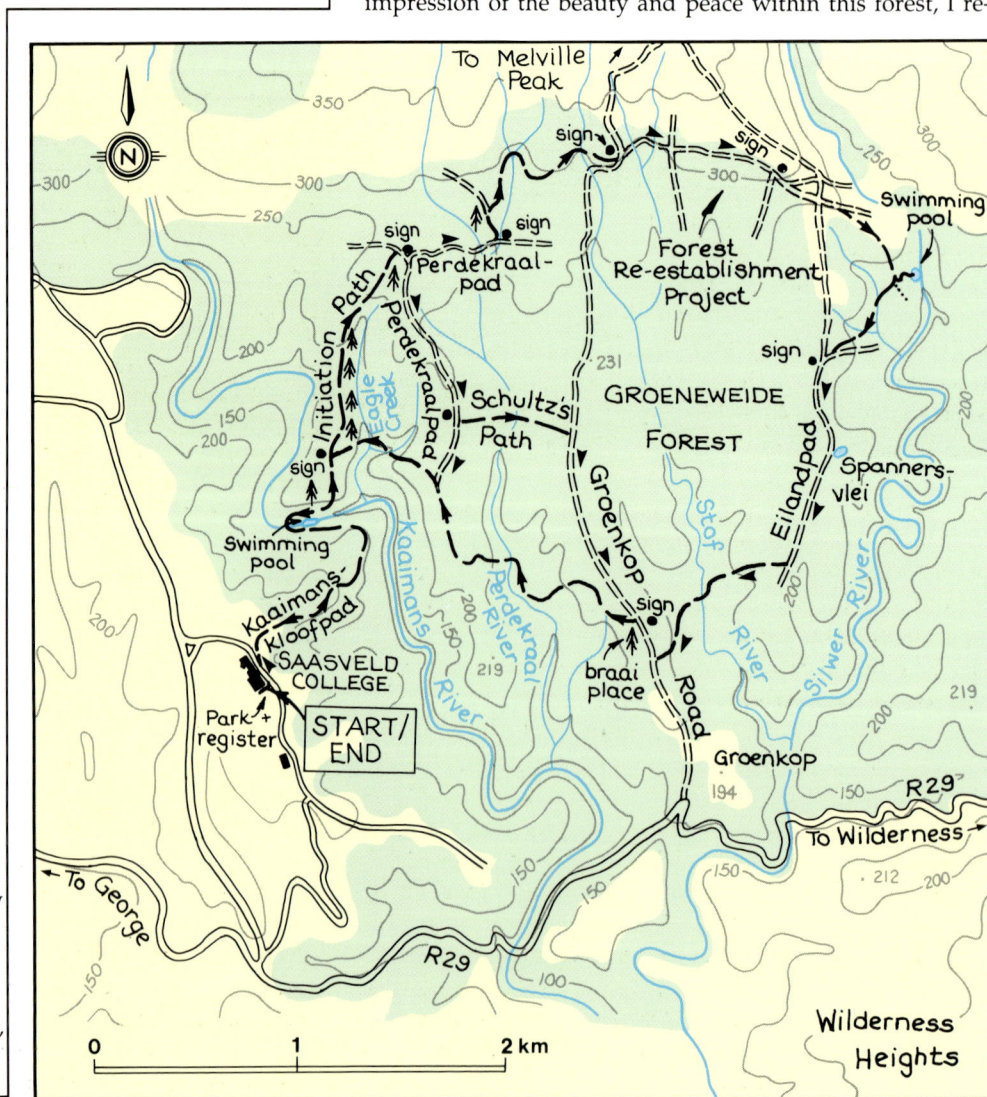

commend that you take the longest trail, if you have the time, since this covers the widest range of forest types. An added bonus is that, from it, a short path leads to a lovely swimming place on the Silver River. It is well worthwhile to take with you the tree list available from the Knysna office of the Department of Water Affairs and Forestry, so that you can identify the many tree species that have been numbered along the way.

The trails begin to the east of the Saasveld Forestry College's main building, where there is a register to complete before setting out. The maps of the walks available here are photostat copies of a colour map and can be confusing since roads and rivers, originally red and blue, are now indistinguishable. The trails enter the forest at a point clearly sign-posted `Forest Walk', where the forest edge forms a corner, across the lawn from the front of the main building.

In the forest, the path drops steadily through wet, then very wet, forest, to cross the upper reaches of the Kaaimans River, here not much more than a stream lined with a dense clump of Palmiet (*Prionium serratum*). Not far downstream is a shallow pool where you can take a dip if the season and weather are favourable. The river provides a brief break in the forest canopy before the path re-enters the trees, following a valley called Eagle Creek. Just beyond an opening in the canopy which reveals some large Outeniqua yellow-woods (*Podocarpus falcatus*) on the opposite bank, the return leg of the trails comes in from the right, where a sign points back to Saasveld and a `Forest Walk' sign points to the left. The latter is to the Initiation Path - which is not the scene of sadistic ritual but a short route used to familiarize students at the College with some of the forest trees. The path ends at a crossroads where a sign, again `Forest Walk', points to the right. Some 50 m down this track is the split to the two shorter trails. Clearly marked `Short Route - 8 km', the short cuts lead to the right, down Perdekraalpad.

To take the 7-km route, simply continue along this branch of Perdekraalpad until it intersects with the path which is the return loop of the 15-km trail, and turn right. The 11-km trail leaves Perdekraalpad about 700 m from the intersection, opposite a tree on the right of the track labelled `B30' and marked with a white shoeprint. This is Schultz's Path, and it is marked by another white shoeprint. After descending to a stream-crossing, the trail climbs gently up the opposite bank and meets a gravel road, the Groenkop Road. Turn right here and follow the road to a braai area, where you can join the return leg of the 15-km trail as it enters the forest at the now-familiar `Forest Walk' sign.

ABOVE TOP: *The colour of a Long-horned grasshopper (* Katydid *) merges with the green foliage of its wet forest habitat.*
ABOVE: Dietes iridioides *flowers irregularly, but mainly in spring and summer, in evergreen forests and on their margins.*

Schultz's Path is lined with a dense growth of Onderbos (*Trichocladus crinitus*) which forms a major component of the understorey of moist and wet forests. This shrub, which can become a small tree, grows in the low light under the forest canopy. It was only when photographing in the forest that I appreciated just how little light is available on the forest floor - less than one per cent of what the trees above receive. Low light intensity is not the only adversity that plants in the forest have had to overcome. Saplings of several trees, including the Bastard saffronwood (*Cassine peragua*), at first produce large leaves with sharp spines on the margins to deter browsing bushbuck; as the trees grow taller, leaves

ABOVE: *A group of vervet monkeys weighs down the branches of a camphor tree on the edge of the Groeneweide forest.*
OPPOSITE: *A scene along the Perdekraalpad in the Groeneweidebos.*

that develop beyond the reach of the buck are the normal size and shape for that species.

If you are walking the 15-km trail, turn onto the left-hand leg of Perdekraalpad. It was on this track that I came across a magnificent collection of bracket fungi. Some were yellow and brown, some bright red and others dark brown edged with lilac, and all were growing on felled wood, each type on a separate piece. Just beyond a stream-crossing, the trail leaves Perdekraalpad at a `Forest Walk' sign on the left. Seven-week's ferns are plentiful along this stretch of the path. This fern species is being researched to determine the best way to manage its harvesting for the export cut-flower market so as to provide sustainable yields.

Ignoring a dead-end forestry track, the path veers right. It passes over two streams then enters a patch of drier forest before crossing the gravel Groenkop Road. On the other side it climbs through pines and meets a plantation track, where a`Forest Walk' sign points right. On a gentle descent, the track at first passes young forest on the right - the result of a forest re-establishment research project - then through pine trees. At an intersection where there is a sign reading `Keer-

punt', keep right - there is a yellow shoeprint indicating the 6-km mark on the left and a trail marker a few metres further on. Not far from here, the track splits again; take the left-hand branch which runs parallel to some electricity pylons on the edge of the plantation. The trail leaves this track on a path to the right marked by a white shoeprint; the path drops through some pines to natural forest.

Just before an intersection, keep a sharp lookout for the path to the Silver River which leaves the trail on the left (east) opposite a tree marked with an arrow and a white shoeprint. This path leads steeply down to the river where there is a pool which invites a swim in summer but which in winter light looks black and cold. At all times of the year it is beautiful, though.

At the intersection, turn right. The path drops to a very muddy crossing of a small stream and up the other side. It becomes a track and meets another track at a spot where `B8A' and a yellow shoeprint pointing the way left are painted in the fork of a tree trunk.

It was on my second walk along this track that I heard the gentle knocking of Olive Woodpeckers and, after finally finding the source of the noise, spent an hour watching a group of these beautifully marked birds going about the task of probing the bark of trees for the insects on which they feed. Very soon after this I was delighted to see a pair of Redbilled Woodhoopoes and a Chorister Robin. Regrettably, the latter did not live up to its name and didn't sing a note. Although the forest is full of bird life, forest birds are very difficult to see in the gloom, and patience and quiet are needed. Another bird which is seldom seen is the Cinnamon Dove, which has the disconcerting habit of perching silently and invisibly next to a path until you are close upon it, when it suddenly clatters off through the undergrowth; once it settles again it becomes impossible to see.

Along this section of the trail, ignore paths into the forest to left and right, and follow the trail markers past Spannersvlei (a soggy bit of forest floor on the left of the trail which is the delight of its population of frogs), down to and across the Stof River and up towards the gravel Groenkop Road. Here, turn right to the braai area where the path once again enters the forest at the `Forest Walk' sign, dropping down to the Perdekraal River, which is crossed by means of a small bridge. On the other side, the path meets the incoming leg of the 7-km trail from the right, before traversing two small streams among bracken and meeting the outward leg of the trails. The sign `Saasveld' points you back to the river-crossing and up through the forest to the College buildings.

CHAPTER FIVE

SWARTBERG

The Swartberg is the high range, approximately 200 km long, which separates the Little and Great Karoos. Although this range is not black in appearance, its name distinguishes it from the Witteberg range, which abuts it in the west, and which is made up of distinctly white-looking quartzite rock. The Swartberg consist mainly of Table Mountain sandstone, here often coloured orange by ferric oxide inclusions.

The Swartberg Pass, which links Oudtshoorn in the Little Karoo and Prince Albert in the Great Karoo, is a national monument. The last of the 23 passes designed by the famous Thomas Bain, it was built under his supervision using convict labour and completed in 1887. The narrow, winding road is 24 km long and rises to a height of 1 585 m, on the way passing through some of the loveliest mountain scenery in South Africa. Just below the summit of the pass on the northern side, amidst a stand of pines, are the ruins of the convict labourers' quarters. At the site of the old toll house (now demolished) another 1 km lower down, under more pines, are a mountain hut for hikers to overnight in, and the house of the forest guard. Further down the pass are the ruins of a gaol.

The road from Schoemanspoort to the pass, and the pass itself, give access to the Swartberg Hiking Trail. This trail is not a single route but rather a series of circuits which provide opportunities for several exceptional day-walks. The three routes described in this chapter allow the walker to experience the southern mountain slopes above De Hoek, the summit ridge and the deeply dissected kloofs of the northern face, but there are other possible day-walks. For

The stream in the lower reaches of Scholtzkloof tumbles over boulders that were once part of the orange sandstone krans.

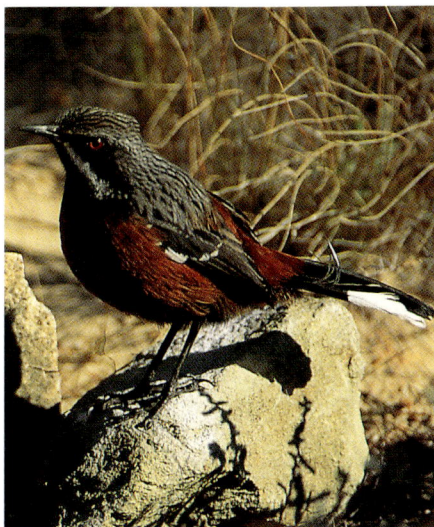

The Cape Rockjumper is one of six bird species endemic to the fynbos.

instance, from the gate next to the picnic site just below the top of the pass on the northern side, you can take the forestry track leading towards Bothashoek; just over 2 km along this, a sign-posted branch leads left to Swartberg Pass North (where you should have a car waiting). This one-way route takes approximately four hours to walk and provides scenery and vegetation similar to that on the Scholtzkloof route. There is also a 5,6-km long path linking the Cango Caves with De Hoek which is an optional extension of the De Hoek Circuit, but this path can be very hot in summer.

Except on the lower slopes (where shale soils predominate) and the watercourses below, the mountains are covered with fynbos. On the summit ridge, which is often blanketed with snow for days and sometimes even weeks, and where strong, cold winds blow, a variety of low restios, proteaceous species and ericas grow.

The climate on these mountains is characterized by extremes. The *average* minimum temperature at the Ou Tol during July and August is below -5 °C. The *average* maximum in January, February and March is above 29 °C. However, snow is possible in any month of the year.

The weather on the mountains can change dramatically and rapidly; a freezing wind can be blowing on the slopes above De Hoek, for example, when below them conditions are sunny and still. Do not attempt to walk when the mountains are in cloud, nor when they are covered in snow (when the pass will in any event be closed). Avoid walking the lower routes on hot days, when they can be very warm indeed. It is essential, even on short routes and even if you set out in perfect weather, to be properly equipped with warm, water- and wind-proof clothing, as well as suitable footwear and head-gear.

DE HOEK CIRCUIT

A strenuous circular route on the southern slopes of the Swartberg through beautiful fynbos and breath-taking mountain scenery.

Time: 5 - 5 1/2 hours.

Distance: 12 km.

Exertion: High.

Controlling authority: Cape Provincial Administration: Department of Nature and Environmental Conservation - Oudtshoorn office.

Permits: Issued at gate of privately owned De Hoek camp.

Maps and information: Swartberg Hiking Trail map, sold by the controlling authority.

How to get there: From the centre of Oudtshoorn, take the road through Schoemanspoort in the direction of the Cango Caves; 28,1 km from Oudtshoorn, take the left-hand branch signposted 'To Prince Albert' and drive 4,9 km to the turn-off to the De Hoek camp. Turn in here and drive to the entrance gate. Having acquired your permit, proceed on the tar road and where it swings left, take the short gravel road to the braai area beyond two swimming pools. Park at the far end of the braai area under the large thorn trees (*Acacia karoo*), giving the many small ones a wide berth, as they could cause punctures.

Start/end: At stile over fence on the other side of the river.

Trail markers: White shoe-prints.

Best times to walk: Any time, but avoid climbing during the heat of the day. In summer, plan to complete all climbing before 09h30.

Precautions: Regard the times given on the Department of Water Affairs and Forestry map of the Swartberg Hiking Trail as highly optimistic. Carry warm, wind-proof clothing, and enough water for the climb. Keep to the path and make sure you take the correct route at the two intersections.

Features: Spectacular mountain scenery, beautiful fynbos, birds, and a rock pool for a swim.

The advertising industry has overworked, abused and devalued every superlative in the English language, but nothing less than a superlative will do to describe the scenery which surrounds you on this walk on the southern slopes of the Swartberg. In addition, the route traverses the transition from Renosterveld through arid fynbos to the moist fynbos of the middle slopes, in the course of which an enormous variety of beautiful plants can be seen.

This circuit is no doddle; the nett height climbed is about 650 m, which is appreciable - and this does not take into account the extra climb into and out of the kloof of the Perdepoort River on the middle section.

The De Hoek camp and bungalows are privately owned, but access to the mountain slopes through the camp has been negotiated by the CPA with the owners.

The trail leads across the stream, over a stile and through a field to the resort's boundary fence, where there is a turn-stile. When I walked this route in winter, a small flock of Speckled Mousebirds were feasting on one of the bushes next to the stream; they were still feeding there five hours later when I returned. The riverine bird life is rich and quite distinct from that of the slopes above.

Through the boundary fence is an old Department of Environment Affairs/Forestry notice, marked by white shoeprints, which represents the meeting of the outward and return legs of the circuit. It does not matter which way round you do the walk; I chose the eastern leg, straight up the ridge, so that I could tackle the climbing first.

The silver foliage of Leucadendron album *bushes gleams on the slopes above De Hoek. The peaks of the Swartberg lie behind.*

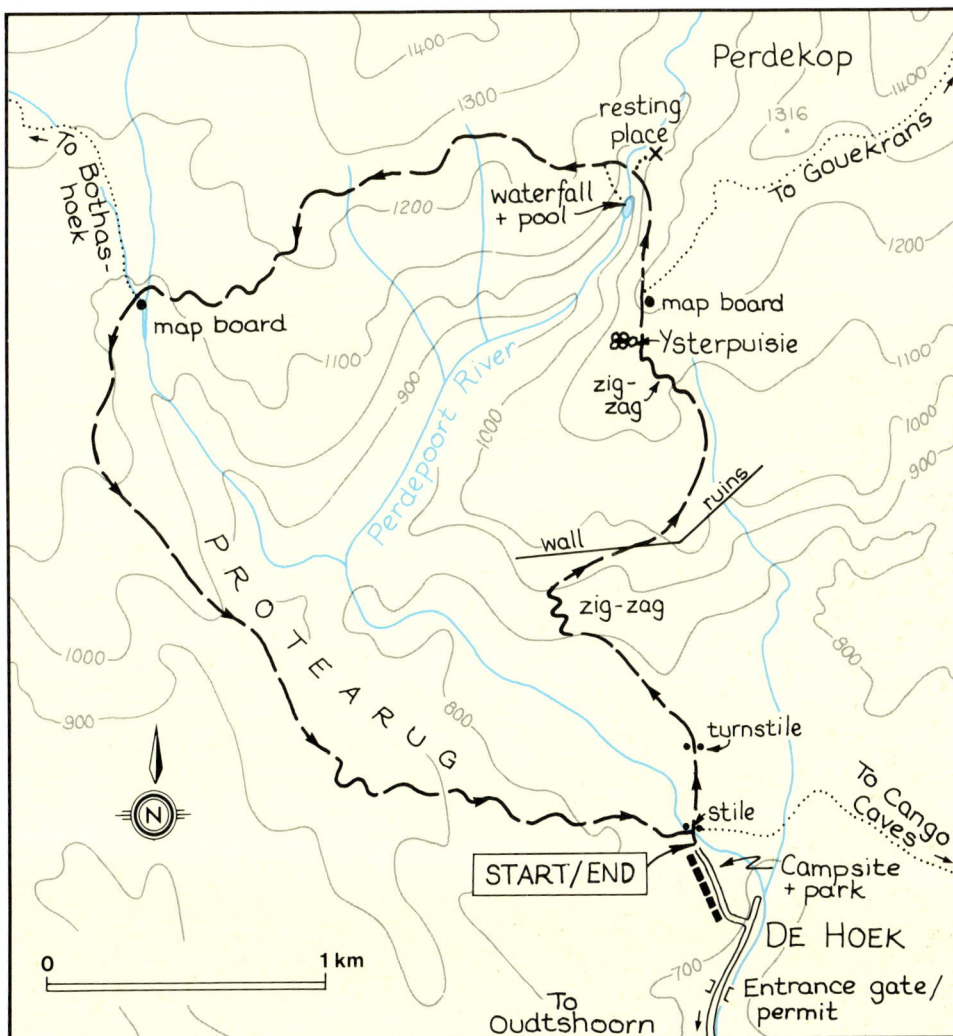

Small populations of Leucadendron tinctum *are found on the south slopes of the Swartberg.*

The route is well marked and, provided you make sure that you keep left at each of the two path junctions encountered on the way, you cannot lose your way anywhere.

Most of the climbing is done on the first leg of the route, which leads from the Renosterveld above the stream through arid fynbos, where Waboom (*Protea nitida*) bushes are prominent, and zigzags steeply up the spur. On top of the spur, you continue to climb, more gently now, through proteaceous fynbos and past the ruins of a stone wall.

As you cross the ridge, vast views of the mountains above and to the east are revealed; the resort of De Hoek nestles in the valley below and behind you. Cape Sugarbirds call and display amongst the fronds of the restio *Cannomois virgata* which lines a small kloof through which the path now climbs. At the top the way swings right, through a dense stand of the same restio species, growing to an impressive height and mixed with proteas here. The path veers left again, to head directly towards Perdekop. Here the views become even grander, with Grootkloof dropping precipitously to the right and the high peaks of the Swartberg visible. Behind you, the distant Outeniqua Mountains appear beyond the hills of the Little Karoo. The slope becomes

steeper again as you zigzag up to the nek below Perdekop, where a path comes in from the right. (This leads up to the hut at Gouekrans on the Swartberg Hiking Trail.) The junction is well marked. On the slopes to the left is a pile of chocolate-brown boulders quite unlike the surrounding Table Mountain sandstone. This is the Ysterpuisie, an isolated outcropping of manganese- and iron-bearing rock.

From the nek the path drops steeply into the kloof below. Look out for a side branch, marked with blue shoeprints, just before the crossing of the Perdepoort River: it leads to a pleasant resting place, equipped with table and benches, next to the stream. Downstream, beyond the river crossing and soon after the path begins to rise, there is another side-path marked with blue shoeprints, this time to the left. It leads to a small waterfall, cascading into a lovely pool which is ideal for a swim in the right season.

A short, steep climb takes you out of the kloof. On the left of this higher point you can see the steep rock faces, covered with orange and lime-green lichens, above the Perdepoort River. Where the gradient levels off, there are bushes of what must be one of the most beautiful of all proteas: *Protea punctata*, which flowers in autumn. On the other side of a small nek there is a sizable stand of one of the most spectacular leucadendrons, *Leucadendron album*, its silvery leaves gleaming in the sunlight. Both these species are characteristic of the moist fynbos on the Swartberg range.

The path drops gently and crosses two more flowing streams (a third is usually just a dry bed). Just beyond the second, you come to another path junction, again well marked, where there is a second map of the route. The path to the right leads up to the Bothashoek hut on the Hiking Trail. From the junction, the path down to De Hoek follows Protearug all the way. The transitions in the vegetation now occur in reverse order, as the path descends steadily and the slopes become increasingly dry. The views on this last section of the route are no less wonderful than on the first, with a rugged kloof to the left appearing below the distant, high peaks of the Swartberg.

Fairly low down on the right, next to the path, is a small population of *Aulax cancellata*, a member of the protea family which has separate male and female plants, the latter with cones. This is the only known population of this species on the Swartberg, although it occurs in some abundance in the south-western Cape. The path crosses a trickle of water at the base of Protearug. There is just a small rise to climb on the other side before you reach the stile on the De Hoek boundary fence, near to the spot where your car is parked.

OU TOL CIRCUIT

A short but challenging circuit through high-alpine vegetation, to the top of the Swartberg, from where there are unsurpassed views. This would make an ideal morning or afternoon outing.

Time: 3 1/2 - 4 hours.

Distance: 8 km.

Exertion: High.

Controlling authority: Cape Provincial Administration: Department of Nature and Environmental Conservation - Oudtshoorn office.

Permits: From the controlling authority.

Maps and information: The current Swartberg Hiking Trail map available from the above office does not show this route, but does show the area and also contains much useful and interesting information.

How to get there: From the centre of Oudtshoorn take the road leading through Schoemanspoort in the direction of the Cango Caves. Take the turn-off to Prince Albert, 28,1 km from Oudtshoorn. Drive 12 km (past the turn-off to the De Hoek resort) to the Calitzdorp turn-off. Continue for 14 km up and over the Swartberg Pass to the Ou Tol and park under the pines next to the Hiking Trail overnight `hut' (actually a bungalow).

Start: Find the beginning of the path on the southern edge of the clearing around the buildings at the Ou Tol.

Trail markers: White shoeprints.

End: The Ou Tol.

Best times to walk: Late summer, when most of the high alpine plants are flowering.

Precautions: At this height, be prepared for dramatic and rapid changes in the weather. You must carry water as well as warm, wind- and waterproof clothing.

Features: A vast panorama from the top ridge of the Swartberg; alpine vegetation characteristic of the Swartberg peaks.

The Ou Tol Circuit is a new route which includes a path leading from the top of the Swartberg Pass up to a small nek just below an unnamed peak (height 1 948 m) and down again to Otto du Plessis Road (which leads to Gamkaskloof). At its highest point - just over 1 900 m - the path is essentially on the same level as the highest peaks of this part of the Swartberg range. Conditions at this height can change drastically in the space of a few minutes, so it is imperative to take warm, windproof clothing, even in mid-summer. Do not be lulled into a false sense of security by fine, warm weather. Snow is possible in any month of the year.

The views, on this route, of the mountains, the Little Karoo and the Outeniqua Mountains to the south, and of the Great Karoo and far-off Nuwekloof Mountains to the north, are incomparable. In addition, the path passes through some of the alpine vegetation unique to the peaks of the Swartberg.

From the start, the path climbs steadily. At the top of the Swartberg Pass, follow the white shoeprints up through the rocks. Very soon you will reach a branch to the right which leads to a weather station. The Ou Tol trail zigzags on up the slope through low restioid and ericoid growth to a small nek, from which you can see down over the south side of the pass. By means of a gentler slope it reaches a second

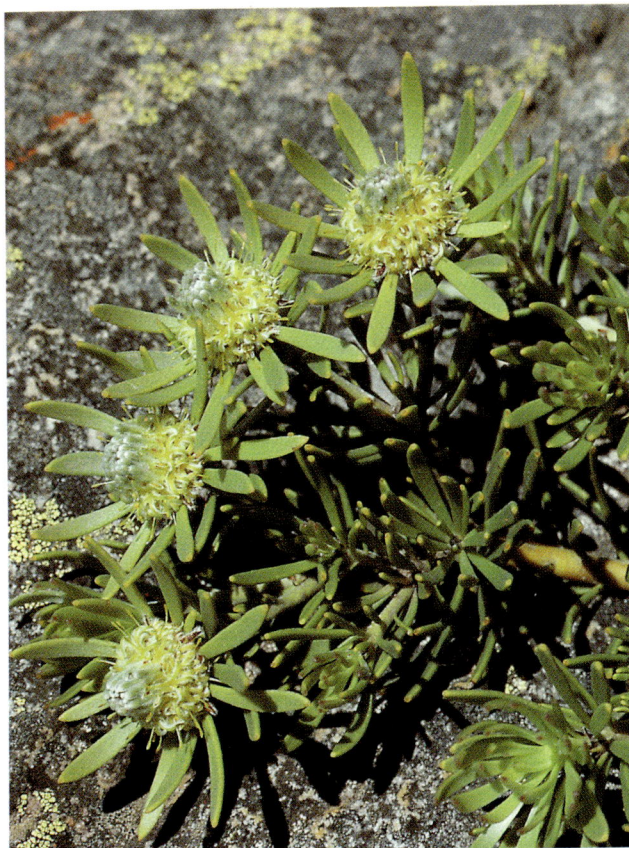

A branch of a male Leucadendron dregei *sprawls over a rock; this habit is typical of the high-alpine plants of the Swartberg.*

nek, just to the west of a small peak (1 709 m) where, from a certain point, you can see right across the Little Karoo to the long line of the Outeniqua Mountains in the south, and over the winding Swartberg Pass to the Great Karoo and the far-off Nuwekloof Mountains in the north. From here the path climbs steeply to its highest point, a third, small nek between the 1 948-m peak and a rocky peaklet just to the south of it.

To stop on the nek and gaze east and west along this mighty range of mountains is a compelling experience. I know of no other place on the Swartberg which can be reached so easily yet provides such impressive views. Take time, too, to explore the rocks above the nek. You may find yourself being watched by Cape Rockjumpers and Cape Siskins, both bird species endemic to the fynbos. Here grow *Leucadendron dregei*, *Protea venusta* and *P. montana*, and *Spatalla confusa*, all low-growing members of the Proteaceae and characteristic of these high peaks. A wealth of ericas is also found here. Because of the extreme cold in winter at this elevation, most of these plants flower in summer.

From this high point, the path drops steeply down the west-facing slope, then swings onto the northern slopes on the level before zigzagging down to the pine arboretum on the Gamkaskloof road. On the way are fine stands of protea-ceous plants characteristic of the drier northern slopes - *Leucospermum wittebergense*, *Protea lorifolia*, *P. repens* and

Paranomus dregei. The arboretum is maintained to test the adaptability of a variety of exotic pine species to the local rigorous climate. At the road, turn right and walk for a few hundred metres to the point where it intersects with the Scholtzkloof path. Here you can take the path to the right over the rise and back to the Ou Tol or, if you wish to extend the walk a bit, continue on the Gamkaskloof road to its junction with the Swartberg Pass and follow this back to the Ou Tol.

From the koppie next to the highest point on the Ou Tol Circuit, there are uninterrupted views east and west along the peaks of the Swartberg.

DIE HEL

In the early 1800s the animals of a party of *trekboers* disappeared into the kloof in which the Gamka River flows through the Swartberg. Next morning, the *trekboers* tracked them to a well-watered valley and decided to settle there. This was the beginning of a small farming community which became virtually self-sufficient. Its members had no contact with the outside world apart from an occasional visit to Calitzdorp to trade some of their produce for essentials such as salt.

During the Anglo-Boer War a commando under pursuit by British troops became lost in cloud on top of the Swartberg. After spending a cold night there, the men were amazed, when the cloud cleared next morning, to see huts in the valley below. When they reached the valley floor the men were greeted by the head of the community, a large, bearded man, named Cordier, dressed in goat-skins and speaking a strange form of Dutch. The commandos spent two days as guests of the farmers before being guided out of the kloof to the Karoo.

In 1962 Gamkaskloof's isolation ended when the Otto du Plessis road was built to link it with the Swartberg Pass. The community gradually dispersed and only one farmer, a descendant of the original group remains. The entire valley, apart from two farms at its western end, is now a proclaimed Wilderness Area belonging to the Cape Provincial Administration's Department of Nature and Environmental Conservation.

SCHOLTZKLOOF WALK

This easy one-way route down rugged Scholtzkloof offers a fine experience of the `other face' of the Garden Route.

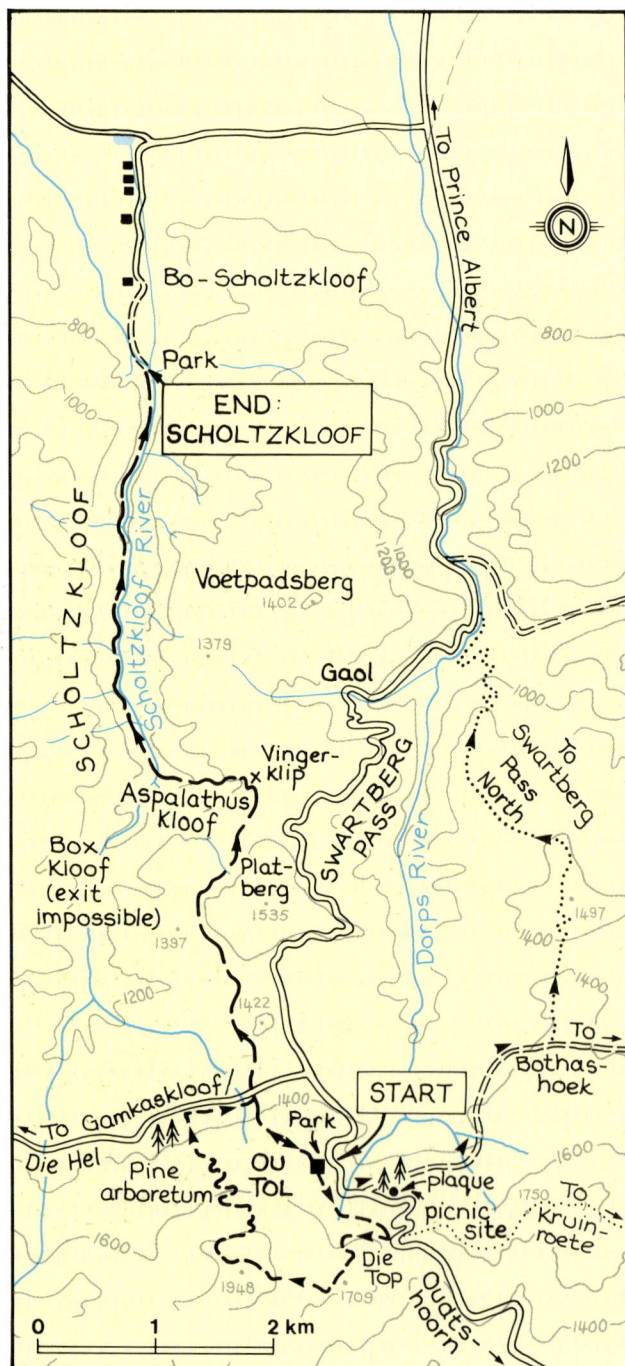

This kloof path runs roughly parallel to the Swartberg Pass on the northern side of the mountains above Prince Albert. The two routes are separated by Platberg and Voetpadsberg. No-one can deny the splendour of the scenery on the pass, but Scholtzkloof is even more rugged and impressive, a deep kloof with steep sides through which there are distant views of the mountains in the Great Karoo. The route can be walked in either direction, but for the sake of the views and because it is a little less strenuous, I prefer to walk down the kloof.

From the Ou Tol (old tollhouse), on the northern side of the pass just below the summit, it is a relatively easy walk to the parking spot at the northern end of the kloof, where you

Time: 4 - 4 ½ hours.

Distance: 10,3 km.

Exertion: Light.

Controlling authority: Cape Provincial Administration: Department of Nature and Environmental Conservation.

Permits: Issued by the Oudtshoorn office of the above authority.

Maps and information: Swartberg Hiking Trail map sold by the above office.

How to get there: From the centre of Oudtshoorn, take the R328 leading through Schoemanspoort in the direction of the Cango Caves. Take the turn-off to Prince Albert 28,1 km from Oudtshoorn. Drive 12 km (past the De Hoek turn-off) to the Calitzdorp turn-off. Continue for 14 km up and over the Swartberg Pass to the Ou Tol and park under the pines.

Start: On the path behind (to the west of) the forest guard's house at the Ou Tol.

Trail markers: White shoeprints.

End: The end of Scholtzkloof, where it opens out.

How to get to end: To leave a car at the end of the walk, drive 20 km from the Ou Tol down the north side of the pass to the signposted turn-off to Scholtzkloof. Drive 2,3 km along the road and turn left into the farm Bo-Scholtzkloof. Continue past three lots of farm buildings and park under the trees. This is private land which should be respected.

Best times to walk: Any time, but avoid hot summer days.

Precautions: Carry warm, protective clothing at all times.

Features: Magnificent wild mountain and rocky kloof scenery, fynbos and riverine vegetation.

will need to arrange to have transport waiting (see 'How to get to end' above). If, on the other hand, you decide to walk the complete route in both directions, be prepared for a very long day's hike (10-11 hours).

The northern slopes of the Swartberg can be very hot in summer. I do not recommend walking Scholtzkloof - particularly up it - in hot weather. The route is exceptionally well marked and the path obvious; you cannot lose your way as long as you stick to the path.

The route starts behind (on the western side of) the Swartberg Hiking Trail hut and guard's house at the Ou Tol. (The other path to the south of the hut leads to the top of the pass.) Keep a lookout here for Cape Rockjumpers, beautifully marked birds endemic to the fynbos. From the buildings, the path leads over a low rise and down the other side through a stand of *Protea eximia*, to cross the Gamkaskloof road just to the right of a small copse of pine trees. One of the taller plants growing in this flattish, sandy area is an Everlasting (*Syncarpha milleflora*), a robust, erect shrub with terminal bunches of white or pink flowerheads in spring and summer.

While the path continues more or less on the level, the ground begins to fall away to the left. Along this stretch of the route you encounter some of the proteaceous plants characteristic of these drier slopes, including *Paranomus dregei*, which grows only on the Swartberg and Witteberg ranges and has cream-coloured flower spikes, and *Protea canaliculata*, one of the 'mountain roses'. Further along, as you skirt the top of a kloof to the left, you will pass a good stand of *Leucadendron tinctum*, within which are a few examples of *L. comosum* subsp. *comosum*. The female of the latter Tolbos has very large cones; these plants, with their narrow linear leaves, are endemic to the Swartberg. *L. tinctum*, on the other hand, has a wide distribution, ranging from here to the coastal mountains of the south-western Cape with their relatively high winter rainfall.

The path skirts the first kloof, which is separated from Aspalathuskloof by a spur. Between the restios are examples of *Agathosma capensis*, known around here as Steenbok buchu, a low bush with yellow-green needle-shaped leaves which give off a powerful aniseed smell when crushed. When I walked this route with CPA Nature Conservation officers Jan Vlok and Dave Osborne, Jan noticed a small erica growing in the rocks above the path. This was a previously unrecorded and unusual locality for this species (*Erica carduifolia*), and was the first of three exciting botanical discoveries that day.

ABOVE TOP: *Hikers head towards Scholtzkloof.*
ABOVE: Erica insignis, *wedged into a crevice in an exposed Table Mountain sandstone rock face.*

ABOVE: *A klipspringer doe in characteristic pose on the north side of the Swartberg Pass.*
LEFT: *Aspalanthuskloof leads into Scholtzkloof.*

Aspalathuskloof owes its distinctive beauty to the dense population of *Aspalathus hystrix* on its lower slopes. The plant, which is a legume, has clusters of silvery-grey needle leaves and yellow flowers in spring.

As the path starts its steep descent into the kloof, it passes just to the left of Vingerklip, a large rock which stands nearly vertical. To the left of the path above Vingerklip Jan Vlok made his second discovery of the day: on the almost bare surface of a slab of rock, a small population of a very rare erica, *Erica insignis*, not previously recorded from here. It is worth looking for (without disturbing!) these small plants wedged in the crevices, which produce uniquely lovely long green and pink flowers in late winter. One can only marvel at their ability not only to grow on exposed, north-facing rock faces that are freezing in winter and baking in summer, but to produce spectacular flowers from a substrate apparently without nutrients. On the path just above the rock face, keep a sharp lookout for a tiny orchid, *Schizodium inflexum*, which bears pink flowers in September and October; its leaves lie flat on the ground and are dark green, spotted purple.

It is a steep climb down Aspalathuskloof. At the bottom, the path turns right to follow the course of the stream down Scholtzkloof. Just above the stream-bed, the ground changes to shale-derived soils and there is a matching change in the vegetation cover. The riverine vegetation here is tall and dense. Towering stands of the restio *Cannomois virgata* that look almost like clumps of bamboo grow alongside the Waterwitels (*Brachylaena neriifolia*), a shrub characteristic of watercourses and one of the few woody plants of the daisy family, the Asteraceae. Also abundant here are *Empleurum unicapsulare*, a willowy small tree with tiny pink flowers and aromatic leaves typical of its family, the Rutaceae, and a legume, *Psoralea affinis*, another large shrub or small tree with sprays of blue flowers in spring.

As you proceed downstream, the sandstone rock of the sides of the kloof becomes increasing red in colour. The last botanical find of our walk that day was a small *Nemesia* sprawled among the rocks next to a small cave on the left above the stream; this is probably a new species.

Despite the rugged terrain, this is an easy walk without any difficult or daunting places to negotiate. The interesting and varied plant life on this route is matched by the magnificence of the scenery.

83

CHAPTER SIX

WILDERNESS

O f all the scenic attractions along the Garden Route, the lakes area is, perhaps, the most quintessential. There are estuaries, lagoons and freshwater lakes elsewhere in South Africa, of course, but nowhere such a concentrated collection of varied types of waterway as here. The loveliness of these is enhanced by the proximity of the edge of the coastal plateau and the backdrop of the Outeniqua Mountains.

The town of Wilderness is the gateway to the lakes area, which embraces the Wilderness Lagoon, the aptly-named Serpentine, Eilandvlei, Langvlei, Rondevlei and Swartvlei. The greater part of this region is managed as a National Park, with the aim of conserving it as a functioning ecosystem while allowing for its human habitation and use for recreation. The Park includes the lower reaches of the Touw and Duiwe rivers, which feed the Serpentine and Eilandvlei respectively, but excludes Groenvlei, which is part of the Goukamma Nature Reserve.

Two lovely walks, described in this chapter, have been laid out along river courses. The Giant Kingfisher Trail (originally named the Touw River Trail) traverses natural forest and reaches a waterfall above a steep slope on which huge boulders enclose several rock pools; the Brownhooded Kingfisher Trail runs through similar country alongside the Duiwe River to a picturesque rock pool under a little waterfall. There is a short (3 km) walk, the Halfcollared Kingfisher Trail, in the forest along the western bank of the Touw River; it begins at the gate to the Ebb and Flow campsite. The oldest walk laid out in the area is the Pied Kingfisher Trail (previously known as the Kingfisher Trail). Those who

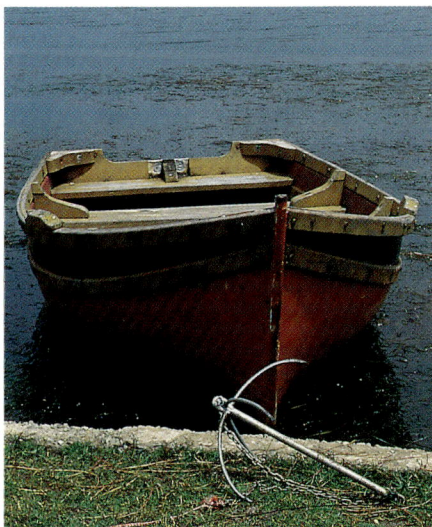

The evening sun silhouettes a variety of bird life below the bird-hide on Rondevlei.

A boat anchored at the edge of Swartvlei makes a tranquil scene.

prefer natural surroundings will find this walk rather like the parson's egg: `nice in parts'. Specifically, these parts are the section on the floodplain next to the Serpentine and the boardwalk along Wilderness Lagoon (a must for bird-spotters), while the sections that pass through suburbia are not of great interest. Another boardwalk, this one on the coast near to the Holiday Inn, provides a short stroll and easy access to Flat Rock - a delightful viewpoint and spot for sundowners.

The bird sanctuary at Rondevlei, the management of which was recently transferred from the Cape Provincial Administration to the National Parks Board, forms the starting point of the Cape Dune Molerat Trail, which is also described here. Because the Wilderness district is a conglomerate of different habitats - forest, rivers, the lakes with their floodplain, and the sea - it is utopia for anyone interested in birds. The Touw River, for instance, offers a delightful introduction to forest birds: Knysna Louries and Blackheaded Orioles make no secret of their presence and are commonly spotted. In the wetland vegetation fringing the lakes and in the scrub forest on the neighbouring slopes lucky bird-watchers may see all five species of kingfisher.

The rapidity of the development of Wilderness into a residential and holiday town is a testament to the area's unique beauty and an on-going headache for those entrusted with conserving its natural features. It is sobering to think that this sprawling town and the roads, railway line and bridges around it have all sprung up in little more than a century. When one George Bennet bought the land which Wilderness now occupies in 1877 for £500, it truly was a wilderness. Mr Bennet literally had to hack an access road from the Passes Road through forest and coastal bush to reach the spot where the Wilderness Hotel now stands.

GIANT KINGFISHER TRAIL

A pleasant and undemanding walk in the forest along the eastern bank of the Touw River to a waterfall and pools amongst tumbled sandstone boulders.

Time: 3 hours.

Distance: 7 km there and back.

Exertion: Light.

Controlling authority: National Parks Board.

Permits: None required; there is a fee to enter the Ebb and Flow campsite.

Maps and information: Sketch map available from Parks Board office in George or at Wilderness Rest Camp.

How to get there: Take the road along the northern side of the Wilderness Lagoon, pass the Faerie Knowe turn-off and, just beyond the combined road and rail bridge over the Touw River, turn in at the entrance to the Ebb and Flow campsite.

Start/end: The far (north) end of the Ebb and Flow campsite.

Trail markers: None.

Best times to walk: Any time.

Precautions: Care is needed when crossing a steep rock face near the turning point, using the two pipelines.

Features: Waterfall and pools, riverside forest, bird life along the river and in the forest.

At the northern end of the Ebb and Flow campsite a sign marks the start of the Giant Kingfisher Trail, which runs along the eastern side of the Touw River valley. The path enters the forest immediately. A few metres from the start, a branch to the right leads steeply up the slope to a cave, while the main trail continues along the river.

Along the first part of the trail, the path climbs up and down through the low forest that covers the sheer slopes above the river. Large exposed rocks along the way provide breaks in the forest canopy and convenient viewpoints from which to look down on the river and its forested banks. They also create a habitat for the aloes (*Aloe arborescens*) which are characteristic of these sites; their scarlet flowers, produced in mid-winter, provide a startling contrast to the green of the surrounding forest. Also growing on these damp rock faces are a variety of bulbous plants, including *Ornithogalum longibracteatum* which produces flowering stems up to a metre long in spring and early summer from large bulbs growing half out of the ground; its flowers are white with green stripes down the centre of the tepals. A jarring note in the otherwise natural surroundings is a large building with rather unsympathetic architecture which dominates the skyline above the slope to the north.

Further along the path the precipitousness of the slope is emphasized by a barrier erected next to the path above an almost-perpendicular drop. After crossing a small stream, the path climbs slightly, divides around a large rock, drops and then runs alongside to the river on a gentler gradient. Here several openings in the undergrowth give access to the river bank and provide views across the river to the high forest, dominated by lichen-festooned Outeniqua yellow-woods (*Podocarpus falcatus*), on the opposite bank. You are likely to hear the raucous call of Knysna Louries, and you stand a good chance of seeing them too. A constant accompaniment to the walk is the call (willie!) of the Sombre Bulbul. Past an ancient Outeniqua yellowwood and a large Wild grape (*Rhoicissus tomentosa*, a woody climber of the grape family Vitaceae), the path emerges onto a flat area covered with ferns where arums flower next to the river.

Back in the forest, the path skirts another Outeniqua yel-

At the turning point, huge boulders surround rock pools, some large enough for a dip.

ABOVE: Plectranthus fruticosus *is common on streamsides in the forest; it flowers mainly in autumn.*
RIGHT: *High upstream on the Giant Kingfisher Trail the pipelines cross a rock cleft where there is a log ladder down the rock face.*

lowwood and a White stinkwood (*Celtis africana*). It is here that the original purpose of this route becomes evident; the path now follows a pipeline which carries water from the upper reaches of the Touw River to the campsite. The pipeline is very obvious along the rest of the trail, becoming something of an eyesore at two points on the route: where there are the remains (and smell) of a diesel pump station, and at a spot where bits and pieces of plastic piping and sheeting line the path. Another, less immediately obvious but far more insidious, ecological problem is a dense tangle of black wattle (*Acacia mearnsii*) which chokes the riverbed in its upper reaches. The overall impression along this section of the route is still, however, the beauty of the natural forest. Because of the gentle slope on this stretch, the trees are large and the forest canopy high above you. I was delighted by the contrast in size and noise level between a flock of louries, calling harshly and clattering about in the tops of the trees high above me, and a pair of Barthroated Apalises (beautifully marked and comparatively tiny birds with an altogether sweeter call) which were hopping around in a bush beside the path.

After keeping on the flat for some time, the path rises suddenly up some steps, crosses a bridge which spans a gap between rocks and reverts to the level for a short while. The reason for the abrupt climb is that the river bank drops sharply to the water at this point. Eventually, the path

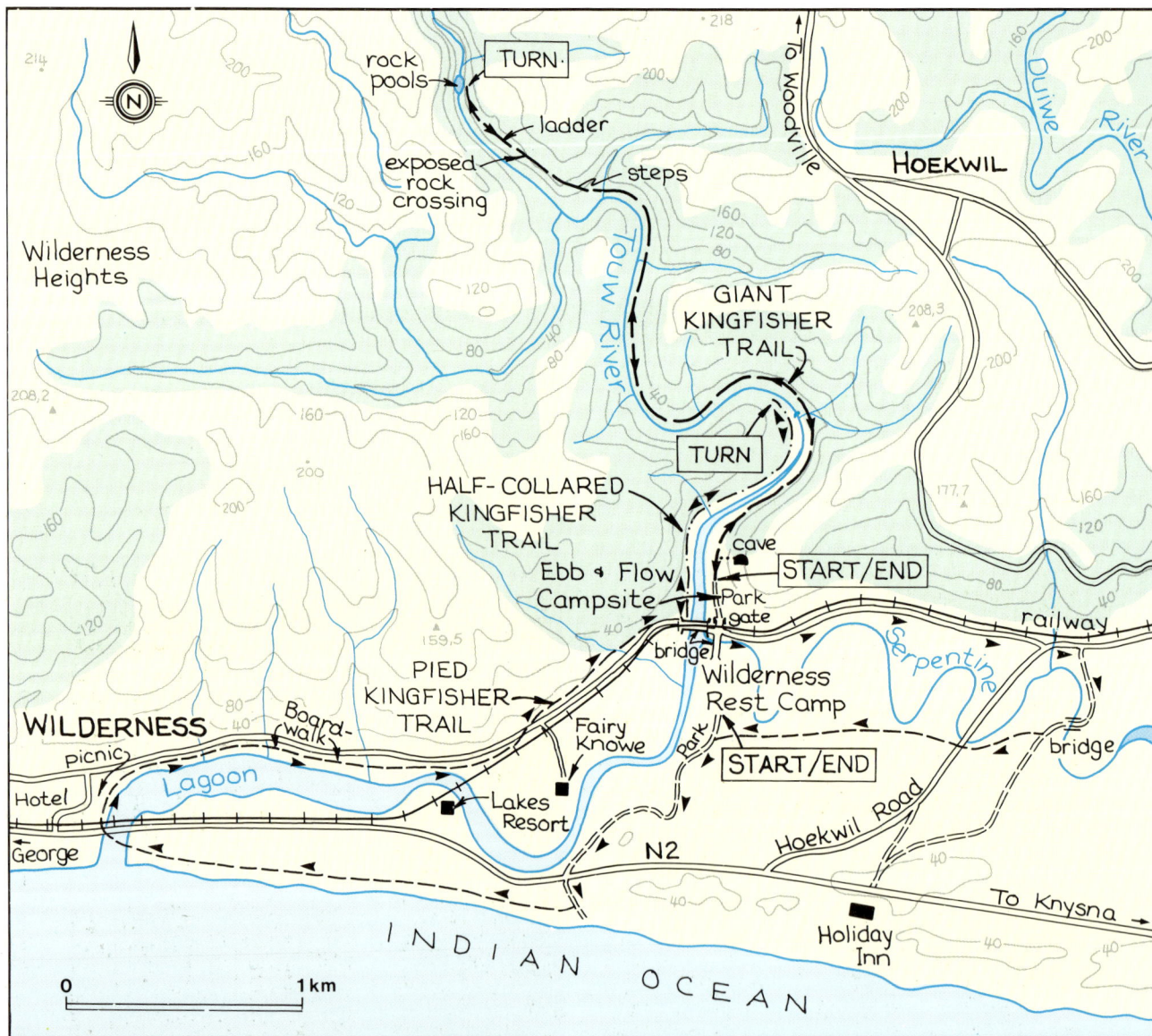

reaches a spot where only the two pipes lead across an exposed rock face. For those who may be fazed by the prospect, the best way to cross this section is to sit down on the top pipe with feet on the lower pipe, and shuffle across sideways. However, it is worth simply sitting here for a while and enjoying the view across the river to the pastures on the other side.

A short distance beyond this hazard there is a sturdy fixed wooden ladder down a vertical rock face. Once this has been negotiated, the path leads you through the trees to the huge tumble of Table Mountain sandstone rocks which marks the end of the trail. Besides a small waterfall there are several rock pools which you should allow yourself time to explore and enjoy.

It takes about 1 $\frac{1}{2}$ hours to reach this spot from Ebb and Flow, and the same back.

KINGFISHERS

Of the 10 species of kingfisher which occur in South Africa, five are found in the southern Cape. Despite their name, not all of these birds actually catch fish.

The largest of the species, the Giant Kingfisher, is 45 cm long and is often seen perched over a river or lagoon on a branch or a convenient telephone or power line, from which it plunge-dives to catch a fish or frog. The prey is held in its strong beak and beaten senseless before being eaten or taken to the nest. The colouring of the female's breast and belly is the reverse of the male's.

The Pied Kingfisher is smaller and entirely black and white, the sexes differing only in the banding on the breast. These commonly seen birds, which frequent pools on the seashore as well as inland waters and estuaries, generally hover in search of prey, and plunge after it. The Pied Kingfisher has an unexpectedly high-pitched twittering call.

Usually seen away from water in a wooded environment, the Brownhooded Kingfisher is an insect eater. The females of this fairly common species differ from the males only in having brown, not black, wings.

The most beautifully coloured of the five species is the Malachite Kingfisher. This common, diminutive bird (only 14 cm long) is a gem. The flash of brilliant blue as it flies low and fast over the water is always a thrilling sight. These are fish eaters which perch in all their tiny glory on reeds, branches or rocks alongside the water.

Seldom spotted and uncommon is the Halfcollared Kingfisher, another spectacularly coloured bird which is larger than the Malachite Kingfisher and differs from it in having a white breast and black beak. This is a fish eater, found on heavily wooded fresh-water bodies and estuaries.

All kingfishers nest in holes in mud banks or tree trunks.

Malachite Kingfisher

Pied Kingfisher (female)

Giant Kingfisher (male)

Brownhooded Kingfisher (male)

Halfcollared Kingfisher

BROWNHOODED KINGFISHER TRAIL

A short, easy walk through forest and riverine bush up the valley of the Duiwe River and a tributary to a waterfall and pool, and back down again.

Time: 3 hours.

Distance: 6 km there and back, including detours on side-paths to viewpoints.

Exertion: Light, except for the short climb to one of the optional viewpoints.

Controlling authority: National Parks Board.

Permits: None required.

Maps and information: Sketch map available from Parks Board office in George or at Wilderness Rest Camp.

How to get there: In Wilderness take the minor road which runs east along the north side of the lagoon, passes the entrances to the Wilderness Camp and Ebb and Flow, and meets the tarred road to Hoekwil. Turn left here, and 800 m further on, at a sign to Langvlei, right onto a gravel road. The parking area for the trail is 3 km further along this road.

Start/end: At the gate, 200 m back along the road, where there is a sign 'Brownhooded Kingfisher Trail'.

Trail markers: Perspex signs carrying Brownhooded Kingfisher motif mounted on low posts, and yellow (occasionally white) arrows; there are three maps of the trail on boards at strategic points along the way.

Best times to walk: Any season.

Precautions: Avoid very wet weather when the river can come down in flood.

Features: Beautiful stream-side forest and bush, a waterfall and pool, and prolific bird life.

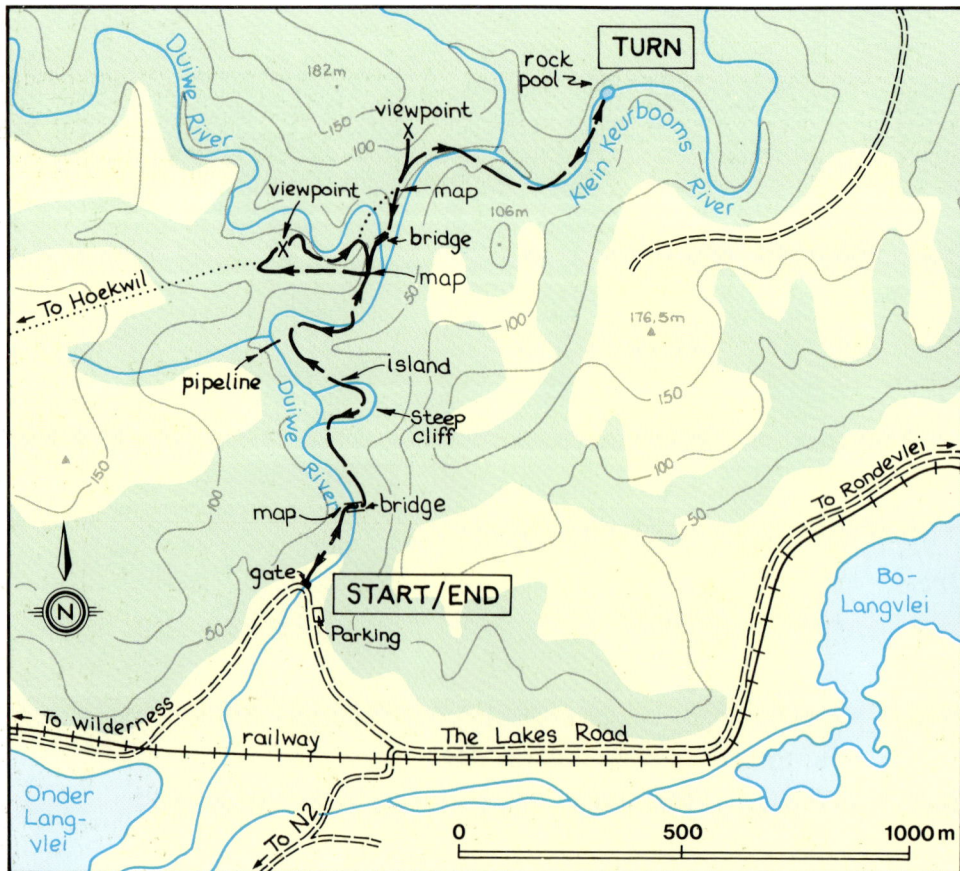

RIGHT: *A typical view of the Duiwe River in summer; this picture was taken just above the second crossing.*

This newly established, roughly 6-km long trail runs first along the Duiwe River (a stream which feeds Eiland-vlei), then up a tributary to a rock pool, and back again. It is not strenuous, although there are short, optional climbs to viewpoints. The low effort demanded by this walk is well rewarded by the beauty of the tree-lined stream and the impressive setting of the rock pool at the turning point.

I haven't been lucky enough to see, here, the birds which give the trail its name, but they certainly are resident in the area. What I have seen and what any walker on the trail can expect to see, is a large variety of bird life associated with the riverine vegetation and the forest. Right at the beginning of the walk, I saw a Burchell's Coucal in the reeds next to the river, and a Cape Robin perched on a fence-post allowed me to come right up close. In the forest, Knysna Louries and Cape Batises are common. On a fine day, the valley is alive with birdsong.

From the steel gate at the start, a grassy track runs along the left-hand bank of the stream, which is lined with river-ine bush. Some of the indigenous plants growing here whose names will be familiar to gardeners are Sagewood (*Buddleja salviifolia*), Num-num (*Carissa bispinosa*) and *Polygala myrtifolia*, which has bright, purplish flowers; creepers such as the Wild grape (*Rhoicissus tomentosa*) and Black-eyed Susan (*Thunbergia alata*) - probably a garden escapee - drape a few of the shrubs.

At the first stream crossing, there is a slatted wooden bridge and the first of the maps of the trail mounted on a pole. A short distance further on, the path recrosses the stream on stepping-stones, then runs beside it, permitting a fine view of the other bank, where aloes (*Aloe arborescens*) and bulbous plants cling precariously to the vertical cliff face. Blackwoods (*Acacia melanoxylon*) and bluegums (*Eucalyptus* sp., probably *E. globulus*) - the first of many growing along the stream course - are encountered as the path curves left. Here the trail crosses the rocky bed of the rivulet onto an island dominated by several enormous bluegums. Despite the fact that they do not really belong here, it is dif-

ficult not to admire the beauty of these giants; near the base of their trunks the thin, cinnamon-coloured outer bark had invariably peeled back to reveal pastel shades of blue and green, interspersed with cream. Another rocky crossing takes you to the opposite bank of the stream, where an arrow points the way up a damp and slippery bank. A few metres on, where the path takes a right turn, you can see, on the left, a bridge carrying a pipeline over the stream. The fact that the route follows the course of a pipeline is not as obvious as it is on the Giant Kingfisher Trail.

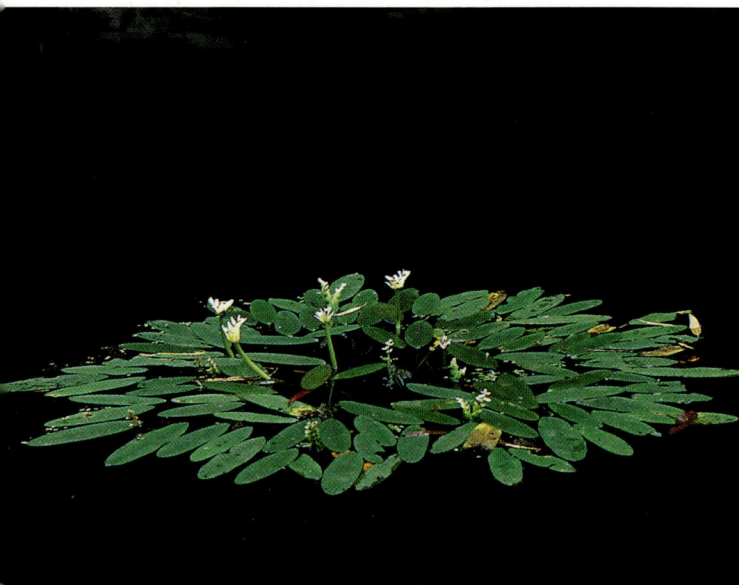

ABOVE: *Waterblommetjies on the peaty water in a placid stretch of the Duiwe River.*
OPPOSITE: *The stream, overgrown by the forest, is sunlit only at midday.*

The trail now follows the course of the Duiwe River through scrub dominated by blackwoods and bluegums. As the stream curves right, you cross it on a low bridge of concreted rock. Shortly thereafter you will come upon a meeting of four paths, where the second map of the trail is mounted alongside the path. The two left-hand paths are the outward and return legs of a short loop to a view site.

If you decide to explore the loop, take the path furthest left, labelled Hoekwil, and make the short, steep climb through low forest to a T-junction on the crest of a ridge. The path to Hoekwil, which continues up the ridge, is the left-hand branch; take the right-hand fork, which heads

down. The north slope of the ridge plunges almost vertically to the forest lining the Duiwe River below.

Soon you will arrive in a small clearing which provides a clear view of the forest on the opposite slope. The stony floor of the clearing is home to aloes and many low succulent plants, which may look out of place here but in fact are not, and also, on the edge of the thicket, to some examples of *Tritoniopsis caffra*, a bulbous plant with spikes of brilliant orange-red flowers in winter. The reason for the apparently anomalous vegetation is that this ridge is of quartzite rock, which is not as fertile as the soils of the valley below. Having descended to the river's edge, the path follows the course of the Duiwe River back to the junction.

At the junction, take the path labelled `Pool', which leads to another concrete-and-rock bridge (built for the pipeline) across the Duiwe River at its confluence with a tributary. Halfway along the `bridge' the path deviates at an arrow pointing up into the trees on the left bank of the tributary. Past more enormous bluegums there are directions on a stone and the last of the trail maps: left is a short cut back to the view site loop, and right is the way to the pool and another viewpoint, the path to which is some 50 m on, to the left. It is a brief scramble up onto another quartzite outcrop, much lower than the first, from which there are views over the wooded valleys along the stream. The main path continues along the course of the stream, crossing it three times at places well marked with yellow arrows. This is a very beautiful part of the walk, with the scenery downstream straight out of a Turner painting.

Shortly after the last crossing, the path comes abruptly to the pool - an eerie place. In summer, during the short period of the day when the sun is over the water, it is a magnificent spot for a swim. In winter, the sheer rock walls surrounding the pool prevent the sun from reaching it and the combined effect of the black water, the dark, vertical cliffs and the lichen streaming from the plants which maintain a precarious foothold in the rocks is impressive but somewhat sombre. This scene is rather more reminiscent of a Japanese brush drawing. The pool is the turning point of the trail and you must follow the path back the way you came.

Back at the start, as a contrast to the forest and riverine bird life on the trail, you may like to drive a further 3 km along the gravel road in the direction of Rondevlei, to where the National Parks Board have built a hide on the edge of Langvlei. You may need a key - available from the office at the Wilderness rest camp - to get in.

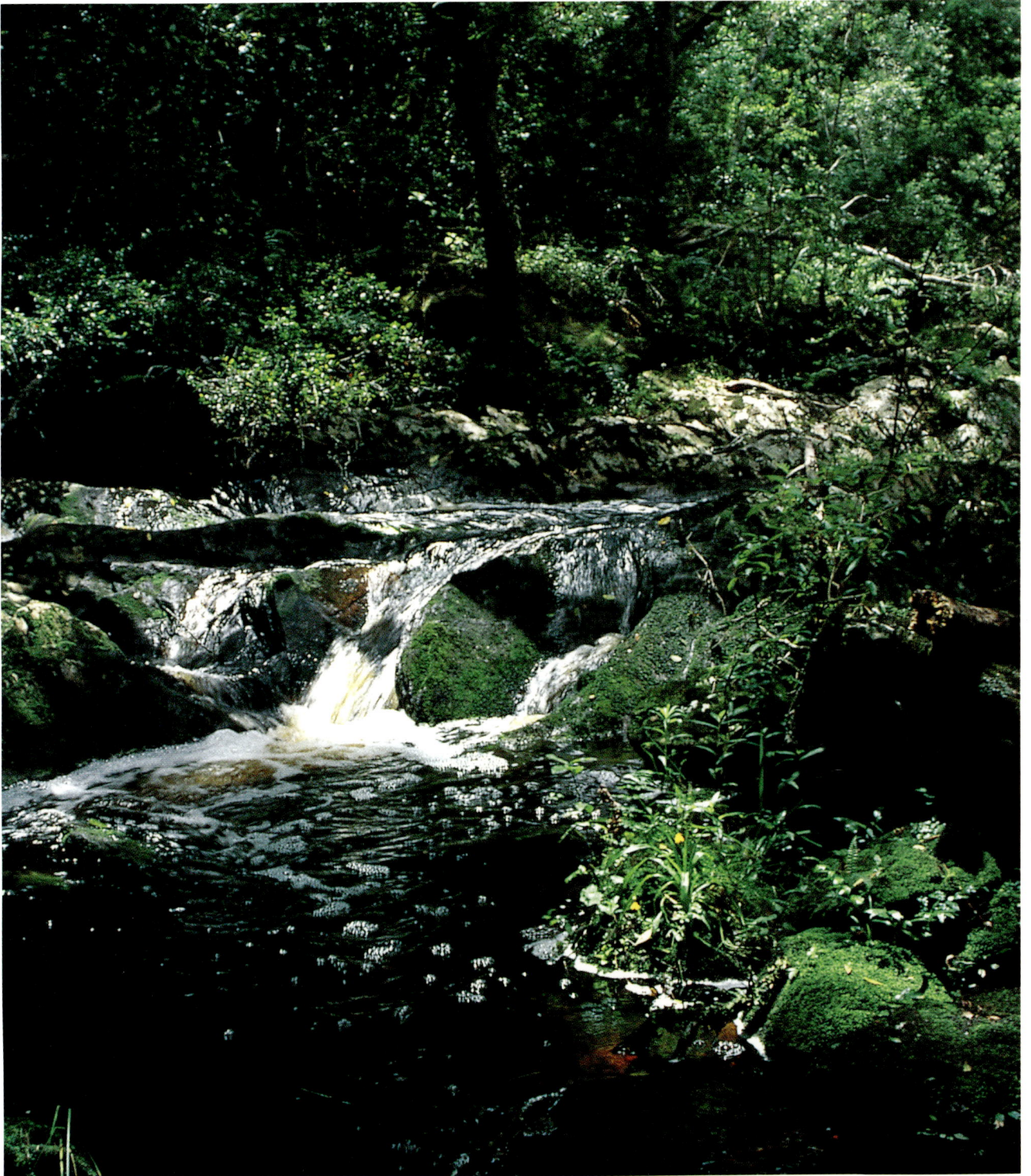

CAPE DUNE MOLERAT TRAIL

A short circuit on the dune overlooking Rondevlei and Swartvlei; it includes some brief, steep climbs. This is a must for bird enthusiasts.

Time: 2 $\frac{1}{2}$-3 hours.
Distance: 6 km.
Exertion: Light to moderate.
Controlling authority: National Parks Board.
Permits: None required; register at start.
Maps and information: An informative map is available at the start; general environmental information is available at the office.
How to get there: 16 km east of Wilderness (6 km west of Sedgefield) on the N2 is the turn-off to the Lakes Nature Conservation Station, also signposted 'George via the Lakes'. Drive 2,8 km along this gravel road and turn right to the conservation station, which is another 1,1 km further on.

A parking area is indicated.
Start/end: The wooden hut containing the register just across the railway line; follow the yellow footprints from the parking area.
Trail markers: Molerat motif on green perspex signs mounted on posts.
Best times to walk: Winter and spring for the flowers.

Precautions: Take water with you, as there is no drinking water along the way. The trail is undermined by the molerats - wear proper hiking boots so as to avoid twisting an ankle.
Features: Extensive views of the lakes, dune fynbos, prolific bird life and a bird feeding-table.

Rondevlei is famous as a bird sanctuary. Most people who visit Lakes Nature Conservation Station do so to view the wealth of bird life associated with the lake and its fringing vegetation from the birdhide on the edge of Rondevlei. On the northern edge of the vlei, separated from it by the railway line between George and Knysna, is a long dune. The Cape Dune Molerat Trail crosses this dune, runs alongside the Wolwe River and Swartvlei and returns along the ridge of the dune.

The flanks of the dune are covered with Milkwood (*Sideroxylon inerme*) forest. Higher up, this gives way to dune fynbos interspersed with scrub forest. The trail provides an opportunity to experience more than just the sanctuary's plentiful bird life: the different vegetation types also comprise a wealth of beautiful plants. Another feature that makes this short trail well worth walking is that the dune provides a superb vantage point for viewing the lakes area.

The trail begins just across the railway line at a walk-through hut where you must fill in a register and issue yourself with a permit. Although you are most unlikely to see the animal which gives the trail its name, you cannot fail to notice the mounds which mark its activity. Anyone who can complete the trail without treading into several mole holes will have achieved something, as the entire dune surface is undermined. In summer, when the dune can be hot, you will be glad of the drinking water you have taken with you.

A Blackwinged Stilt foraging in the shallow water in front of the birdhide at Rondevlei.

There are a series of seven strategically placed benches along the route, so there is always one handy when you need a rest or simply wish to sit and enjoy the scenery.

To begin with, the trail runs alongside the railway line for a little way; then it climbs fairly steeply, through the trees, up the side of the dune. From the top, which is flattish, there are views of Rondevlei and the birdhide as the path winds westwards through a mixture of fynbos and scrub forest. The second bench faces west, and from this you can also see Langvlei. Here the path swings right and crosses the dune. The vegetation along the ridge is dune fynbos. Soon you meet a management track; follow it for a few metres as it makes a steep descent of the dune's north side. The trail leaves the track and veers right, down another track next to the reed beds fringing the Wolwe River. The vegetation here is completely different - the flat, sandy areas are carpeted with Suurvy (*Carpobrotus* spp.) and other vygies; clumps of *Aloe arborescens* beside the track provide a colourful nectar source in winter for Greater Doublecollared Sunbirds. A host of other birds live in the adjoining riverine scrub. You can enjoy the tranquillity of this environment from a bench set under a Milkwood tree a few metres off the track just beyond the overgrown ruins of a cottage.

As the trail rounds the eastern end of the dune next to Swartvlei, there is a bird feeding-table. If you have remembered to bring along some crumbs, worms or other avian delicacies, you can sit here and enjoy watching a sample of the bird life of the riverine scrub and Milkwood forest.

Further on, the trail abruptly leaves the vlei-side and climbs steeply up the eastern end of the dune. Next to the path the sandstone which makes up the core of the dune is exposed: a very soft, friable rock carved into rounded folds by rain and wind. Past two well-placed benches looking out over Swartvlei, the path reaches the beacon at the highest point on the dune. It then runs almost the complete length of the ridge on a track. The views from all along the top are excellent. Just before the path leaves the track and descends to the buildings at the start, the dune narrows and provides, from a single spot, extensive views of Swartvlei to the east, the Wolwe River to the north and Rondevlei and Langvlei to the west, with the mountains behind George just visible. In winter and spring, the fynbos which covers the top of the dune is bright with colour.

The circular route can be completed easily in the three hours specified, leaving ample time for the almost obligatory visit to the birdhide. In the hide, read the comments of previous visitors - they may alert you to a species you otherwise might have missed.

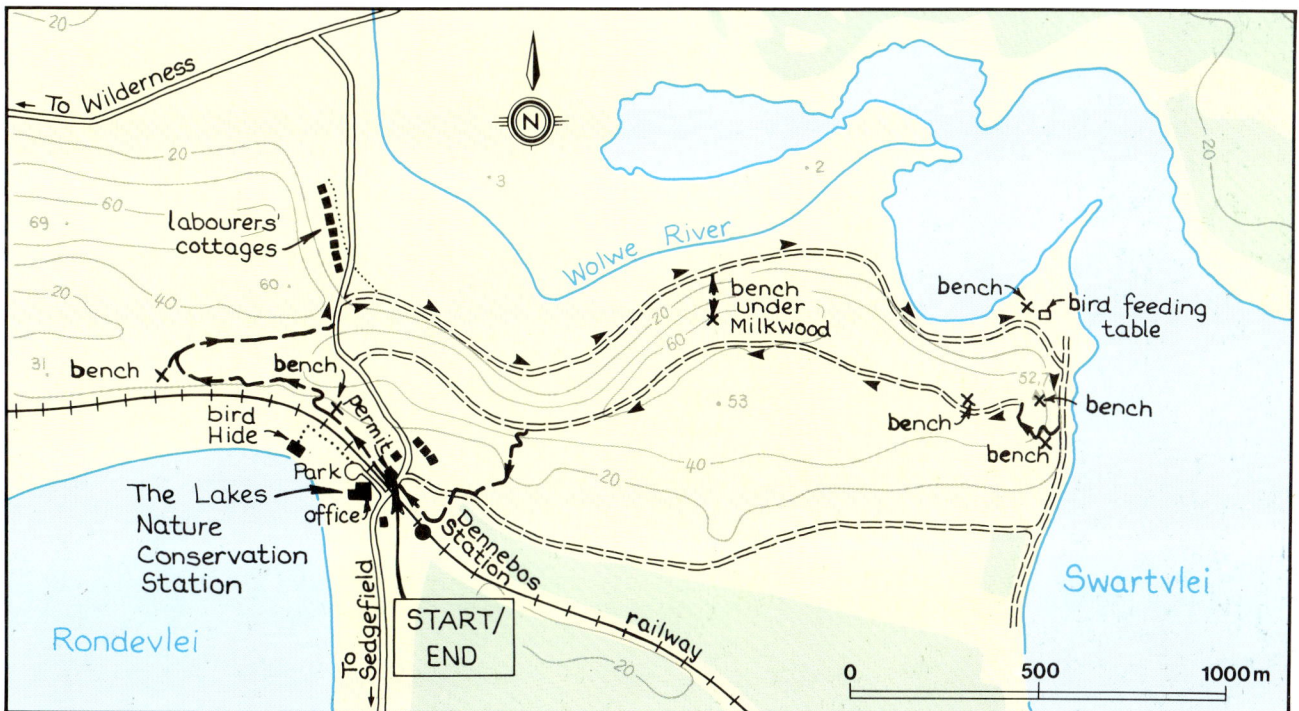

LEFT: *Seen from the Cape Dune Molerat Trail, the Wolwe River meanders into Swartvlei.*
RIGHT: *Hottentot Teal are easily recognizable by their blue bills and black caps.*

OUTENIQUA CHOO-TJOE

In the 1970s South Africa had the distinction of being one of few remaining countries where `steam' enthusiasts could still come to see steam-powered locomotives of all types in daily use. Gradually these were replaced by electric and diesel-electric locomotives, but the route between George and Knysna has been preserved as the exclusive domain of steam locomotives. A most pleasant

The Choo-Tjoe draws into Knysna station.

way to view the countryside in the heart of the Garden Route is at the leisurely pace of the Outeniqua Choo-Tjoe. This mixed-train service (of freight trucks and passenger coaches) runs from George to Knysna and back again every day except Sundays. Most often one of a team of beautifully dec-

orated and maintained Class 24s is used, but occasionally the Garratt GO is used.

The railway line from George reaches the coast at Victoria Bay and plunges into a short tunnel before crossing the spectacular curved Kaaimans River bridge (a favourite spot for steam-train photographers). After passing through a second tunnel, it reaches Wilderness, the first stop. From here it crosses lagoons, lakes and rivers (including the Touw River, where rail and road traffic share the same bridge) *en route* to Sedgefield. It finally reaches Knysna station after crossing the Knysna Lagoon over a long bridge. The route has become a magnet for train-buffs from all over the world.

CHAPTER SEVEN

SEDGEFIELD

Sedgefield lies at Swartvlei's outlet to the sea at the eastern end of the complex of vleis which begins at Wilderness. Only Groenvlei (also known as Lake Pleasant), once part of Swartvlei, lies further east, in the Goukamma Nature Reserve.

The beaches on either side of Sedgefield Lagoon mouth offer delightful walking opportunities. To the east, towards Platbank, are spectacularly eroded sandstone cliffs on which sea birds roost. To the west is Gericke Point, a dramatic rocky headland, but you can walk beyond this all the way to Wilderness if you have the time and inclination. A 6-km (4-hour) walk from Montmere Resort (just north of the N1 highway, on the eastern edge of Swartvlei), up on to the ridge behind it and past the Veld and Vlei camp, provides good views of Swartvlei; this route is equally popular with joggers and cyclists. The best walking, however, is in the near-natural surroundings of the Goukamma Nature Reserve.

The reserve was established in 1960 to conserve a portion of the sand dune and lake complex which elsewhere between Wilderness and Knysna has been extensively modified by housing, agriculture and other human activities. It encompasses, in a relatively small area (1 456 ha), a freshwater lake (Groenvlei), a stretch of coastline backed by a system of high, stable dunes, part of a small river (the Goukamma) and its opening to the sea. For the walker, this provides the chance to view strikingly varied scenery and to enjoy the wealth of bird, animal and plant life associated with these different habitats.

The word `Goukamma' probably derives from the Khoi-

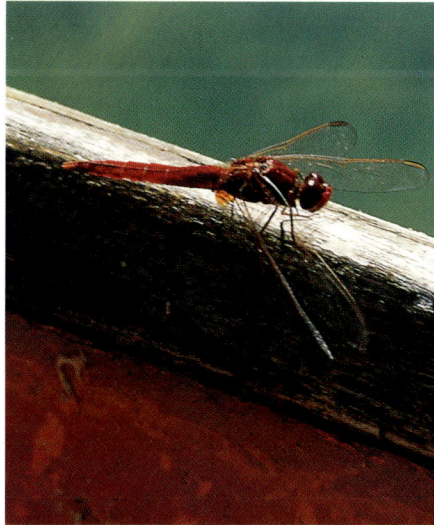

The delicacy of a dragonfly counterpoints the sturdiness of an old rowing boat.

khoi word `ghaukum' for the plant *Carpobrotus deliciosus*, a member of the Mesembryanthemaceae family, which has fleshy leaves on sprawling stems. The name is a reminder that the nomadic Outeniqua tribe of the Khoi-khoi were here long before permanent settlements were established.

Groenvlei, at the western end of the reserve, is a freshwater lake, its level maintained more or less constant by seepage from and to the surrounding dunes. It became cut off from the Swartvlei/Sedgefield Lagoon complex thousands of years ago by the movement of the dunes. It is a bird sanctuary, home to some 75 bird species. Bass have been introduced to the lake and angling is popular; no petrol-powered boats are permitted. There is no shortage of bird life in other parts of the reserve: African Black Oystercatchers breed along the coast and can often be seen on the rocks. African Fish Eagles breed along the Goukamma River. The Milkwood forests host many species, including Paradise Flycatchers, Black-headed Orioles and Knysna Louries.

The three walks described in this chapter provide an experience of the littoral, the dunes and the Milkwood forests. If your time is limited, you may like to take the short walk from the Nature Conservation Station at Groenvlei through the Milkwood forest and alongside the lake itself, where the animal and bird life is especially rich and interesting. To get there, turn off the N2 National Road to Groenvlei 5 km east of Sedgefield, drive past the hotel up onto the dunes and turn left at the sign indicating the CPA Nature Conservation Station. Just before the buildings there is a parking area; opposite this is the start of the trail, where there is a register which should be completed before setting out. Although this walk provides views of Groenvlei, the lake is probably better explored by boat.

The Redknobbed Coot builds its nest of broken reed stems, which it stamps noisily into a floating platform, anchored to the reeds.

GOUKAMMA NATURE RESERVE CIRCUIT

A short, fairly easy circuit from the Goukamma picnic site up and over the dunes, returning through Milkwood forest alongside the river.

The picnic site and the reserve's buildings lie on the estuary of the Goukamma River.

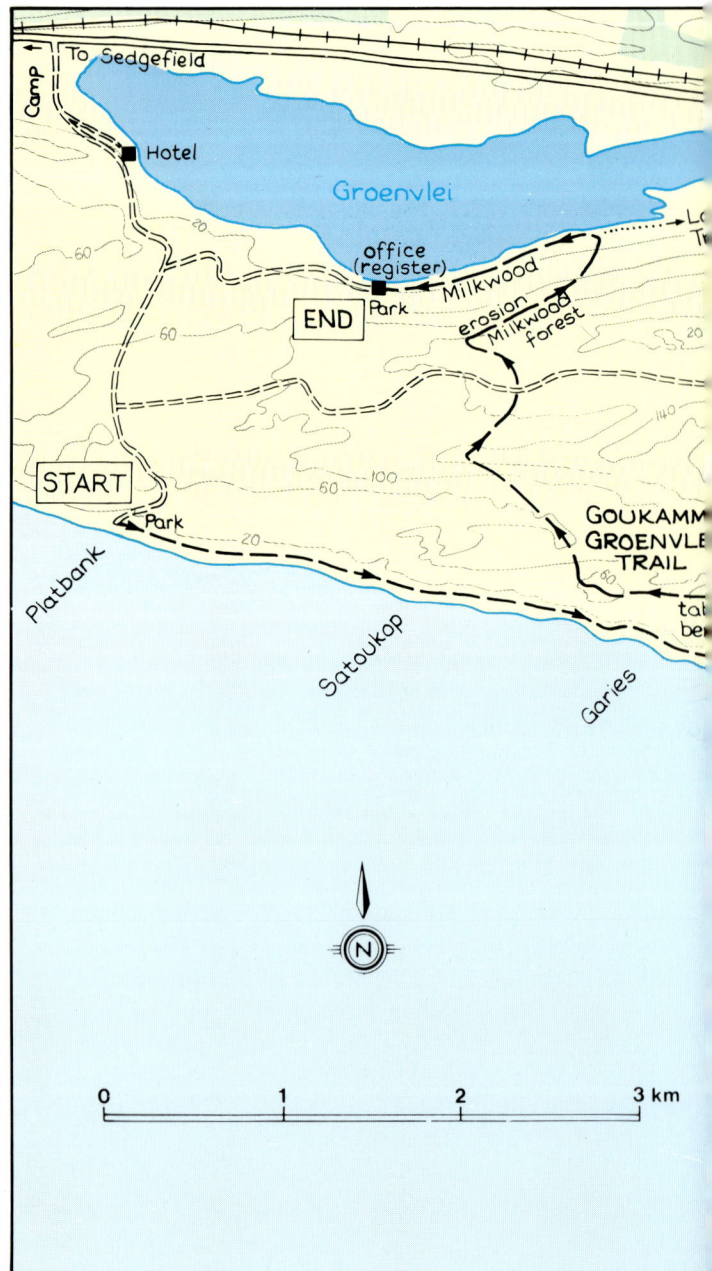

Time: 3 1/2 hours.

Distance: 8 km.

Exertion: Light to moderate.

Controlling authority: Cape Provincial Administration: Department of Nature and Environmental Conservation - Goukamma.

Permits: An entry fee is payable at the gate of the Goukamma picnic site. Fill in the register at the start of the trail across the suspension bridge over the river.

Maps and information: A sketch map is available at the picnic site entrance; further information can be had from the office there.

How to get there: From Sedgefield, drive 13 km along the N2 in the direction of Knysna and take the turn-off to Buffelsbaai on the right. The entrance to the Goukamma Nature Reserve is 6,1 km from the N2.

Leave your car near the gate at the northern end of the picnic area, 800 m from the entrance to the reserve.

Start/end: Walk up the track (closed to public vehicles) parallel with the river and cross the water on the suspension bridge. The register which marks the start and end of the trail is on the other side.

Trail markers: None; arrows mark changes of direction or indicate the correct route to take at intersections.

Best times to walk: Spring - for the dune fynbos flowers.

Precautions: Watch out for puff adders on the dunes. The mosquitoes in the Milkwood forest can be voracious, so you will need an insect repellent.

Features: Suspension bridge, dune fynbos, coastal scenery, Milkwood forest, the Goukamma River and birds.

This route is a well-planned introduction to the variety of scenery and interest that the Goukamma Reserve has to offer. Although it is not a strenuous walk, there are some short, fairly steep climbs up the dune, on which the loose sand proves more tiring than a firm footing would be.

Crossing the suspension bridge spanning the Goukamma River can be fun, as your steps may start the bridge oscillating. It is perfectly safe but, if the movement gets too much for you, stop halfway for a while and enjoy the lovely views up and down the quiet waters of the river. On the other side there is a register to fill in before setting out.

The path climbs steeply through some dense riverside

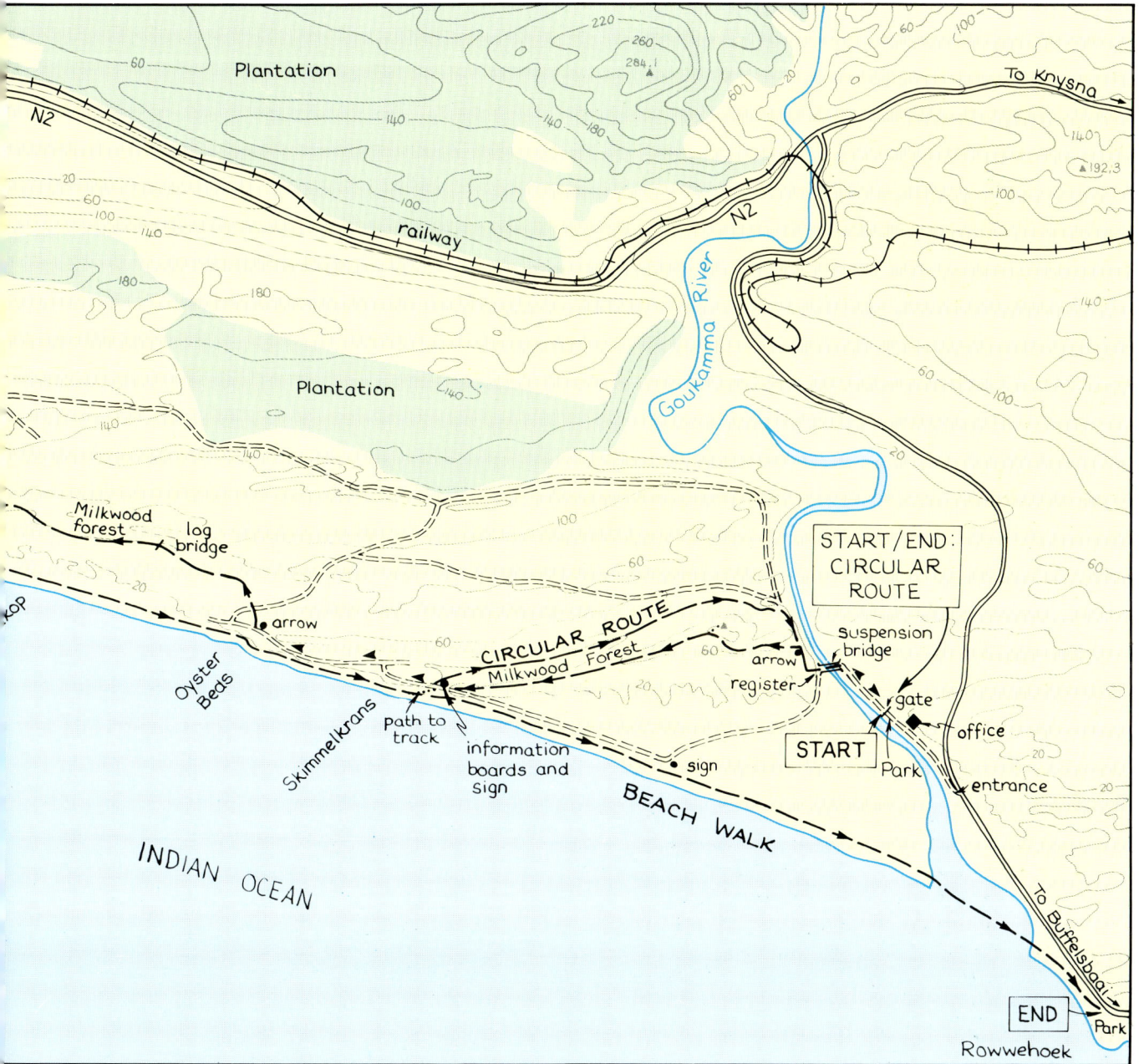

101

vegetation onto a low ridge of a dune. From this point there is a clear view to the river mouth. You can also see up-river, where the brilliant green of a Kikuyu pasture next to the river on a farm adjoining the reserve contrasts with the muted colours of the dune vegetation and the purple-blue silhouette of the Outeniqua Mountains in the distance.

On the sea side of the dune dense piles of dead rooikrans (*Acacia cyclops*) and Port Jackson (*Acacia saligna*) trees attest to an ongoing effort by the reserve's management to eradicate these invasive aliens. Many years ago the former Department of Forestry was responsible for planting these trees, as well as Marram grass (*Ammophila arenaria*), to stabilize drift sand on the beach side of the dunes. The legacy of this misguided policy is the dense thicket of acacia which can be seen adjacent to the beach further along the trail, where it has smothered the natural vegetation.

An arrow on a board indicates that you must take the left-hand branch at a junction - the right-hand path is the return route. Higher up, Camphor bushes (*Tarconanthus camphoratus*) mark the fringe of the forest of Milkwoods (*Sideroxylon inerme*) that covers the dune's northern side. At the top of the dune a short turn-off to the right leads to a beacon from where there is a fine 360^0 view. From this point the path runs along the ridge of what is now revealed as one of a sea of dunes stretching westwards along the coast. Beyond the dunes, Cradock's Berg rises above George on the horizon. The path drops steadily, through dune fynbos where the Candelabra flower (*Brunsvigia orientalis*) flowers in March, into scrub forest. At the end of the dune, the path, which is now at beach level in low forest, meets a track; 10 m to the right are information boards describing porcupine, bush pig, bushbuck, grysbok, honey badger and Cape clawless otter, all of which, depending on your luck and the time of the day, can be seen in the reserve. Here, too, is a sign show-

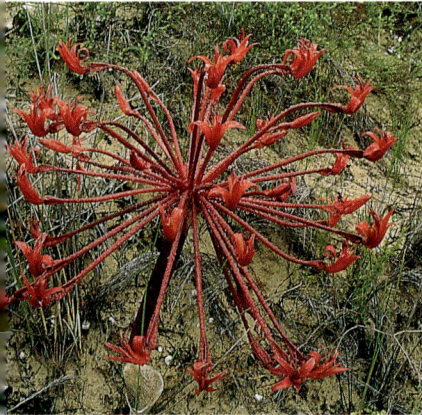

LEFT: *Candelabra flowers are a striking sight in March against the flat colours of dune fynbos.* BELOW: *The path runs down the ridge of the dune on the first leg of the Circuit.*

ing the direction to Skimmelkrans and the beach (left), the way to Groenvlei (ahead), and the path into the forest you will take for the return leg of the circular route (right).

The Milkwood forest is a very different environment from the dune fynbos. In among the trees, some of which are named, both the light and sounds are muted. Although you can hear birds, they are difficult to spot and patience is required to identify them in the semi-gloom. When I walked the route, it was at once thrilling and frustrating to hear the cry of an African Fish Eagle from here and not be able to see it. The sombre colours beneath the trees were relieved by splashes of orange where filtered sunlight caught the colour of the bark of Bastard saffronwood (*Cassine peragua*) trees. These trees form one of the major components of this forest-type. The Milkwoods themselves are unmistakable; some have massive trunks. Droppings along the path indicate the presence of bushbuck. Keep a watchful eye out for the arrows that show the way where the trail is a bit faint.

This stretch of the path runs in a valley between dunes. This becomes evident when the path emerges from the forest and continues, now in fynbos, alongside the trees. The beacon on top of the dune appears to your right. At an arrow, the path turns right, back into the trees, for the last part of the walk alongside a curve of the Goukamma River, which can be glimpsed through the trees from time to time.

When the path emerges from the forest it meets the outward leg of the circuit, and you have a clear view of the river below. As I walked down this section, a grysbok doe was browsing alongside the path below, oblivious of my presence. Grysbok are shy animals and will disappear quickly on sighting people. As I watched (and before I could photograph it), this one ambled off quietly into the thick riverine vegetation in front of the suspension bridge. This undisturbed natural scene was a fitting end to my walk.

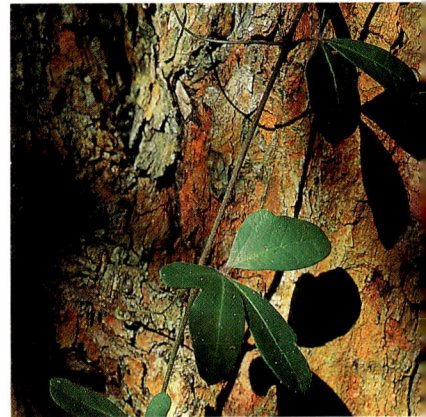

RIGHT: *The brilliant orange bark of Bastard saffronwood; the tree's leaves are reputed to be toxic.*
BELOW: *Conservation and agriculture exist side by side: pasturage on the far bank of the Goukamma marks the boundary of the reserve.*

GOUKAMMA-GROENVLEI TRAIL

A moderately arduous walk over the dunes from the Goukamma River, finally descending through a Milkwood forest to the shores of Groenvlei.

Time: 5 hours.

Distance: 13 km.

Exertion: Moderate.

Controlling authority: Cape Provincial Administration: Department of Nature and Environmental Conservation - Goukamma.

Permits: An entry fee is payable at the gate of the Goukamma picnic site. Fill in the register at the start of the trail across the suspension bridge over the Goukamma River.

Maps and information: A sketch map is available at the picnic site entrance; additional information can be had from the office there.

How to get there: Leave one car at the Conservation Station at Groenvlei. To get there, drive down the Lake Pleasant road which leaves the N2 5 km east of Sedgefield (or 8 km west of the Buffelsbaai turn-off) past the caravan park and hotel up onto the dune. Turn left at a sign to the Conservation Station and follow this road to its end. To get to the Goukamma Nature Reserve itself, drive 13 km out of Sedgefield along the N2 in the direction of Knysna and take the turn-off on the right to Buffelsbaai.

The entrance to the Goukamma Nature Reserve is 6,1 km from the N2. Leave your car near the gate at the northern end of the picnic area, 800 m from the entrance.

Start: Walk up the track (closed to public vehicles) parallel with the river and cross the water on the suspension bridge. The register which marks the start and end of the trail is on the other side of the river.

Trail markers: None; arrows mark the route at intersections or where there may be uncertainty over the route.

End: The Conservation Station at Groenvlei, where you must have transport waiting.

Best times to walk: Spring - for the flowers in the dune fynbos.

Precautions: Puff adders are common on the dunes, so watch where you place your feet. The mosquitoes in the Milkwood forest can be troublesome, so use an insect repellent. There is no water en route, therefore be sure to take liquid with you, especially in summer when the dunes can be hot.

Features: Grand coastal scenery, dune fynbos, Milkwood forest, a wide variety of bird life and buck, including bontebok.

This one-way trail (*see* map, page 100) is not so strenuous that you cannot afford time to make a detour to the beach if you start out early enough. As it crosses the dunes, the route involves some short climbs. The only places you could possibly stray off the path are in the scrub forest, so keep an eye on the path there; elsewhere the route is obvious. The attractions of the trail are the scenery - fine views of the Goukamma coastline and the countryside inland - and the vegetation (dune fynbos, and scrub forest) and associated fauna that make up the unique environment of the dunes themselves.

The first part of the trail is common to the Goukamma Nature Reserve Circuit; from the suspension bridge over the Goukamma River, the path winds up to the top of a dune next to a Trigonometric Survey beacon, then runs down the ridge of the dune through fynbos and scrub forest to meet a track. Just beyond this, there is a signposted path to Skim-

RIGHT: *The Rameron Pigeon's yellow eye-surround is distinctive. These pigeons gather in small flocks to feed in fruiting trees.*
FAR RIGHT: *Afternoon sunlight filters through the twisted branches of the Milkwoods above Groenvlei.*

melkrans which provides an easy route for a detour to the beach. On the opposite side of the track, next to information boards that give details of some of the reserve's animals, is the path which is the return leg of the Goukamma Circuit.

The trail to Groenvlei continues along the track westwards through scrub forest, where we saw signs of porcupine. Bark had been scraped off the bole of a Bastard saffronwood (*Cassine peragua*) tree, and there were indications that the animals had been rooting in the leaf litter on the forest floor nearby. Rameron Pigeons which had been feasting on the fruits of the Kershout (*Pterocelastrus tricuspidatus*) clattered off through the trees as we approached. On the track were spoor of bushbuck and bush pig droppings. The animals featured on the information boards are certainly there but are not often seen in daytime.

Over a rise, the track comes to the edge of the dunes, where there is a clear view westwards of the coast. At low tide you can see, along the beach, the flat rocks of the intertidal zone known as the Oysterbeds. From this spot, the track swings away from the coast to a T-junction 30 m inland; you must take the indicated track left. Over the next rise, another arrow shows the way off the track onto a path which heads further inland through low fynbos, then swings left on the ridge of a minor dune. On the right is a high dune, the slopes of which are covered with scrub forest. You enter the forest where the path drops to the bottom of a small valley across a log bridge. The path here is a tunnel cut through the trees where, on a hot day, there is welcome shade and cool air. Enjoy this, because soon the trail turns abruptly right, out of the trees, and begins to climb steadily up to the ridge of the high dune. Beyond some Milkwoods (*Sideroxylon inerme*) on the slope, the path traverses fynbos. In spring this veld is full of colour; particularly beautiful are the flowers of *Freesia alba* and the Riversdale bluebell (*Gladiolus rogersii*) which grow larger here than I have seen elsewhere.

The path runs along the ridge to a high point where a table and benches invite you to stop and rest. From here you can enjoy clear views of the dune country you have crossed and of the distant coastline to the east; the nearer coastline is hidden by neighbouring dunes.

Now the path drops into forest where there are some siz-

able Milkwood trees. Emerging on the other side, it follows the ridge of a short dune - back into forest; once through these trees, the path descends to the sandy base of a wide valley. In this area there are some fine examples of Camphor bushes (*Tarconanthus camphoratus*) - small trees here, and the largest bushes of the Blombos (*Metalasia muricata*) I have ever seen. These had stems like the trunks of small trees, and must be very ancient plants. Also visible were large hoof-marks, possibly those of the small herd of bontebok resident in the reserve.

Once across the valley bottom, through which a track runs, you begin a steady climb up the side of the next high dune. At the top, the trail swings inland again and crosses a flattish area of fynbos dominated by *Passerina rigida* but including small, colourful herbs such as *Geranium incanum*, and geophytes (among which are more *Gladiolus rogersii*). The path skirts a fence and reaches the top of the dune over-looking Groenvlei. From this point there are magnificent views westwards to the coast near Sedgefield and to Swartvlei and Rondevlei inland. Below you lies Groenvlei.

The last leg of the trail takes you steeply down, at first over the ridge, then the flank, of the dune into the Milkwood forest above the lake. In the forest we were lucky to see the courting display of a pair of Bluemantled Flycatchers, birds not often encountered. At the bottom of the dune the path runs for a short way between the reeds fringing the vlei and the trees before it skirts the ranger's house under the Milk-woods and reaches the parking area at the end of the trail.

ABOVE: *Moorhens are common in the reeds on the vlei's edge; a sighting of a Little Bittern* (RIGHT) *is rare, however.*
ABOVE RIGHT: *The Aandgonna on a dune above Groenvlei.*

GOUKAMMA BEACH WALK

A walk between Platbank and Rowwehoek, at the mouth of the Goukamma River, along the magnificent beach in the Goukamma Nature Reserve.

The coastline which stretches from Platbank in the west some 14 km to Rowwehoek in the east forms both a distinct ecological unit of the Goukamma Nature Reserve and one of its boundaries (*see* map, page 100). I have walked the beach many times, and each time it has been a different and memorable experience. It is one of the loveliest, least-spoilt stretches of coastline along the Garden Route.

You can walk in either direction, but you will have to arrange to have transport waiting at the other end. If the Goukamma River is open to the sea, it is easier to end (or begin) the walk at the picnic site alongside the river rather than at Rowwehoek; from the suspension bridge across the river a track leads directly to the beach on the western side of the river mouth.

If you start walking not later than 3 hours before low tide, you will be in no danger of being cut off. If you are beginning the walk from Platbank as suggested, head down onto the beach and turn left (east).

The long sweep of sand is broken by several headlands where wave action has undercut the dunes over millennia to expose the sandstone core. Because this rock is generally very frail and brittle, slabs of sandstone have tumbled down onto the beach, leaving exposed faces which have been eroded by the rain, wind and salt spray to show their stratification. Skimmelkrans is the most easterly of these headlands. Some of the rock faces here have a most peculiar, contorted appearance and reveal what appear to be pipes.

Time: 3 1/2 hours.
Distance: 14 km.
Exertion: Light.
Controlling authority: Cape Provincial Administration: Department of Nature and Environmental Conservation - Goukamma.
Permits: None required.
Maps and information: There is a sketch map available at the gate to the Goukamma Nature Reserve on the Buffelsbaai road; additional information is available from the office there.
How to get there: To leave a car at Rowwehoek, on the eastern side of the Goukamma River mouth: Drive 13 km out of Sedgefield along the N2 in the direction of Knysna and turn off right to Buffelsbaai; the entrance to the Goukamma Nature Reserve is about 6 km down this road and Rowwehoek is 1 km beyond that. To reach the start: From the N2, take the turn-off to Lake Pleasant (Groenvlei) 5 km east of Sedgefield and follow the unsurfaced road past the caravan park and hotel over the dunes to the parking area above the beach at Platbank.
Start: On the boardwalk down to the sand at Platbank.
Trail markers: None.
End: Rowwehoek on the rocks on the eastern side of the Goukamma River mouth, next to the Buffelsbaai road.
Best times to walk: At low tide in any season.
Precautions: Unless you walk this route at low tide, you will be cut off, particularly during spring tides. On no account try to climb the soft, friable sandstone cliffs of the dunes, as rock falls are common. The wind can blow strongly along the beach; it is preferable to walk with the wind behind you.
Features: Unspoilt beach; mussel beds and other life in the intertidal zone; sandstone cliffs and birds of the littoral.

A Kelp Gull makes off with a live octopus taken from a rock pool.

One of the pleasures of walking this route at very low tide is the sight of thousands of mussels, packed tight together on the temporarily exposed rocks. The Oysterbeds to the west of Skimmelkrans are formed by a long, wide stretch of flat rock at sea level below the cliffs. This is an ideal spot to spend a bit of time exploring the life in the intertidal zone. A feature of this beach are the small, flattened and beautifully rounded pebbles which dot the sand at low tide. These come in a remarkable range of colours, from grey through green, beige and brown, and some are attractively patterned.

Jellyfish stranded on the beach are the target for hundreds of *Bullia* plough snails which doggedly fight the undertow of an occasional wave to reach their prey. Kelp Gulls take advantage of low tides to go hunting in the exposed rock pools. You will see African Black Oystercatchers along the beach, but they are wary birds and will not permit you to come too close. Almost invisible on the sand are tiny White-fronted Plovers with their delightful habit of running up the sand to escape an incoming wave. If you are lucky, you might see an African Fish Eagle soaring over the dunes next to the beach: there are two breeding pairs along the Goukamma River and they can sometimes be seen early in the morning on the dunes at the river mouth or perched on a log midstream. The river estuary is home to a large variety of water birds.

In summer the sea invites a swim, but be careful - the sidewash and undertow can be savage. There are several places among the rocks where you can swim safely or just float lazily on the swell - possibly at eye level with an octopus in a crevice.

If you are walking in an easterly direction and are running out of time, there is an obvious path, made of logs to prevent erosion of the sand, which leaves the beach 50 m or so beyond Skimmelkrans. This leads to a junction where the Goukamma Nature Reserve Circuit turns to commence its return leg, and the Goukamma-Groenvlei Trail continues along a track which runs along the low dunes next to the beach from the Goukamma River mouth.

ABOVE: *Plough snails make a meal of a beached jellyfish.*
RIGHT: *The view west from Platbank towards Sedgefield Lagoon mouth and Gericke Point.*

108

CHAPTER EIGHT

KNYSNA FORESTS

The visitor who drives into Knysna on the modern coastal road from Sedgefield can have little appreciation of the enormous difficulties experienced by early settlers in reaching the area. A drive along the Passes road between Saasveld and Knysna might give him some inkling of the formidable barriers presented to those pioneers by the uninterrupted stretch of natural forest and the steep-sided valleys of the several rivers which run from the Outeniqua Mountains to the sea. Despite these obstacles, however, several families had settled in the area around Knysna Lagoon towards the end of the 18th century.

In 1804 there arrived in Knysna - at the head of a procession which included his family, friends, retainer and possessions - a man whose origins are still disputed. Allegedly the illegitimate son of the teenage British monarch, George III, and Hannah Lightfoot, a Quaker, George Rex certainly did not suffer from a lack of funds. Shortly before his arrival in Knysna at the age of 39, he had bought the farm Melkhoutkraal on the eastern side of the lagoon; later he expanded his holdings to include the whole lagoon area and the Heads. Melkhoutkraal was developed into a fine estate and George Rex and Knysna became virtually synonymous.

The answer to the difficulties of transport to and from Knysna appeared to lie in developing the lagoon into a harbour. To this end the lagoon was surveyed and, although the first vessel to attempt the passage through the Heads - the *Emu*, a naval brig - was wrecked, the harbour was established. An Admiralty scheme to establish a Royal Navy shipbuilding yard at Knysna never materialized, but a ship-

Bracket fungi - a decorative and vital component of the forest ecosystem.

building industry was established nevertheless by another family whose name is inextricably associated with Knysna. The Thesen family left Norway in 1869 intending to emigrate to New Zealand but, as they tried to round Cape Agulhas, their ship was blown back by a gale and they put into Cape Town. One of the sons sailed to Knysna and his enthusiasm for the place persuaded the family to settle there and start a boat-building and joinery business, which soon flourished. By the early part of this century the Thesens had built up a small fleet of coasters.

The port of Knysna remained busy until the construction of the railway between George and Knysna (opened in 1928) put an end to maritime trade with the town. The harbour was finally deproclaimed in 1954, and only yachts use it now.

Apart from wool produced on local farms, the main produce of the area was timber. During the 19th century the forests to the rear of Knysna, which formed part of the broad belt of forest on the coastal plateau between George and Humansdorp, were ruthlessly exploited. Some of the timber was used locally but by far the larger part was transported to Cape Town by ship.

The remaining large area of indigenous forest behind Knysna is one of the town's greatest natural assets. In the forests have been laid out several trails, described below, which allow the walker to enjoy the timeless peace and beauty of this unique environment. Two easy walks provide delightful yet contrasting views of the Goudveld Forest and are also of historial interest. The short trail at Millwood evokes the days of the brief gold-rush which had the place in turmoil at the end of last century, and at nearby Jubilee Creek you can take a stroll in beautiful forest that was the scene of past alluvial mining.

Bucolic reflections in Knysna Lagoon on a still summer morning belie the urban activity a stone's throw away.

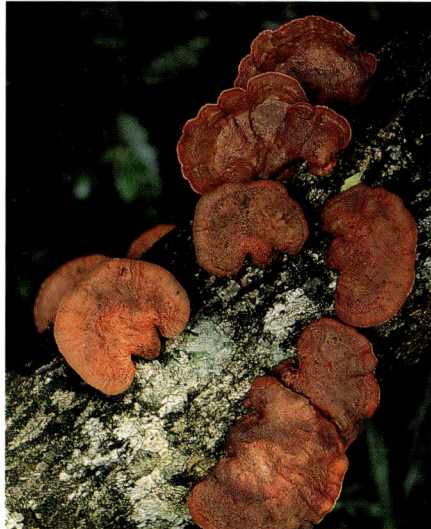

JUBILEE CREEK WALK

A short walk in enchanting forest surroundings which were the scene of alluvial gold mining in the past. It begins and ends at an idyllic picnic spot.

Time: 1 - 1 1/2 hours.

Distance: 4 km.

Exertion: Light.

Controlling authority: Goud-veld Forest Station.

Permits: No permit required; register at the entrance to the forest station.

Maps and information: Available where you register; there is an informative display on the southern Cape forests here.

How to get there: Drive 7 km west from Knysna on the N2 to the Rheenendal turn-off. The turn-off to the Goudveld State Forest is found 13 km along the Rheenendal road; it is also signposted 'Millwood Gold Fields'. The entrance, where you register, is 2,3 km up this road and 5,1 km further on, in the forest, is the signposted turn-off to Jubilee Creek picnic site and walk.

Start/end: The eastern side of the bridge at the picnic area.

Trail markers: None.

Best times to walk: Any time.

Precautions: Enter the old mining shafts at your own risk and carry a torch; the shafts, as well as parts of the paths, can be slippery when wet.

Features: Historical interest, natural forest and stream.

Jubilee Creek is close to Millwood and you can do the walks at both venues on the same day. The picnic area at the Creek is a delightful place to rest between walks and is deservedly popular. Lush green, man-made meadow studded with yellow daisies in spring lies on both sides of a gently flowing stream. The gloom in the encircling natural forest hides mosses, fungi, flowers and birds as colourful, in their way, as the flowers in the bright sunlight.

At one time the creek teemed with life of another kind - miners bent on making their fortunes. Whereas the mining of the mountain slopes around Millwood followed quartz reefs, Jubilee Creek yielded mostly alluvial gold. Some 200 m along the stream from the start of the route you will find the first evidence of past mining activity here in the form of a pit to the left of the path signposted 'Old alluvial gold diggings'. To reach this point, you will have passed through a beautiful section of forest containing a variety of ferns including Tree ferns (*Cyathea capensis*). It was on this initial stretch that I spotted a Chorister Robin in the undergrowth. The sound of forest birds is all around, the liquid call of the Blackheaded Oriole unmistakable.

The path continues on the south bank of the stream, some-

The placid waters of Jubilee Creek at the first crossing.

times breaking out of the forest into riverine vegetation where tall plants of *Wachendorfia thyrsiflora* show off their spikes of yellow flowers in early summer.

Some way beyond the first stream crossing, as the path climbs a small rise through the trees, there is a sign to the right indicating a water furrow made by the miners, and over the rise are the ring-barked remains of some massive bluegums (*Eucalyptus globulus*) planted by them. Just beyond this, I was alerted by the noise of a flock of frantic Cape White-eyes to the sight of a boomslang draped over a young Outeniqua yellowwood (*Podocarpus falcatus*) across the stream; it was probably intent on raiding a nest. The snake disappeared into the dense undergrowth as I made the second stream crossing. On the other bank of the stream, the path branches; to the left there is a continuation, into Millwood Creek, of the section of the Outeniqua Hiking Trail on which you have been walking, while the right-hand branch leads to the last short section of this walk. Past another digging, you reach a pool and waterfall which mark the turning point. The pool is broad and relatively shallow, but deep enough for an enjoyable dip on a hot day.

When I walked back, I was surprised to see a second boomslang next to the path just beyond the first stream crossing. A magnificent specimen, dark green above and yellow below, this snake tentatively stuck its head out of the grass to check that I was well out of its way before crossing the path into the dense riverside vegetation. This was on a hot October day when the snakes were probably newly active after winter. These tales of reptilian encounters are not intended to deter you from walking this beautiful path, but rather to emphasize that boomslang are almost always timid and pose no danger to anyone who leaves them alone.

A male adult boomslang in one of many possible colour phases.

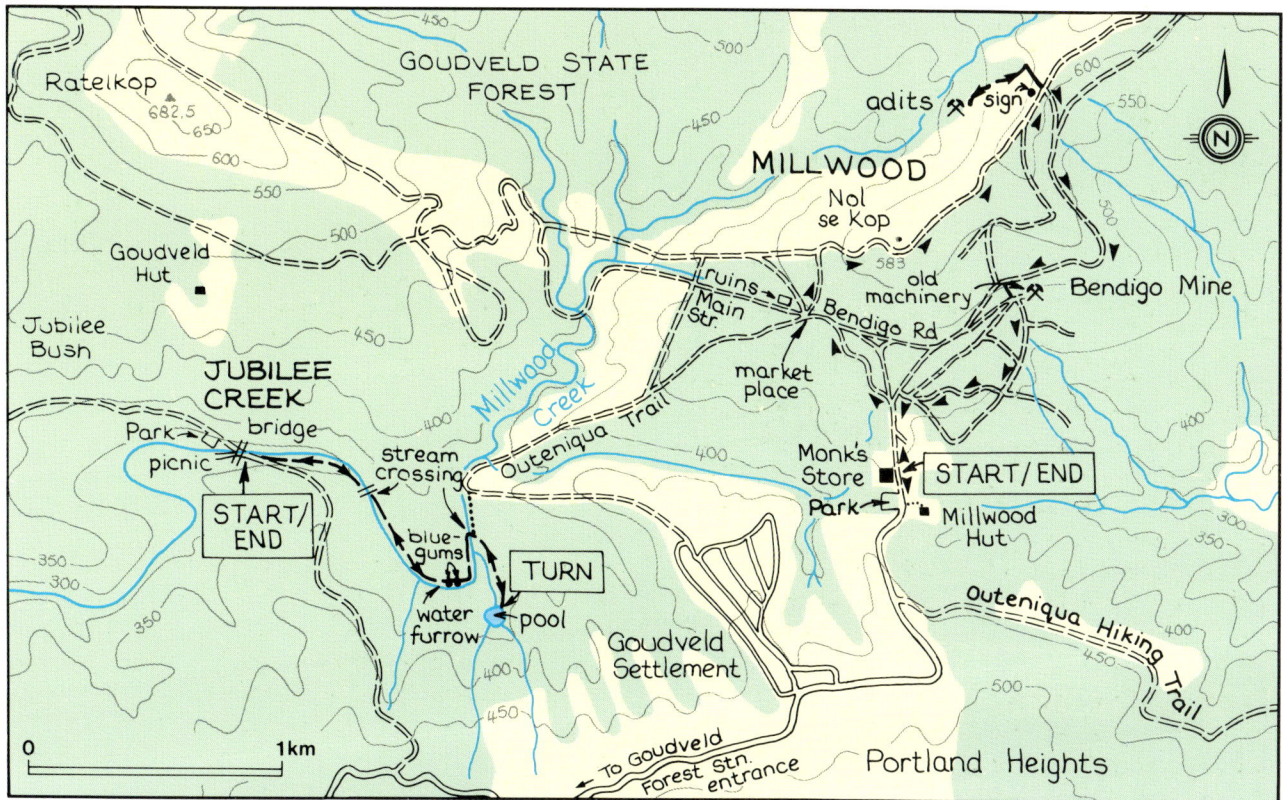

MILLWOOD CIRCUIT

A short, easy walk through the historic gold-mining area on Nol se Kop, a foothill of the Outeniqua Mountains; minor detours offer glimpses of old mines and mining equipment.

Time: 2 - 2 $^{1}/_{2}$ hours.

Distance: 5,6 km.

Exertion: Light.

Controlling authority: Goudveld Forest Station.

Permits: No permit required; register at the entrance to the forest station.

Maps and information: Available where you register; there is an informative display on the southern Cape forests here.

How to get there: Drive 7 km west from Knysna on the N2 to the Rheenendal turn-off. The turn-off to the Goudveld State Forest is found 13 km along the Rheenendal road; it is also signposted `Millwood Gold Fields'. The entrance, where you register, is 2,3 km up this road. Continue another 8,6 km to the parking area next to old Monk's Store.

Start/end: Monk's Store.

Trail markers: yellow perspex squares with a black circle enclosing a pick and shovel.

Best times to walk: Any time.

Precautions: Enter the old mining shafts at your own risk and carry a torch; the shafts, as well as parts of the paths, can be slippery when wet.

Features: Historical interest, fynbos and mountain scenery.

The area where gold was mined briefly in the 1880s is the venue for two short walks. One of these, the Millwood Circuit (*see* map, page 113), begins at the only building still standing at what was the mining settlement of Millwood. This is Monk's Store, otherwise known as Materolli (a corruption of the store's original name, `Mother Holly'), which now houses mementoes of the town's heyday. It is well worth spending some time here before setting out.

In all truth, there is very little on the walk itself that provides any inkling of the activity in and around the town during the gold-mining boom years. Its only other surviving building is in Knysna. Millwood House, as it is known, is a museum whose exhibits recreate the atmosphere of the time.

From Monk's Store the route follows a track through a pine plantation. There are some street signs which indicate where the old town's roads ran, and the ruins of some foundations, but this is all. The buildings of Millwood were of

LEFT: *Spring daisies at Jubilee Creek's picnic site.*
BELOW: *Monk's Store exhibits memorabilia of mining madness.*

wood with roofs of corrugated-iron - materials easily reused elsewhere. From the crossroads signposted 'Market Place', the track runs through the plantation behind Millwood and then next to the trees along the ridge of Nol se Kop. From here, there is a view west, of the wooded valley below (the Millwood Nature Reserve) and the Outeniquas. At a point where the main route turns right, back into the plantation, there is a path to the left and down the slope, signposted `To mines 530 m'. This branch leads past the fern-fringed edge of natural forest to the entrances of two old mine shafts, reached by a short, steep climb down.

Back in the plantation, the forestry track leads down the eastern slopes of Nol se Kop towards Millwood again. Shortly before it leaves the pines, a signposted path drops straight down the slope to the entrance to one of the best-known mines, the Bendigo, near which has been erected a shed which contains some interesting relics of old mining machinery. From here it is a short walk back to the start.

TOP: *A miner's home rebuilt in Knysna, Millwood House is part of the town's museum.*
LEFT: *In the derelict graveyard at Millwood, this headstone commemorates a young Englishman who died there, aged only 24.*
BELOW: *The view of the Outeniquas from the track on Nol se Kop.*

THE MILLWOOD GOLD RUSH

Gold-diggers take time out from sinking a new mine shaft at Millwood to strike the pose considered appropriate for photographs in the 1880s. The photographer was none other than the Knysna apothecary, Mr Groom.

In 1876 James Hooper, who farmed at Ruigtevlei on the slopes above Swartvlei, picked up what he thought might be a gold nugget in the Karatara River. The Knysna apothecary, William Groom, confirmed that it was indeed gold. Hooper showed the nugget to C.F. Osborne, a Government Roads Inspector who had been on the Californian gold fields and who enthusiastically began to prospect. News of the find spread and other prospectors poured into the area, where promising signs were being found of alluvial gold.

By 1885 there were 200 diggers living in tents around Millwood. In 1886, by which time encouraging traces of gold had also been found in quartz reefs in the nearby mountain slopes, Millwood's population had swollen to about 1 000, including 600 prospectors from as far away as California,

Australia and Cornwall. Companies were floated and Millwood grew into a thriving town of wood and corrugated iron houses, with shops, a post office, a bank and six hotels. In 1888 as many as 1 400 claims were being worked all over the difficult terrain around Millwood, including the famous Bendigo mine whose shaft can still be seen near the site of the town.

Although substantial amounts of gold were recovered at Millwood (about £11 000 worth in all), the workings soon gave out and by 1890 most of the companies were bankrupt and the diggers had migrated to the gold fields on the Witwatersrand. By the end of the century, when only a handful of prospectors remained, Millwood no longer existed, its buildings dismantled and re-erected elsewhere.

TERBLANS TRAIL

A short circuit through natural forest at Gouna which provides a perfect introduction to the forest environment. Grootdraai picnic site is the starting point.

Time: 2 1/2 hours.

Distance: 6,5 km.

Exertion: Light to moderate.

Controlling authority: Gouna State Forest Station.

Permits: None required; register at the picnic site.

Maps and information: Colour map with information on sale at Department of Water Affairs and Forestry in Knysna.

How to get there: Take the well-signposted road to the Gouna State Forest which leaves the N2 as it skirts the Knysna Lagoon. Past the entrance to the Gouna State Forest Station, 17 km from Knysna, is the well-marked Grootdraai picnic site, where you park.

Start/end: Across the road (Kom-se-pad) from the Grootdraai picnic site.

Trail markers: Bushpig motif on yellow perspex squares.

Best times to walk: Summer if you wish to swim; a delightful, shady haven on any warm day.

Precautions: Keep to the path in the forest.

Features: Magnificent natural forest, swimming spot and forest birds.

The Terblans Trail involves a short, fairly steep climb into and out of the valley of the Rooiels stream, but elsewhere the route is more-or-less level. Many of the trees are numbered, so take with you a copy of the National Tree List available at the Knysna office of the Department of Water Affairs and Forestry. In particular, keep an eye open for the tree after which the walk is named - the Terblans (*Faurea macnaughtonii*). It is a straight, upright tree which can grow to 25 m and which has the distinction of being the tallest-growing member of the Protea family in southern Africa. The species' rather unusual geographical distribution comprises small isolated areas of the Knysna forests and forests in the Transkei, Natal and Transvaal. To the layman the long, pendulous, pink or white flower spikes look nothing like a protea, although they are in fact typical of a large number of the genera of this plant family.

Indigenous forest rises above Kom-se-Pad, the public road linking Diepwalle and Gouna, which the Terblans Trail shares.

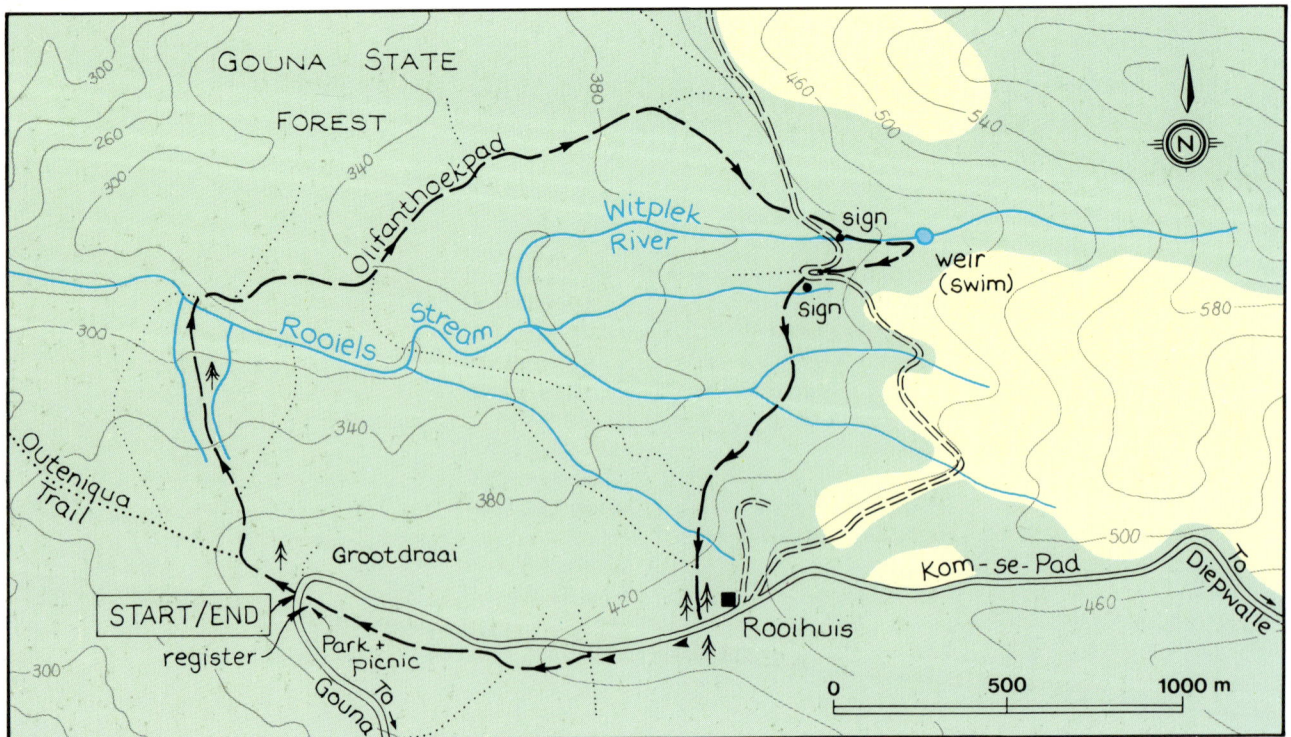

THE INDIGENOUS TIMBER INDUSTRY

Virtually all the timber of indigenous hardwoods is produced in the state forests of the southern Cape. At Witelsbos in the Tsitsikamma area and at Diepwalle in the Knysna area, auctions are held once or twice a year. The local furniture industry takes about 75 per cent of production, and the balance goes to timber merchants and private craftsmen. The logs on auction are pre-graded: only some 2 per cent is prime grade; average grade accounts for about 20 per cent; merchantable grade for about 50 per cent, and serviceable grade (poor quality) for the balance.

The woods most in demand for furniture are stinkwood, yellowwood (both *Podocarpus falcatus* and *P. latifolius*) and blackwood – in that order. To date, the top price paid for a single stinkwood log was R9 600 per m^3; that was in 1985. Yellowwood and blackwood average R750-R800 per m^3. Blackwood (*Acacia melanoxylon*) is not an indigenous tree, but an alien which has invaded the forests. The demand for blackwood timber has two conflicting consequences for forest management: its market value makes the removal of mature blackwood trees from infested forests economically viable, but the total elimination of this exotic from a stretch of natural forest would not only be expensive but would reduce its potential economic yield.

Blackwood logs await auction at Witelsbos depot.

The tree's common name apparently refers to the woodcutter (one Terblanz) who first realized the quality of the species' wood and exploited the timber. (The species is named after C.B. Macnaughton, Conservator of Forests at Knysna at the beginning of the century.) The tree is seldom felled now, but the timber is valuable - hard and dark brown in colour, with a beautiful grain and a characteristic sweetish smell.

From the Grootdraai picnic site, cross Kom-se-pad and find the well-signposted start of the path into the forest. For 200 m or so, the route follows part of the Outeniqua Hiking Trail before turning right off this path and gradually dropping to a stream which feeds the Rooiels River. On the banks of the stream, some lovely ferns grow. The path takes a right turn and climbs fairly steeply up the opposite bank before levelling off in a tract of moist forest. When I walked the trail, I saw the signs of a felled tree having been dragged along one of the slippage paths (the Olifanthoekpad), probably by the Percheron horses used for this purpose because they make less impact on the forest than would mechanized traction. Near the path in this section of moist forest there are still many fine, large examples of Real yellowwoods (*Podocarpus latifolius*).

The path meets a forestry road; turn right and walk for 10 m or so along this road; the path heads back into the forest on the left, along the bank of a small stream, to a point where a cement weir provides a perfect place to swim if the weather is suitable. You can sit next to the pool under a large Kershout (*Pterocelastrus tricuspidatus*) or Witels (*Platylophus trifoliatus*) and admire the opposite slope, which is covered with Tree ferns (*Cyathea capensis*). You will also see a small tree (or large upright shrub, really) named the Cape stock-rose (*Sparmannia africana*), which has soft, hairy leaves and, in spring, trusses of showy white flowers with a tuft of gold and purple stamens. This plant, which is typically found on forest margins, can be processed to provide a soft fibre and was exploited in the 19th century; Japanese researchers are currently re-evaluating the use of its fibre for special applications.

From the weir, the path doubles back to the road, which it crosses and re-enters the forest. After crossing two small streams, it comes to the edge of the natural forest and runs next to a pine plantation to Kom-se-pad. Turn right and follow the public road for a short way, along which are several good-sized *Kalanders* (*Podocarpus falcatus*). The trail leaves Kom-se-Pad and cuts through the forest back to the Grootdraai picnic site.

ELEPHANT WALK I

An easy circular walk in the Diepwalle Forest, passing, on the way, the arboretum, old railway line, depot and King Edward VII tree.

Time: 3 ¹/₂ hours.
Distance: 9 km.
Exertion: Light.
Controlling authority: Diepwalle State Forest station.
Permit: None required; sign the register on the verandah of the office building.
Maps and information: A black-and-white map (a photocopy of limited use) is free at the start; a detailed colour map with information on its reverse is on sale at the Knysna office of the Department of Water Affairs and Forestry.
How to get there: From Knysna, drive east on the N2 for 5 km and take the turn-off to Uniondale (R339); 17 km along this road is the clearly signposted turn-off right to the Diepwalle Forest Station. Park in the designated area behind the Outeniqua Hiking Trail `hut'.
Start/end: At the large `Elephant I' sign outside the office.
Trail markers: Elephant motif, either painted in white or appearing on yellow perspex squares, on tree trunks.
Best times to walk: Any time.
Precautions: Keep to the route; becoming lost in the forest is no joke. Some of the side-paths marked on maps or referred to here will be obvious, while others may be overgrown.
Features: Magnificent moist and wet indigenous forest, an arboretum, forest birds, fungi and the wood depot.
Note: This route can be extended to 13,5 km by continuing on Elephant Walk II at the 7,5-km mark at the Diepwalle picnic site near the depot - this is well signposted. A long (19,6-km) route can be made by including Elephant Walk III from the point where this route crosses the Uniondale road.

Most of this circuit (*see* map overleaf) lies east of the Knysna-Uniondale road. Apart from the road crossings, the route runs entirely in the forest, mostly following old woodcutters' paths now used by forestry staff in managing the forest. If you are as susceptible to the seduction of forest birds, trees and fungi as I am, you could stretch this walk out to a day and even find yourself having to hurry for the last stretch so as to leave the forest before dusk, as I had to. Be sure to take with you a National Tree list or, more conveniently, the partial list available with the map of the area at the offices of the Department of Water Affairs and Forestry in Knysna. A very large variety of trees have been numbered along the route, allowing you to become familiar with the trees which grow in different forest types.

Having signed the register near the `Elephant Walk I' sign, take the steps down to the road. A few metres along this road there is a large hanging sign depicting an elephant in white. The elephant points you down the path through the forest to the arboretum, where there are labelled stands of different tree species, planted to test their suitability as plantation trees. Although they are indigenous in the sense that they occur in South Africa, some of these trees do not grow naturally in the forests of the southern Cape.

In the arboretum the path takes a sharp left turn, then

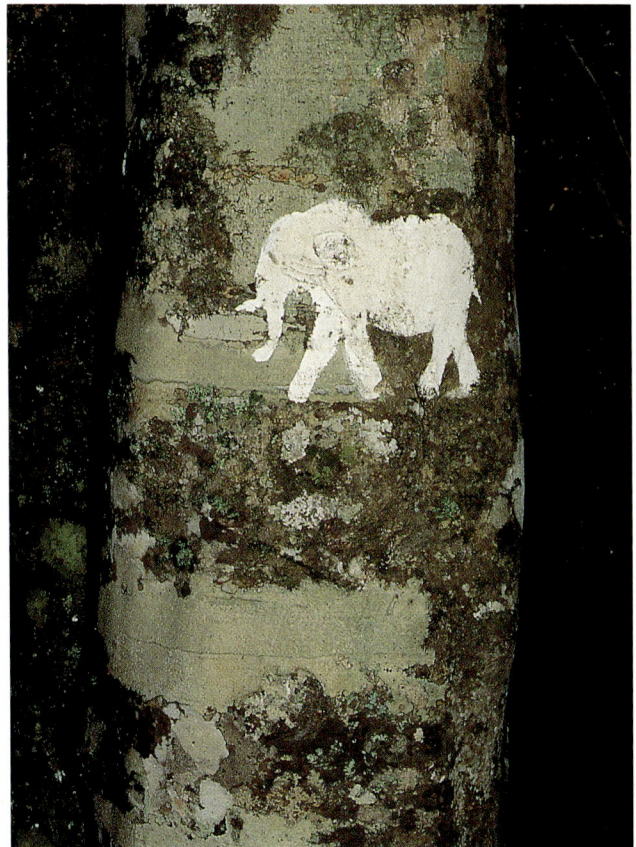

*A trail-marker for Elephant Walk I is conspicuous against the trunk of a White pear (*Apodytes dimidiata*).*

121

leads into natural forest. In a stream bed there is a fine stand of Tree ferns (*Cyathea capensis*), where I encountered my first protracted distraction - a pair of Knysna Louries in the forest canopy above. The path shortly meets another from the left and then swings right into moist forest. The canopy here is fairly open and you can hear domestic noises from the forestry labourers' cottages nearby, but these become muffled as you carry on down the Kalanderpad. This is aptly named as, just to the left of the path, there is a huge Outeniqua yellowwood (*Podocarpus falcatus*).

It was just as I had stopped to admire the size of this forest giant that the tranquillity of the forest was shattered by the hysterical cackling of two pairs of Redbilled Wood-

hoopoes high up in the branches of the trees above the path. I watched their peculiar, rapid bobbing-up-and-down display while an Olive Woodpecker, quite unaffected by all the commotion, quietly went about its business of picking insects from the bark of a tree not more than a metre from one of the pairs. To add to the excitement, I saw more Louries and a Blackheaded Oriole, all in the same area.

Further on, the Kalanderpad swings right, drops and crosses a stream; a fascinating variety of mosses grow on some old logs among the Tree ferns alongside. Up the other

The canopy of ancient trees towering over Kalanderpad is home to numerous colourful forest birds.

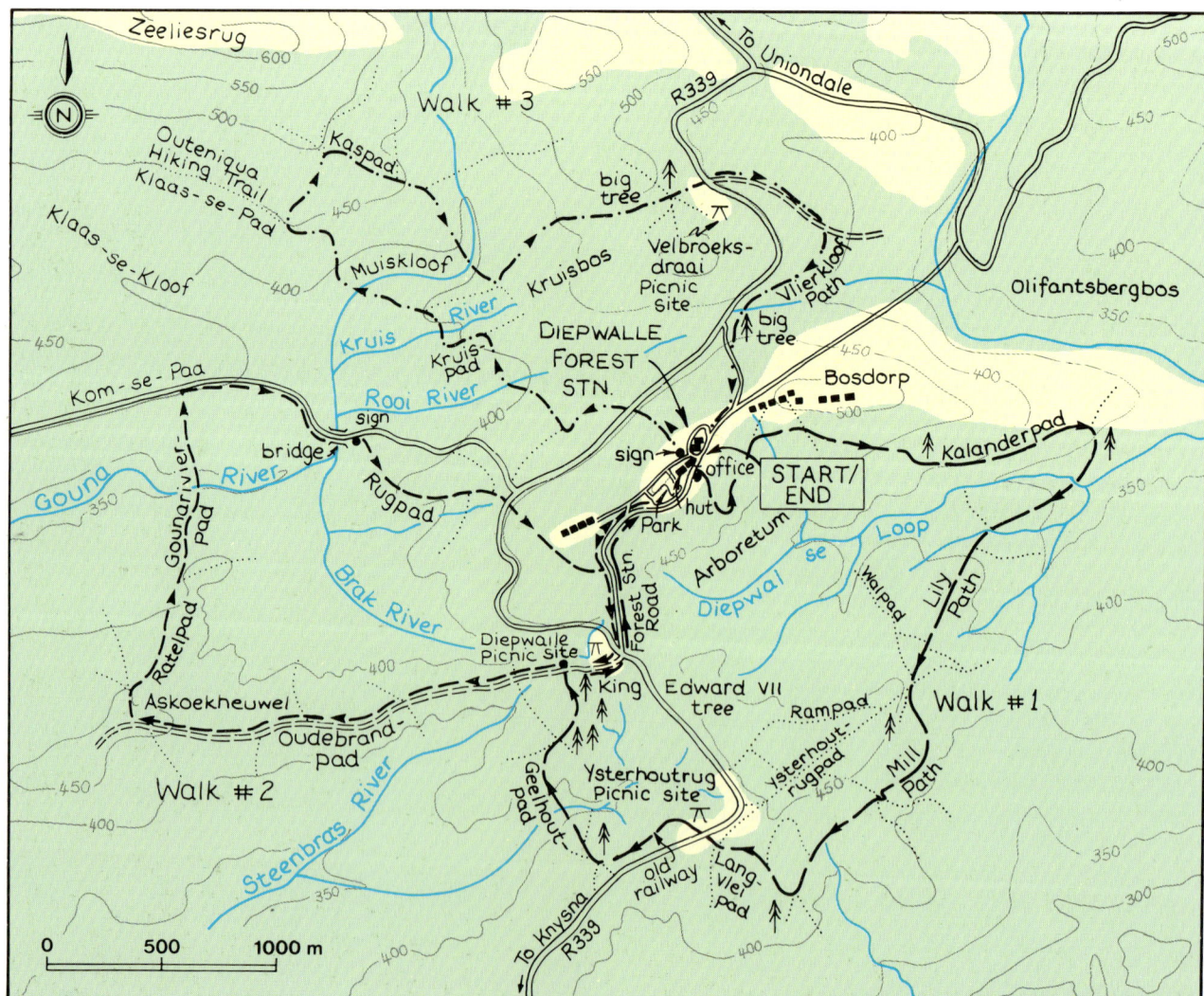

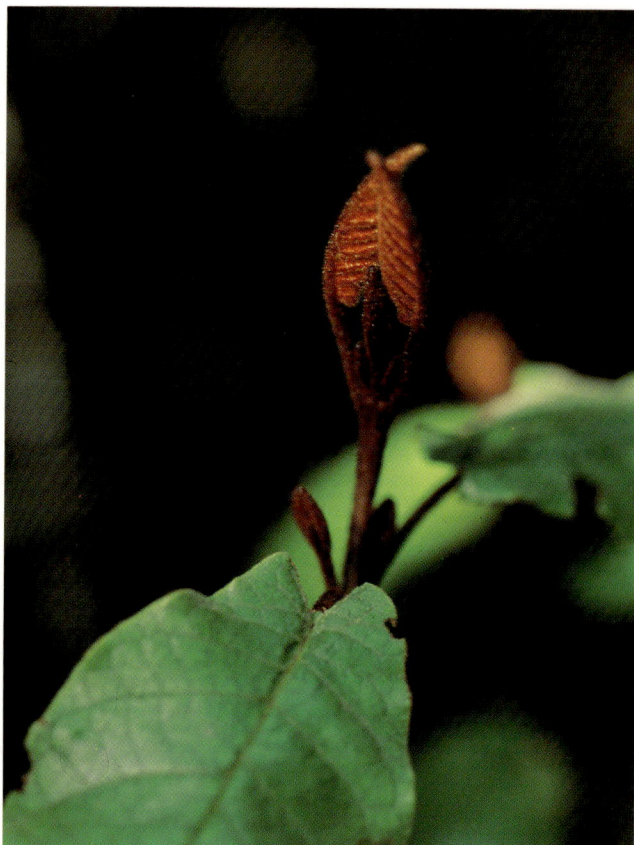

ABOVE: *Knysna Louries can be heard long before they are seen feeding in high branches.*
RIGHT: *Onderbos* (Trichocladus crinitus) *is the major component of the understorey in moist and medium-moist high forests.*

bank, a notice proclaims this `Wet high forest'. The path climbs steadily and gently along the Lily Path, with Onderbos (*Trichocladus crinitus*) on either side. A path (the Walpad) and then a forestry track (the Ysterhoutrugpad) join from the right. Cross the track and re-enter the forest, following the markers carefully. The path now drops fairly steeply through dense Onderbos. At the bottom of the slope it swings right onto the Mill Path, a broad, wet path which in several places is lined with logs. The damp provides the conditions for a fascinating variety of maroon and yellow mushrooms to grow. It was here that I first saw a Horse's foot bracket fungus (*Phellinus igniarius*), a woody brown mass, with white faces top and bottom.

From the Mill Path, the way to the Uniondale road is not very well marked and can be confusing. At a T-junction, where the path meets a track, turn left and a few metres further on, at a branch in the track, turn right. A small stream bed is crossed just before a path from a depot on the main road comes in from the right. A little further on you reach another T-junction where you must turn right on the track up the hill; a second track intersects at an angle from the left.

At the next branch, keep left; at a crossroads, ignore the path to the right and the track to the left. The route emerges on the main road at the Ysterhoutrug picnic site.

The main road provides a short cut, if necessary, to the turn-off to the Forest Station. The trail continues where an elephant marker at the Ysterhoutrug picnic site points the way back into the forest (passing the toilets on the left) at the start of a small loop to the Diepwalle picnic site. The path initially runs along the course of an old railway line - of which nothing is now visible - then swings right, drops down and crosses a beautiful stream lined with Tree ferns in very wet forest. Up the other side it passes some fine old Kalanders. Just after the first of these, on the right of the path, you reach a crossroads. The path left, marked with the now familiar sign, is the continuation of the trail on Elephant Path II. If you do not intend combining these two walks, turn right past the huge King Edward VII tree to the picnic site and the main road. Across this is the turn-off back to the Forest Station.

THE WOODCUTTERS

Woodcutters (one of them apparently holding a pet vervet monkey) pose on a pile of handsawn yellowwood.
The timber at centre back was probably destined for railway sleepers.

It would be facile to blame the woodcutters entirely for the despoliation of the southern Cape forests. The root causes were the insatiable, ever-increasing demand for timber, initially from the Dutch East India Company's settlement at the Cape and later, when it was under British administration, from the Cape Colony in general, coupled with decades of public indifference to the fate of the forests.

The D.E.I.C. set up woodcutters' posts where George now stands in 1776 and in Plettenberg Bay in 1787. The woodcutters' activities were destructive and wasteful, to the extent that when Governor van Plettenberg visited Plettenberg Bay as early as 1778, the men were reported to be causing `reckless forest destruction'. This continued virtually unchecked (apart from some half-hearted, ineffectual official attempts at control) until the 1880s, when Comte Médéric de Vasselot introduced a successful system of forestry management which put an end to the unthinking and rapid devastation.

The woodcutters themselves had become an isolated, inbred, uneducated and poor rural community who led hard lives in the permanent twilight of their environment. (Dalene Matthee gives a vivid and sympathetic description of their lives in her novels *Circles in a Forest* and *Fiela's Child.*) By the time several government commissions were sent to investigate the plight of the woodcutters, their numbers were already on the decrease. The more easily accessible timber in the forests had been worked out and control (which included the lottery system instituted in 1913) over the tree-fellers' activities was effective.

In March 1939 the government passed the Woodcutters Annuities Bill and the remaining woodcutters were pensioned off. Thus passed into history one of South Africa's more colourful communities.

ELEPHANT WALK II

A very easy circuit which runs in natural forest – home to forest birds and vervet monkeys – and crosses the Gouna River.

Time: 3 hours.

Distance: 8 km (from the forest station); 6,5 km (from Diepwalle picnic site).

Exertion: Light.

Controlling authority: Diepwalle State Forest Station.

Permits: None required; sign the register on the verandah of the office building.

Maps and information: A black-and-white map (a photocopy of limited use) is free at the start; a detailed colour map with information on its reverse is on sale at the Knysna office of the Department of Water Affairs and Forestry.

How to get there: From Knysna, drive east on the N2 for 5 km and take the turn-off to Uniondale (R339); 17 km along this road is the clearly signposted turn-off right to the Diepwalle Forest Station. Park in the designated area behind the Outeniqua Hiking Trail `hut'.

Start/end: From the office, walk back down the forest station road (Stasiepad) to the main Uniondale road opposite the depot; at the end of the walk you return on the Stasiepad via a branch from higher up the main road. You can also start and end this circuit (after registering at the office) at the Diepwalle picnic site, in which case you return either on the main Uniondale road or cross it, to meet the Stasiepad.

Trail markers: Elephant motif, either painted in white on tree trunks, or on yellow perspex squares.

Best times to walk: Any time.

Precautions: Keep to the route, as it is easy to become disorientated and lost off the path in the trees.

Features: Beautiful wet and very wet natural forest types, the Gouna River, forest margin vegetation, the wood depot and forest birds.

Note: This route can be extended to a 12,5-km route by continuing on Elephant Walk III from the point at which this route crosses the Uniondale road.

This route (*see* map, page 122) can be followed as an extension of Elephant Walk I from the Diepwalle picnic site. By itself, however, it provides a satisfying half-day circuit starting and ending at the Diepwalle Forest Station or the picnic site. Most of the walk is on forestry management tracks, above which the tree canopy is broken. There are no rough, difficult or steep parts anywhere on the circuit.

If you drive to Diepwalle from Knysna early in the morning, keep a look-out for bushbuck on the edge of the natural forest - they often graze at the forest margin at this time.

Anyone interested in horses will enjoy seeing the forest station's Percheron workhorses grazing in a paddock next to the road. These huge, stocky white animals are used to drag felled timber from the forest, as they do little damage to the forest floor in the process. Percherons are not often encountered in this country and are increasingly uncommon in Europe, where their numbers have steadily declined because of farm mechanization.

Having filled in the register, take the Forest Station road you drove up from the Uniondale road. The stretch of forest on either side is full of birds, and you are likely to hear the raucous calls of Hadedas above the canopy and the noisy cackles of Redbilled Woodhoopoes in the trees. Knysna Louries can often be spotted here too. Across the main road is the Diepwalle picnic site. Pass the depot where logs of yellowwood, stinkwood and blackwood are stored in preparation for auction and continue through the picnic area and a steel gate onto the Oudebrandpad. The path joining the track from the left is that of the Elephant Walk I; a large yellow sign clearly indicates the directions of the two walks.

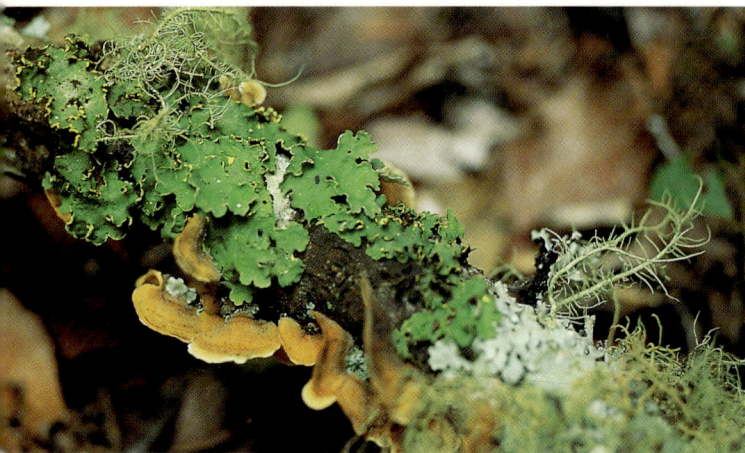

LEFT: *Lichens are using this log only for support, whereas the bracket fungi are feeding off it.*
FAR RIGHT: *The elegant flowers of the Cape stock-rose, a shrub found in wet situations.*

The Oudebrandpad runs through medium moist forest for about 2 km, before it comes to a well-marked and obvious clearing on the right called `Askoekheuwel'. Here the trail leaves the Oudebrandpad and turns right into the forest on a path known as the Ratelpad. A few metres into the trees there is a three-way split - keep right, following the elephant trail markers along the steadily dropping path. On both occasions I walked this trail, I saw Knysna Louries here. On the second outing I also watched a troop of vervet monkeys performing their arboreal acrobatics in the trees just off the path.

The path splits again; keep left on what is now the Gounarivierpad. It drops a bit more steeply, through obviously very wet forest, to the river. There is permanent running water here and it a good place for a drink. The river itself is overgrown with vegetation and presents a sombre appearance, but a few metres upstream from the crossing is a small series of cascades which are pleasant to explore on a fine, warm day. Across the stream is a large stand of Tree

COMTE MEDERIC DE VASSELOT

The Comte Médéric de Vasselot de Régné, a graduate of the renowned School of Forestry at Nancy in France, was 43 years old when he arrived in Cape Town on 17 March 1881 with his wife and eight children to take up the position of Superintendent of Woods and Forests for the Cape government.

De Vasselot was a man of vision with an incisive mind. Building on the experience of Captain Christopher Harison, Conservator of Forests at Knysna (who had introduced the so-called `section system' in an attempt to control the over-exploitation of the natural forests), he rapidly introduced a new system which proved effective. This system was based on the preservation of the Cape forests in a healthy, balanced state in which they could be exploited for their timber on a sustainable basis. In other words, it allowed for timber to be removed at a rate which matched the growth of the indigenous forest.

In 1888 the Cape Parliament passed the first Forest Act, by which demarcated forest became inalienable. Under De Vasselot's auspices a Forestry Department was built up with professional, trained officers on its staff, among whom were H.G. Fourcade, the renowned botanist and surveyor, and C.B. Macnaughton, who began forest research in this country and drew up a scientific plan for forest management.

When De Vasselot left the Cape at the end of his 12-year contract, this remarkable man had laid the foundations of a policy of protection and management of the southern Cape forests which is still employed today.

ferns (*Cyathea capensis*) through which the path meanders before climbing up through wet forest to Kom-se-pad. This road, which links the Gouna and Diepwalle forests, is open to public vehicles. Turn right along Kom-se-Pad and follow it over a bridge across the Gouna River; 60 m beyond the river a yellow sign points the way off the road back into the forest on a path which climbs steadily and finally meets the main Uniondale road. Cross the Uniondale road to the forestry road which eventually meets the Forest Station road. Turn left and continue back to the car park.

If you wish to continue your walk on the Elephant III route, turn left along the Uniondale main road and follow it for 700 m, keeping a careful watch for the path into the forest on the new route. This junction is easily missed, although it is marked by a small yellow elephant sign. Directly across the Uniondale road at this point there is the path which comes from the forest station.

The moss on the trunks and branches of these trees identifies the environment as wet forest.

THE KNYSNA ELEPHANTS

Of all the animals found in the southern Cape forests, none excites such passionate interest as the elephants. Thirty or forty years ago the sight of elephant crossing the main road near Harkerville was not uncommon. Today a sighting anywhere in the forests behind Knysna, the last refuge of the remnants of a once huge herd, is extremely rare.

Before 1870 there were an estimated 400-600 elephants in the Knysna forests, together with huge herds of buffalo. The brief frenzy of gold-mining at Millwood which started in 1886 was accompanied (to complete official indifference) by uncontrolled hunting, for sport and ivory, which contributed to the decimation of the elephants and the elimination of the buffalo. Other enemies of the elephants were farmers whose crops were regularly damaged by the animals. By 1908, when the government at the Cape eventually proclaimed them Royal Game (protected from being hunted by all except royalty), only about 20 elephants remained. In 1920 Major Jan Pretorius, a famous hunter who the year before had been hired to eliminate the elephant herd at Addo and came within an ace of doing so, was granted a licence to shoot one bull in the Knysna forests for the South African Museum. The hunt was a disgraceful fiasco and five animals were shot. The herd never recovered from this blow. When the Wildlife Society carried out detailed surveys in 1968 and 1969, the herd's numbers averaged about 10. Today there are only four known survivors - a bull, a cow, a juvenile bull and a calf (sex unknown).

There is evidence that the original herds spent only some of their time in the forests and moved freely to browse open veld to the north (Addo) and south (coastal plain). As these areas with their richer soils were settled and farmed, the elephants were forced to spend more time in the forests, to the detriment of their nutrition and, hence, breeding potential.

It has been proposed that four young elephants from the Kruger National Park be introduced to the Knysna forests to boost the breeding rate of the remnant herd. It is not certain, however, that the new animals, even if they were able to adapt to a sudden, massive change in habitat, would fare any better than the existing elephants. The sad truth is that man has so limited and damaged the Knysna elephant herd's environment that there is no going back. *Requiescant in pace.*

TOP: *This old Knysna bull, known as Aftand, was photographed in May 1969 in the Garden of Eden. The animal had a broken right tusk, the result of an argument with a tractor.*
ABOVE: *This cow was photographed a year earlier on the Graspad in the Harkerville forest reserve.*

ELEPHANT WALK III

A fairly easy circular route, on which there are two Outeniqua yellowwood giants, in the shaded depths of the natural forest at Diepwalle.

Time: 3 hours.

Distance: 6 km.

Exertion: Light to moderate.

Controlling authority: Diepwalle State Forest Station.

Permits: None required; sign the register on the verandah of the office building.

Maps and information: A black-and-white map (a photocopy of limited use) is free at the start; a detailed colour map with information on its reverse is on sale at the Knysna office of the Department of Water Affairs and Forestry.

How to get there: From Knysna, drive east on the N2 for 5 km and take the Uniondale turn-off; 17 km on is the turn-off right to the Diepwalle forest station. Park here.

Start/end: At the large 'Elephant III' sign on the road past the northern wall of the office.

Trail markers: Elephant motif and arrows in white or on yellow perspex squares; white shoeprints (pointing in the opposite direction to which you are going) on a short section of the route which is common with the Outeniqua Hiking Trail.

Best times to walk: Any time.

Precautions: Keep to the route and the path, as it is easy to get lost in the forest.

Features: Splendid wet and very wet forest types, forest birds, tree ferns and forest streams.

Although all of the Elephant Walks are forest walks, each has a distinctive feel. Elephant Walk III (*see* map, page 122) traverses larger areas of forest which is wetter than that on either of the other two circuits; much of the route lies along narrow paths in deep forest where the tree canopy overhead is dense. Furthermore, the terrain is more hilly than on the other two routes. Like Elephant Walk II, this is a good half-day walk, but it can also be combined with Elephant Walk II for a full day's outing.

From the Forest Station's office where you fill in the register before starting out, a large yellow perspex sign points the way down the forestry road just north of the office. A few metres along the road there is a sign where the path leaves the road and enters the forest. This path runs steeply down the slope in low forest to meet the Uniondale road.

As I walked this part of the route, I was delighted to see - for the first time - a Narina Trogon, which is a rarely spotted forest bird. The bird (a female, which lacks the male's green chest but is splendidly coloured with a brilliant emerald cap and back, and red below the tail) was on the ground next to

Percherons - first bred in France as farm workhorses - are used to slip logs out of the forest.

the path. I watched her for more than half an hour as she flew, fairly unconcerned by my presence, from bush to bush in the undergrowth before disappearing from view. Directly across the main road the path re-enters the forest. A short way in, it turns right at a junction marked by a white arrow and a white elephant. This path drops and crosses the Rooi River, which is lined with Tree ferns (*Cyathea capensis*). A short way up the other bank it meets the Kruispad (a broad path) at a T-junction. A couple of hundred metres to the left this path meets a forestry track, Klaas-se-pad. Here you turn right and follow, for a kilometre or so, the route of the Outeniqua Hiking Trail, which is marked by white shoeprints pointing in the opposite direction to which you are walking. Klaas-se-pad descends to cross the stream in Muiskloof, where there is permanent running water; on the other side, the path narrows and climbs steadily. At the top of the rise, the route leaves Klaas-se-pad (and the Outeniqua Hiking Trail) on a path well-marked with white elephant signs and arrows. This path continues to climb until it meets the Kaspad at a sharp right turn. The Kaspad drops steadily through increasingly wetter forest and crosses the same stream as previously, higher up in Muiskloof. A short way up the other side, at a T-junction marked with two white elephants, you turn left on a path which climbs gently to the Velbroeksdraai picnic area on the Uniondale road.

On the way, you pass a Big Tree, a truly gigantic Outeniqua yellowwood (*Podocarpus falcatus*). The information board beside the massive trunk gives the tree's age at over 600 years. Stop to admire this plant and reflect that it was growing here before any European had seen this land, before hunters eliminated virtually all the animals which had lived in this forest for centuries, and long before the woodcutters came to cut down and remove almost all the trees of any significant size, which they did in the space of a few decades. Why this individual was spared is not clear, but it gives you an inkling of what the Knysna forests must have looked like before they were plundered and raped.

Just 10 m beyond the eastern edge of the grassed picnic area is the main road, on the other side of which a track leads into the trees at a point marked with white elephants and arrows. Some 300 m along the track, take the path to the right. This twists and winds through the trees and a group of Tree ferns fringing a small stream on its way to a second large Outeniqua yellowwood, at least as large as the first. Beyond this, the route uses a forest station road to return to the office and parking area.

ABOVE: *Mosses and small ferns fight for living space on a dead log beside a stream in this moist high forest.*
BELOW: *Narina Trogons are plentiful in the forests but, because they perch inconspicuously, are seldom seen.*

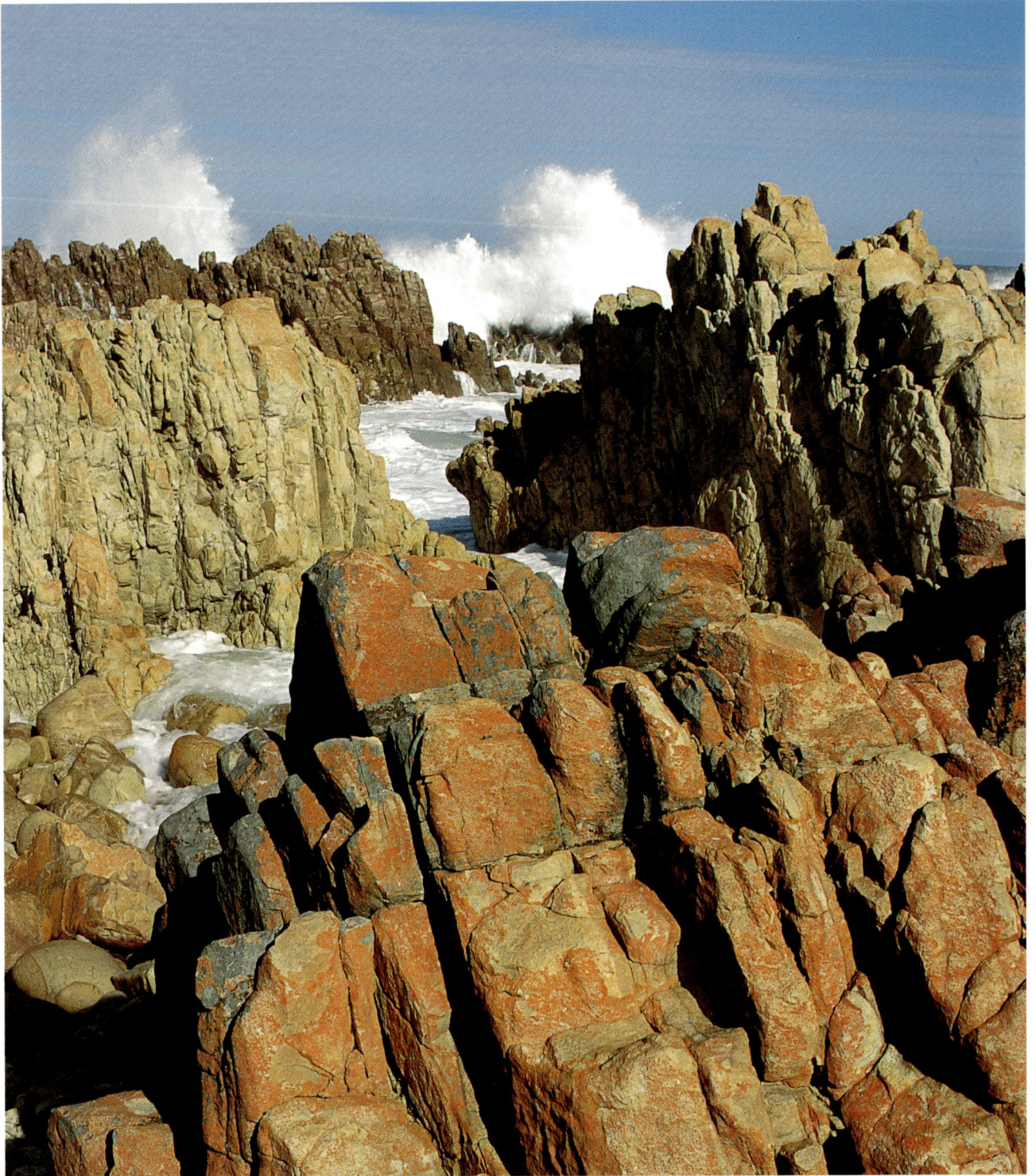

CHAPTER NINE

PLETTENBERG BAY

When Bartolomeu Dias sailed eastward along the coast after his brief landing at Mossel Bay in 1488, he passed another large bay which he named Bahia Formosa - Beautiful Bay. No-one can deny that Dias's name is fitting, for this is indeed a lovely stretch of coast which every year draws hordes of holiday-makers from all four of South Africa's provinces; in the summer season the town's resident population of about 10 000 swells to between four and five times that figure.

The first Europeans to penetrate the dense forests between the Tsitsikam-mas and the coast were parties sent out by the governor of the Dutch East India Company settlement at the Cape to barter for cattle with the Khoi-khoi tribes along the Langkloof. Occasional forays over the mountains were made to hunt the elephant and buffalo which roamed the forests. European settlement from the Cape gradually spread eastwards during the 18th century. In 1778, by which time there was a small communi-ty of Dutch farmers in the area, the governor of the Cape Colony, Joachim van Plettenberg, visited the bay and used the occasion graciously to bestow upon it the name by which it is known today.

In 1787 a woodcutters' post was set up near the mouth of the Piesang River and here timber from the forests was stockpiled before being loaded onto ships for transport to the Cape. In the early 19th century, as the forests became worked out, the importance of Plettenberg Bay diminished and for decades it remained a poor, isolated village which served only the local farming community and fishermen.

In 1912 a Norwegian company leased Beacon Isle from its

A Swift Tern leaves the crowded roost at the rocky Point on Robberg.

owners, the Anglican Church, and erected a whaling station there. For eight years the village had a new lease on life as whaling fleets came and went, but then the company packed up and left. For many years the build-ings were used as a hotel for fisher-men, until they were replaced by the grandiose hotel-turned-timeshare complex which stands there today as a symbol of Plettenberg Bay's new-found prosperity.

The two long sweeps of beach - Robberg Beach between Beacon Isle and Robberg, and Lookout Beach, which fronts the Bietou Lagoon north of the town - provide opportunities for lovely walks. So too does Keur-boomstrand, which adjoins Lookout beach. At Kranshoek, to the west of Plettenberg Bay, there is a magnificent walk, described below, along a rugged stretch of rocky coastline. A new two-day hike, the Harkerville Coast Hik-ing Trail (*see* page 172), also traverses this coast but leads through the Harkerville forests as well.

The Wittedrift High School has laid out a Nature Trail and this circuit, with optional stages allowing for shorter or longer walks, mostly follows the meandering course of the Bietou River. Details of this walk, on which dogs and horses are also allowed, and a walk through the town of Pletten-berg Bay along the Piesang River, Central Beach, Lookout Beach and the Keurbooms Lagoon (the Piesang River Trail), can be obtained from the office of the Plettenberg Bay Pub-licity Association.

The 11-km circular trail in the Nature Reserve at Robberg, described below, provides the walker with a wealth of beau-tiful scenery, including a view of the bay and its beaches which can have changed little from that which met Dias's eyes as he rounded the Point of the Robberg peninsula over five centuries ago.

Vertical strata and varied coloration are the hallmarks of the rocks at Kranshoek.

KRANSHOEK WALK

A fairly strenuous circuit from the Kranshoek picnic site through natural forest down to a magnificent stretch of coastline and back up through coastal fynbos and plantation.

Time: 3 $\frac{1}{2}$ - 4 hours.

Distance: 9,4 km.

Exertion: Moderate.

Controlling authority: Harkerville State Forest Station.

Permits: None required; register at start.

Maps and information: Colour map with information sold at the Knysna office of the Department of Water Affairs and Forestry. There are 8 interpretation boards on the walk.

How to get there: Take the gravel road signposted `Harkerville' off the N2 20 km east of Knysna (12 km west of Plettenberg Bay). Follow the signs for 5 km, past the forest station, to the Kranshoek picnic site and viewpoint. Park at the picnic site under the trees.

Start/end: At the register next to the picnic site.

Trail markers: White shoeprints.

Best times to walk: Summer for swimming, but magnificent at any time.

Precautions: There is an exposed part of the path with a short drop to the sea which can be slippery and requires some care. You must take drinking water with you.

Features: Spectacular coastal scenery, interpretation boards and swimming in a rock pool in the sea and in a pool in Crooks River.

The Kranshoek Walk runs through some beautiful forest, but it is the scenery of the coastal part of the route that is especially memorable. The walk has been well laid out and equipped, at intervals, with interpretation boards (8 in all) which provide, in a reasonably unobtrusive way, a great deal of information about interesting ecological features along the route. For both these reasons the walk is highly recommended. Although the route is not especially strenuous, there are steep climbs from the plateau down to the sea at the start, and later, from the mouth of Crooks River back up to the plateau; there are also several short climbs up and down along the coastal stretch in between. A shorter walk can be done by starting at the viewpoint and using the very steep short cut favoured by anglers to reach the beach. In the forest, several common tree species have been identified by their numbers in the National Tree List - a partial list is issued together with the official map for this walk.

From the picnic site, where there is a register to complete, the path starts into the forest, crosses a stream and leads to the very edge of the vertical cliff above the Kranshoek River.

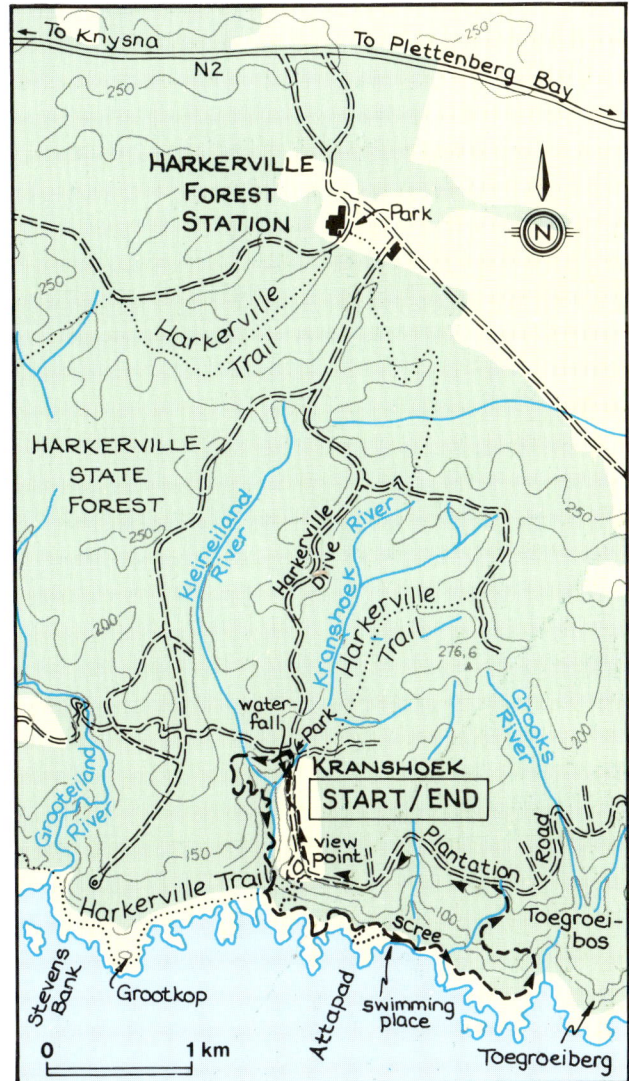

OPPOSITE: *The origins of the pebbly beach at the mouth of the Kranshoek River are explained on an information board there.*
ABOVE: *A gazania grows in a pocket of sand amongst the rocks.*

Here you will find the first of the interpretation boards, which have notes on types of forest, their structure and why they are the way they are; there are also two places where you can view the steep kloof leading to the sea.

From the cliff edge, the path heads into forest, traverses an area of pine plantation and then re-enters indigenous forest, where it zigzags down a steep slope over a small scree belt to the Kranshoek River (most of the time really just a stream). Just after crossing and recrossing the stream for the second time, the path passes through some dense coastal scrub and emerges on a pebble beach in a small cove. The spectacular coastal scenery begins here. This part of the coast must have experienced some enormous geological stresses in by-gone times, as the rock strata here are vertical. As a result, the weathered rocks are particularly sharp and jagged, a feature characteristic of the scenery.

From the cove the way leads east (left) to a second bay past a turn-off left (ignore this, as it is the very steep, erosion-causing, short cut up to the viewpoint), into coastal scrub forest and past a cave. Up the slope on the other side the path swings sharp right and heads towards a promontory and back again before zigzagging up in scrub forest, to cross a scree belt on a steep slope high above the beach. From here the path once again drops to the sea where a safe, natural swimming pool is indicated among the rocks. Beyond this is a tricky spot where the path has been cut into a steep, muddy slope directly above a channel where the sea

ABOVE: Aloe arborescens *in bud at Kranshoek on a warm, misty autumn afternoon.*

runs through the rocks. Take care, as the path is slippery.

The next kilometre or so is easy going in the open and on the level, mostly through dense but low coastal vegetation, to the inlet which marks the mouth of Crooks River. In this lonely and isolated place, it is thrilling to watch the waves smash on the rocks which protrude from the sea below the opposite headland. The scene is duplicated in more rocks and another headland further along the coast, just visible through the sea haze. From here, the route passes over some rocks and heads along the beach into the inlet.

Just before Crooks River runs into the sea, it forms a large pool surrounded by trees - a second possible swimming place on the walk. As I approached the pool, I disturbed a pair of Giant Kingfishers which objected noisily to my arrival as they flew off.

The path climbs steeply from the water, zigzagging through indigenous forest called Toegroeibos to the top of the plateau. As you are now walking along the edge of the plateau in open fynbos above a precipitous drop to the coast, you have spectacular views from the first few hundred metres before the path swings inland and enters plantation. The rest of the walk back along the forestry track on the plateau to the viewpoint is, frankly, an anti-climax. From the viewpoint to the picnic site there is a path, parallel with and slightly lower than the road, which allows a clear view of the waterfall. Several false paths lead to the cliff edge; ignore them, as the almost-vertical face below is dangerous.

ROBBERG TRAIL

A moderately strenuous circular route which leads out high on the northern side of Robberg to the Point, returns along the southern coastline to the Gap and climbs back onto the plateau.

Time: 4 hours.

Distance: 11 km (there is a sign posted short cut across Robberg down the drift sand from the north side to the beach opposite Die Eiland).

Exertion: Moderate.

Controlling authority: Cape Provincial Administration: Department of Nature and Environmental Conservation - Plettenberg Bay office.

Permits: Obtained at the entrance to the Robberg Nature Reserve, or the Plettenberg Bay office; there is an entrance fee.

Maps and information: Map of trail warning of dangers along the route issued at gate or available at the Plettenberg Bay office. General environmental information available at the office.

How to get there: From the centre of Plettenberg Bay, take the road past Beacon Isle towards the airfield. The road to Robberg branches left off this road. From the town centre to the gate is a distance of 7,4 km; it is another 500 m to the parking area at the Information Centre.

Start/end: Next to the Information Centre.

Trail markers: Seal motif on green perspex squares; yellow footprints on the rocks.

Best times to walk: Spring for the flowers, but spectacular at any time.

Precautions: There are several difficult sections along the trail which require care, and anyone who is not sure-footed or who suffers from vertigo should not go beyond the Gap. Walkers of this trail should be aware of the potential dangers of high tides and, in particular, of freak waves on the coastal sections of the route. There are strong currents in the sea off the beaches. Take drinking water with you.

Features: Spectacular coastal scenery and views across the bay, geological and archaeological interest, coastal fynbos and thicket, the intertidal zone, and a wide variety of bird and animal life.

A peninsula is a rare feature on the southern Cape coast. Robberg has only survived aeons of constant battering by large waves from the Indian Ocean swells because the rock underlying it is hard Table Mountain sandstone. Lying on this bedrock are beds of more recent rock, including a noticeable conglomerate rock of rounded pebbles held in a flint-hard matrix of sandstone which has become quartzitic through the deposition of silica. Fossil shell casts have been found in some of the recent (Enon) quartzites.

Human and animals remains in cave deposits have been dated to between 19 and 10 thousand years ago. (As a result, no disturbance of the caves on the peninsula is permitted.) Some fine examples of Stone Age tools and other artefacts made from stone and bone and discovered on Robberg are exhibited at the Information Centre at the car park, which is well worth a visit - preferably before you set out. You will also find information about Robberg's fauna and flora here.

There are two major plant communities on Robberg, namely thicket and coastal fynbos. Over 100 species of birds have been recorded, including those associated with the rocky coastline, the fynbos and the thicket. Dassies are common, but less obvious animal life includes grysbok (the most common buck here), duiker and bushbuck; Cape clawless otters and mongooses are occasionally seen. Seals, whales and dolphins can sometimes be spotted in the sea next to

A seal pup waddles eagerly towards the sea.

Robberg, the ideal vantage point for whale-watching.

Robberg's spectacular scenery owes much to the sheer cliffs which characterize a great deal of its coastline. Their steepness also makes some parts of the trail beyond the Gap difficult and even dangerous in certain conditions.

From the car park, take the path signposted `The Gap' and `The Point' to the left of the Information Centre. The path drops down through a short stretch of fynbos where, in

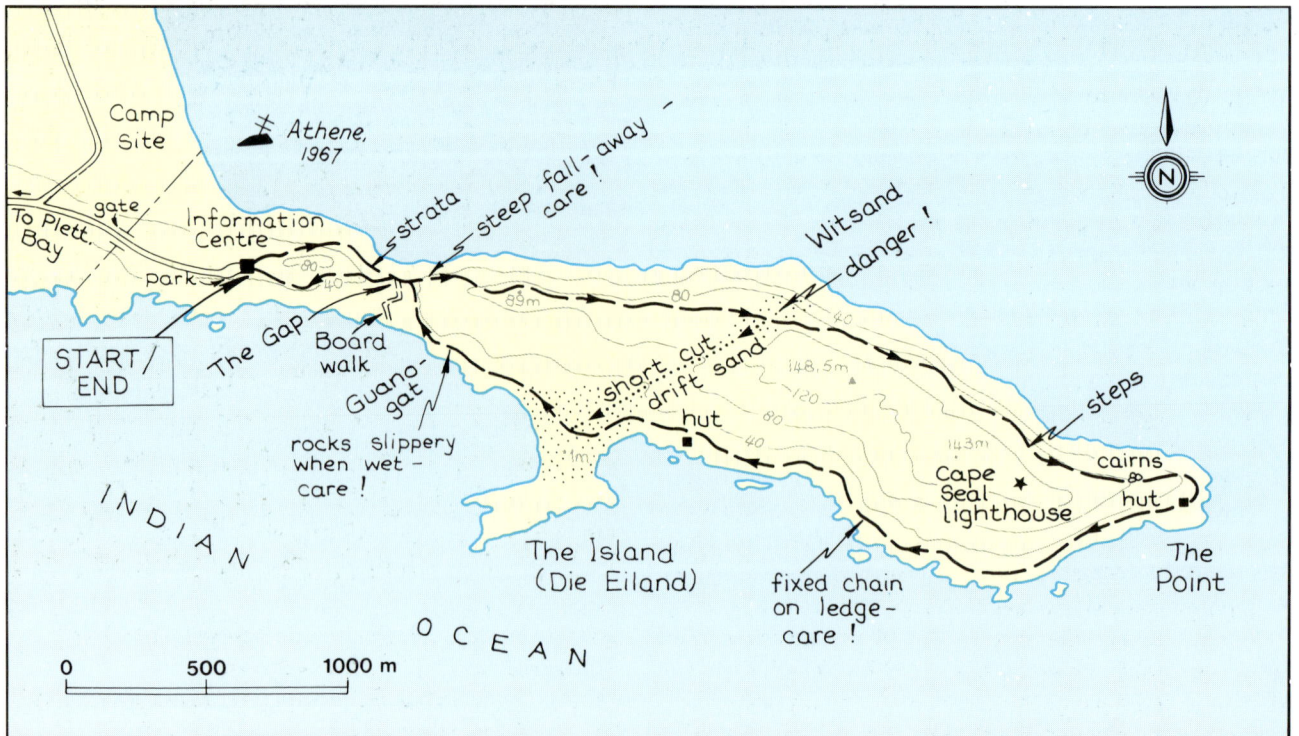

Camp Site

Athene, 1967

To Plett. Bay

gate

Information Centre

strata

steep fall-away - care!

Witsand danger!

park

START/ END

The Gap

Board walk

Guano-gat

rocks slippery when wet - care!

short cut drift sand

hut

Cape Seal lighthouse

steps

cairns

hut

INDIAN

The Island (Die Eiland)

fixed chain on ledge - care!

The Point

OCEAN

0   500   1000 m

the space of a few minutes, I spotted Redwinged Starlings, Southern Boubous, Cape Robins, Orangebreasted Sunbirds, Cape Batises, Speckled Mousebirds, Cape White-eyes, Sand Martins and Sombre Bulbuls.

The trail runs more or less on the level through the thicket above the cliffs on the northern side of Robberg to the Gap. Just before you reach the Gap, notice the rock faces which reveal the layers of different rock types. Dassies like to bask in the sun here on chunks of broken-off conglomerate rock. Across the bay the town of Plettenberg Bay is spread out, with the long line of the mountains behind.

From the Gap itself, where a wooden boardwalk leads down to a small, sandy beach on the southern side, you can take either the path to the Point or that to Die Eiland.

The path to the Point climbs the steep, rocky slope, passing one spot where there is a sheer drop from the path; this is not difficult to negotiate, although it needs care. On top of the ridge, the trail reaches the belt of driftsand which bisects the peninsula beyond the Gap. The top of this plume of sand is unstable over a sheer fall to rocks on the north side of Robberg, and signs warn of the extreme danger of turning left off the path. Down the sandy gully to the right is a short cut to the sand spit linking Die Eiland and the peninsula.

Beyond the driftsand the trail traverses an area where limestone outcroppings in the sand are covered with a great many small herbs and bulbous plants which are colourful in spring. Towards the Point the path descends some steps to the cliff edge, then descends past two large stone cairns, to the rocks at the Point. Here, it is a surprise to find the first of the two huts on Robberg that belong to the Angling Club of Plettenberg Bay. Below the hut, next to the sea, I saw a huge flock of Swift Terns alongside a large number of Kelp Gulls. This must be a favourite roosting place, as the rocks are white with their droppings. The brilliant white plumage of the terns close-packed on the rocks made a stark backdrop for a single pair of African Black Oystercatchers.

Past the anglers' hut is the most beautiful section of the trail, where the tumbled Table Mountain sandstone boulders, brightly coloured by orange lichens, contrast with the dazzling white of the foam from the breakers which pound this exposed coast. Back beyond the point, hovering in the haze above the intense blues and greens of the sea, is the long, purple line of the distant Tsitsikamma Mountains.

From these rocks, the path climbs onto the edge of a dune sandstone cliff. I saw a pair of Cape Rock Thrushes on the rocks next to the path here; the male's rich grey and cinnamon markings blended beautifully with the colour of the rock. Just beyond this, a marker leads to a tricky spot - probably the trail's most daunting - where you have to negotiate a narrow ledge on a vertical rock face above the sea with the help of a fixed chain. There is no way up and over the rock; other hopefuls have worn an apparent path that leads nowhere. From here to Die Eiland is a mere stroll past the other anglers' hut, the last part of which is on the beach at the edge of the sand spit.

On the other side of the spit, the trail crosses the rocks to pass below Guanogat (a large overhang cave which is off limits). You will need to be careful at several spots on this section, particularly if the rocks are wet or the sea is running high. The last short section of the trail leads steeply up the rocks on the south-facing cliffs next to the Gap, onto the plateau, with the aid of steps. From here, there is a level walk back to the car park.

ABOVE: *At the Gap, Die Eiland appears beyond the conglomerate cliffs on which dassies like to bask in the sun.*
FAR LEFT: *The town of Plettenberg Bay is visible above the vertical cliffs of Robberg beyond the Gap.*

CHAPTER TEN

NATURE'S VALLEY

Nature's Valley is a small village, of both holiday cottages and permanent residences, on the floodplain to the west of the lagoon of the Groot River. In December 1987 an area of 2 561 ha around Nature's Valley, including the forested valleys of the Groot River and its western neighbour, the Salt River, as well as the adjacent coastline and a substantial portion of the coastal plateau, was incorporated into the Tsitsikamma Coastal National Park. Some of the natural forest on the east of the Groot River Valley was retained by the Department of Environment Affairs as part of the Bloukrans State Forest.

The De Vasselot section of the Tsitsikamma Coastal National Park and Bloukrans State Forest together offer some of the finest accessible natural settings for walks on the whole southern Cape coast. Some 36 per cent of the De Vasselot section of the Park is covered by the fynbos of the coastal plateau, which makes this an important refuge for this veld type, elsewhere under threat or eliminated by agriculture, forestry and urban sprawl. The remainder of the vegetation, except on the estuaries and the coastline, is indigenous forest, generally in good condition. This is undoubtedly my favourite walking area on the Garden Route. Within the park an extensive network of trails gives the hiker the opportunity to enjoy the coastline, the rivers and their estuaries, the forests and the fynbos. Two fairly long walks which between them combine all these elements are described below. There are a large number of shorter walks in the park, including the Kalander Trail - a short circuit in the small valley next to the northern side of the Groot River Pass, where the beauty of the Outeniqua yel-

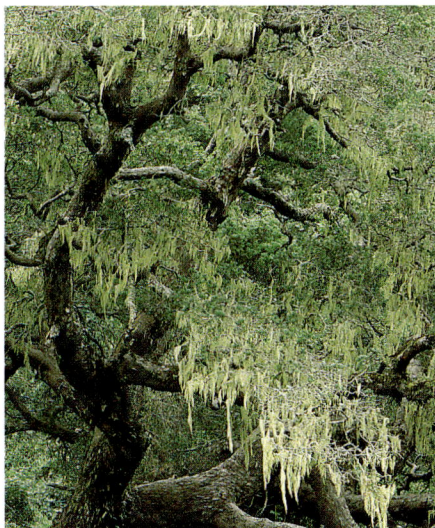

An Outeniqua yellowwood, bearded with lichen, on the Kalander Trail.

lowwoods (*Podocarpus falcatus*) is breathtaking. On the other side of the Groot River Lagoon there is a walk to a viewsite on the bluff overlooking Nature's Valley beach where the Otter Trail ends. The Tsitsikamma Hiking Trail starts at the National Parks Board campsite; the first 8 km also form the outward leg of the Grootkloof Forest Trail (described below) which returns along the stream-side in the forested kloof. The estuary of the Salt River is a place of very special beauty, reached either by a short coastal walk from Nature's Valley (not possible at high tide) or by a path over the intervening ridge. In addition to the walks within the park, there is a wonderful circular trail which passes through the indigenous forest of Stinkhoutkloof in the Bloukrans State Forest. It very soon becomes apparent, when one walks in the Nature's Valley area, that the birds and animals associated with its various habitats are prolific. Bushbuck can sometimes be seen browsing on the edge of forest in the early morning or late evening. Judging from the quantity of their droppings, bushpig must be very common in the forests west of the Groot River but they, like the other nocturnal forest creatures, are shy and unlikely to be seen. The richness of the bird life in the De Vasselot section of the Tsitsikamma Coastal National Park easily rivals that in Wilderness National Park: the full range of forest birds occurs here; fynbos birds can be spotted on the coastal plateau, and coastal birds on the beaches and around the Groot River and Salt River estuaries.

A bonus for walkers is the fascinating marine life to be found in the rock pools along the coast. In fact, the only drawback of the Nature's Valley trails is that each offers so much of interest that it is easy to become absorbed and lose track of time!

Tranquillity reigns in the De Vasselot reserve while storm clouds gather over the Tsitsikamma Mountains.

SALT RIVER VIA KEURPAD TRAIL

A long, fairly demanding circular route which runs through unspoilt forest and fynbos and crosses the Salt River twice.

Time: 5 $\frac{1}{2}$ - 6 hours.

Distance: Approximately 15 km.

Exertion: Moderate to high.

Controlling authority: National Parks Board; the De Vasselot section of the Tsitsikamma Coastal National Park.

Permits: Obtainable at the gate of the De Vasselot campsite.

Maps and information: Obtainable at the gate of the De Vasselot campsite.

How to get there: From Plettenberg Bay, drive east on the N2 for 22 km, past the Crags, to the signposted turn-off to Nature's Valley; turn down the old national road and follow it across the plateau down the Groot River Pass and past the turn-off to Nature's Valley, to the entrance to the De Vasselot campsite on the right. Park inside the gate.

Start: Directly across the main road from the gate.

Trail markers: White footprints.

End: The gate of the De Vasselot campsite.

Best times to walk: Winter, spring and early summer for the fynbos flowers.

Precautions: Don't attempt the coastal route between the Salt River estuary and Nature's Valley at high tide. Keep to the demarcated path, especially in the forests.

Features: Varied, magnificent and unspoilt natural surroundings, the Salt River estuary, indigenous forest, fynbos, birds of these three habitats as well as of the coast, forest animals (if you are lucky) and otters (if you are very lucky).

This longish walk provides a fine introduction to several ecological features which characterize the southern Cape coast: moist, dry and scrub forests, the tall montane fynbos on the dry slopes and plateaux, the kloofs deeply dissected from the plateau, and the estuarine environments of the Salt and Groot rivers.

The route (*see* map, page 145) involves a crossing of the Salt River near its mouth, about an hour short of the end of the walk. Be prepared to wade through the river up to your midriff if your crossing coincides with a high spring tide. At low tide it is a paddle. The trail involves two stretches of sustained climbing and is fairly strenuous.

The first part of the route is on the outward leg of the Kalanderkloof Trail. Once in the forest behind the picnic site at the start, ignore the apparent path that runs beside the telephone line, and continue to a fork where a sign indicates Kalanderpad to the left and Uitsigpad - the one to take - to the right. As I started to climb up the Uitsigpad through the forest one morning, I was lucky enough to see a Barn Owl in plain view next to the path. Higher up the ridge the path emerges from the trees into tall, dense fynbos; typical southern Cape montane fynbos covers the top of the spur you are climbing, as well as the entire plateau area in the De Vasselot reserve. The path swings right, under the telephone line (rather an eyesore) to the edge of a kloof leading into the Groot River Valley. The kloof is laid out below you, with the Tsitsikamma Mountains, a succession of peaks, receding into the distance. To the south, just over the ridge, is a view of the village of Nature's Valley beside the lagoon, with the beach beyond.

On the top of the ridge the path briefly joins a forestry track, passes a signposted turn-off to Kalanderkloof on the left and eventually meets the main road. Head across the road to the picnic site a few metres further along and walk around the boom at the start of a forestry track. A short way along this track, it forks at a sign indicating Salt River (left) and Forest Hall (right). Keep to the right - the left-hand track leads directly down to the mouth of the Salt River. The right-hand track, the Keurpad, crosses a flat plateau flanked on the right by a deep kloof, one of many leading into the Salt River. The track becomes a path and drops increasingly steeply down a spur into the kloof itself. A lovely copse of Keurboom trees (*Virgilia divaricata*), after which the path is named, is traversed before the Keurpad enters natural forest, zigzagging down the slope to the Salt River itself. From the stepping stones that cross the river there is a tranquil view downstream of water and trees, with some large specimens of Outeniqua yellowwood (*Podocarpus falcatus*) prominent. The path follows the southern bank of the stream for 20 m or so before starting the first of the zigzags which take you up the slope through the trees. As you climb, the trees become progressively shorter, because they grow on sites less favourable than the valley bottom. There is the usual evidence of bushbuck and bushpig, but here in greater pro-

ABOVE RIGHT: *The Rugpad descends to meet the Salt River near its mouth.*

RIGHT: *The extensive view to Nature's Valley beach from the viewpoint on the path between the village and the Salt River.*

fusion. You will almost certainly hear Knysna Louries and, if you are fortunate, as I was, see one or two at fairly close range because of the low canopy.

The slope eases gradually and the path, still in the forest, heads straight for the junction of the Forest Hall path and the Rugpad on the left, which is signposted 'Soutrivier'. Some large Outeniqua yellowwoods can be seen along the first part of the Rugpad, which is on the flat and very easy going. Keep a very careful lookout here for a white arrow carved into a tree trunk to the left of the path indicating a sudden right turn. If you miss this, you will continue straight on, as many walkers have clearly done, on what looks like the path but isn't. If you notice an absence of the white footprints which mark the route at regular, brief intervals, retrace your steps until you regain the path.

The path begins to drop gently to the junction with the second route to Forest Hall (right). Keep walking in the direction of Salt River as the path drops more steeply, clears the trees and runs first in tall fynbos with the sound of the sea loud on your right, then into the scrub forest which lines the bank of the Salt River. The path emerges from the trees on the edge of the estuary and traverses a small, flat, vegetated sand spit. Just beyond this, cross the water to the small beach opposite.

There are two routes to Nature's Valley from here. The first is along the eastern bank of the estuary and coastal rocks, and is passable at low tide. The second is signposted Nature's Valley and leads steeply up some log steps and

An opportunistic Kelp Gull rummages in my rucksack on the pebble beach near the Salt River mouth.

joins the forestry track which is the direct route to this point from the picnic site on the main road. Soon a sign reading 'Nature's Valley' leads you off the track onto a path to the right. This tops the rise and drops steeply down the other side. At one spot there is a magnificent view of the beach, bay and lagoon of Nature's Valley. Further on, the path meets the coastal path (signposted 'Salt River/Blue Rocks'), where you turn left to Nature's Valley. At the fence turn right to the yellow-and-green painted bollard which marks the boundary of the reserve and left again along the fence, emerging at the shop in Nature's Valley. There is still a walk of about 2,5 km through Nature's Valley along St George's Avenue, the lagoon road and finally the main road back to the campsite.

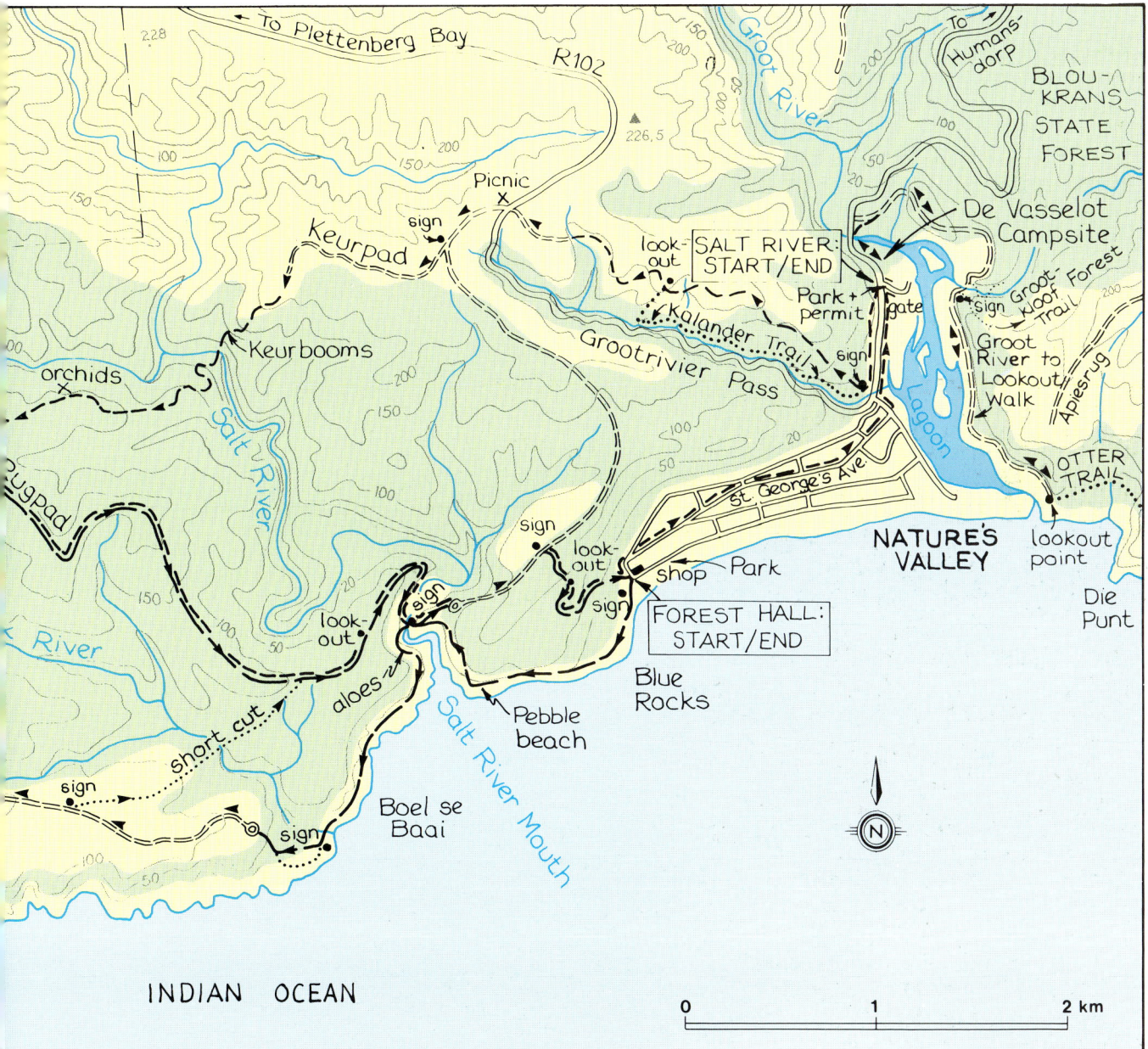

FOREST HALL ROUTE

A lengthy, strenuous circuit along the coast and in the forest of the De Vasselot section of the Tsitsikamma Coastal National Park, twice crossing the Salt River estuary.

Time: 6 - 6 $\frac{1}{2}$ hours.

Distance: Approximately 18 km. (There is a short cut linking the Forest Hall path with the Rugpad which roughly halves the distance.)

Exertion: High.

Controlling authority: National Parks Board: the De Vasselot section of the Tsitsikamma Coastal National Park.

Permits: Obtainable at the gate of the De Vasselot campsite.

Maps and information: Obtainable at the gate of the De Vas-selot campsite.

How to get there: From Plettenberg Bay, drive east along the N2 for 22 km, past the Crags to the signposted turn-off to Nature's Valley. Turn down this road (the old national road) and follow it across the plateau, down the Groot River Pass and past the turn-off to Nature's Valley, to the entrance to the De Vasselot campsite on the right. After obtaining your permit, drive back along the main road, turn into Nature's Valley and drive the length of the town to the shop at the south-western end and park.

Start: Down the path to the beach; turn right to `Blue Rocks'.

Trail markers: White and yellow painted footprints or shoeprints.

End: Back at the shop on the edge of the village.

Best times to walk: Any time.

Precautions: On the way to Salt River from Nature's Valley on the coastal route you cross a ledge with a sheer drop to the sea and rocks below. Consult a tide timetable (available from news agents) when planning this walk, as the coastal sections are not passable at high tide. Keep to the path, especially in the forest. The section of the route along the Forest Hall boundary is very steep and slippery.

Features: Magnificent unspoilt coast and forest, the Salt River estuary, and coastal and forest birds.

This is a circular route (*see* map, page 145) which takes you along the coastline west of Nature's Valley up the boundary of the De Vasselot section of the Tsitsikamma Coastal National Park near Forest Hall, and back via the Forest Hall path and Rugpad to the Salt River. From here you can take the coastal route back to Nature's Valley, or the path over the ridge.

The route allows you to experience most of the different environments offered by the De Vasselot reserve, namely coastline, estuary, forest and fynbos, with their assorted flora and fauna. It is a must for anyone with the necessary time, energy and agility.

Take careful note of the tides and avoid walking the first part of the route when the tide is in, particularly during spring tide. Ideally, start out about three hours before low tide, as this will make the coastal walk easy and both crossings of the Salt River a paddle rather than a wade. The official start is at the National Parks Board camp on the Groot River, but the extra 3 km to Nature's Valley and the same back would make the walk very long indeed - without much reward, since most of this distance is in the village itself.

I would recommend that you begin at the shop and take the path straight to the beach.

I started out on this route one winter's day and was immediately assaulted by a powerful stench. My first thought was that the village had a serious sewage disposal problem but when I reached the beach the reason for the smell became clear: the sand was littered with rotting red bait at the high-water mark. I later learnt from the Parks Board ranger at the camp that a heavy algal infestation in the sea, akin to red tide, had killed off the red bait.

Turn right along the beach to the black rocks at its end. On the rocks, difficult to see at first against this background, were a pair of African Black Oystercatchers. They moved off as I approached and joined a group of at least 15 others congregated on the rocks next to the sea. It is unusual to see so many of these birds together. A little further along the rocks two Pied Kingfishers were fishing the pools and a Grey Heron stalked into the fringing vegetation.

The path runs just above the rocks to begin with, then along them. At one point it climbs to a ledge where there is a 5-m drop straight into the sea below; be careful here. From the rocks you scramble down to a beach of pebbles of all sizes and colours. Distracted by their beauty, you can easily overshoot the path which leads up into the scrub forest a short way along the beach. It runs over a bluff in order to avoid the rocks at the eastern side of the Salt River mouth which would be extremely difficult to negotiate.

In the scrub forest there are several side-paths to fishing spots; ignore these and soon you will find yourself descending to the sand alongside the river. Head upstream around the cove to where the river begins to curve back to the right. Above the rocks on the other side you will now see a clump of aloes (*Aloe ferox*). Cross here (or further upstream if it is easier) and make for the aloes. Next to them, a path leads steeply up into scrub forest again, levels off, then drops and emerges next to the rocks at the western side of the Salt River mouth. The point where this path meets the beach is marked by a pair of shoeprints. If you decide to return this way, take careful note of this spot, as it is not very obvious.

The path leads to the right along the edge of the rocks, then turns up into the trees again, behind large slabs of rock. There is a steep and slippery scramble down into another pebbly cove, from which you can look back and see the sheer rock face which the path avoids. Beyond an easy

West of the Salt River mouth, the trail runs along the shore over the black rocks.

147

stretch across the rocks, there is a rockfall where you must scramble down a cleft to the pebbles below and up the rock on the other side (marked by two white shoeprints). Around the corner there is another steep, 3-m scramble down. From this point, the path runs in the edge of the scrub forest for a while. When it clears the trees, Boel se Baai lies ahead. Here the going is very easy past the blocked-off outlet of a small stream, and you are likely to see the odd fisherman trying his luck off the rocks.

Where the coastline turns away from Boel se Baai, the path comes to a junction. A green perspex notice, next to two white footprints, warns that the trail you have just negotiated is a `Dangerous trail. Caution necessary especially when wet and during spring tide'. The coastal sections of the route do need care and although the total distance travelled is not great, it takes 1 to 1 ¹/₂ hours to get to this point. At the junction, take the route inland into the coastal forest. This is a wide, very obvious path which climbs steeply from the coastline. As it emerges from the trees into fynbos, it meets a track. Continue up the track, which passes a small vlei area on the right and, as it levels out on the ridge, a path to the right marked (when I walked it) by a blank square yellow perspex sign. This is a short cut which drops into the forest, crosses the Brak River, climbs up the other side and joins the Rugpad; if time is short, you can use this path to cut out the long loop that takes in Forest Hall.

Beyond the turn-off to the short cut, the track runs through tall fynbos dominated by leucadendrons, bracken, ericas (*Erica densifolia*, which bears red flowers with green tips, and *E. canaliculata*, which bears dusky pink flowers) and patches of scrub forest. The track enters real forest just before the

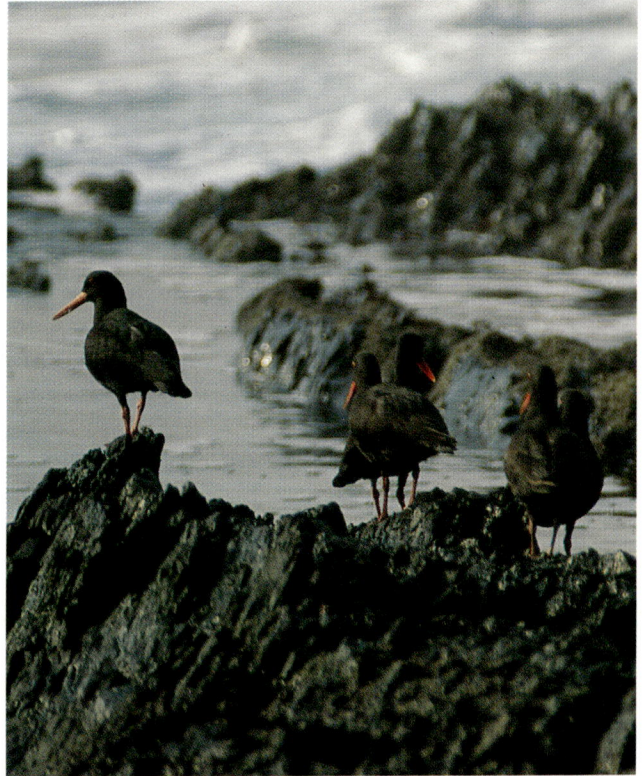

ABOVE: *A group of African Black Oystercatchers - birds usually seen in pairs - on Nature's Valley beach.*
OPPOSITE: *The Salt River estuary seen from the viewsite just off the Rugpad.*
BELOW LEFT: *You are most likely to see a Cape clawless otter either in the early morning or late evening.*

green-and-yellow bollard which marks the boundary corner of the reserve is reached. Through the gate beside the bollard is a right-angle bend to the left on the track which leads to Forest Hall; this is private property. The path you take heads down into the forest at an angle to the right, just before the gate; the junction of this path and the track is marked by white footprints pointing towards you.

The section of the route in wet forest along the boundary of the reserve is heavy going, with very steep and slippery slopes down to two streams and a stream bed, and up the other sides. No concession has been made for the terrain, and the path, which is marked by white footprints pointing in the opposite direction, follows a straight line to the junction with the Forest Hall path. There is a crossroads at this

point. Straight on is a track to a ranger's house; the path on the left leads to Forest Hall. Take the path in the forest to the right - a wide, level one which makes for very easy walking compared with the previous section of the route, and which leads to the well-signposted junction with the Rugpad. Turn right onto the Rugpad (marked `Soutrivier') and follow it all the way down to the river, taking care not to miss an arrow carved into a tree trunk on the left of the path some 15-20 minutes' walk from the junction. This arrow marks an abrupt right turn in the path, beyond which white footprints mark the route all the way down. Look out for a short branch off the path to the right lower down; this leads to an open spot with a magnificent view of the Salt River estuary below.   The second time I walked the Rugpad, I emerged from the trees onto the bank of the Salt River in the early evening and was thrilled to see a Cape clawless otter leave the river, climb the opposite bank and disappear into the

trees. A sighting of this animal is a rare and wonderful treat. To make the experience even more memorable, an African Fish Eagle took off from the trees above the bank and headed upstream, flying over a Pied Kingfisher perched on its customary dead tree trunk on a little sand spit mid-stream.

The National Parks Board have plans to establish a camp with accommodation at this spot on the Salt River. Any such disturbance of this marvellous natural estuarine environment would be a disaster, in my opinion, and would make a mockery of their motto `Custos naturae'. The Salt River estuary is a very special place.

The path follows the Salt River downstream for a short distance to a point where you can cross. On the other bank, in the trees behind the sand beach, is the well-signposted start of the path up and over the ridge to Nature's Valley. Alternatively, you can return along the coastal route if the tide is low enough.

GROOTKLOOF FOREST TRAIL

A circular walk through the forest up to the fynbos on the coastal plateau and back along the stream in forested Grootkloof.

Time: 5 ½ - 6 hours.

Distance: 15,5 km.

Exertion: Moderate to high.

Controlling authorities: National Parks Board - De Vasselot section of the Tsitsikamma Coastal National Park, and the Bloukrans State Forest Station.

Permits: Obtainable at the gate of the De Vasselot campsite.

Maps and information: Obtainable at the gate of the De Vasselot campsite and the office at the Bloukrans Forest Station.

How to get there: From Plettenberg Bay, drive in an easterly direction on the N2 for 22 km, past the Crags to the signposted turn-off to Nature's Valley. Turn down this road (the old national road) and follow it across the plateau, down the Groot River Pass and past the turn-off to Nature's Valley to the entrance to the De Vasselot campsite on the right. Park inside the gate.

Start/end: At the Tsitsikamma Hiking Trail hut in the De Vasselot campsite.

Trail markers: White painted shoeprints (outward leg); yellow painted footprints (return leg). There are distance markers at 1-km intervals.

Best times to walk: Winter and spring for the fynbos flowers, but the environment is beautiful at any time of year.

Precautions: When the level of the lagoon is high, the last river crossing will require wading.

Features: Natural forest beside the Groot River lagoon and in Grootkloof, forest birds and a delightful forested stream in Grootkloof.

Grootkloof Trail is a circuit (*see* map, overleaf), the outward leg of which is also the first 8 km or so of the Tsitsikamma Hiking Trail. It traverses a part of the De Vasselot section of the Tsitsikamma Coastal National Park as well as a section of the Bloukrans State Forest.

From the natural forest surrounding the lagoon, the trail climbs steeply onto the fynbos-covered coastal plateau, before it enters (more-or-less) natural forest, in which it stays all the way down Grootkloof and back to the camp. The initial climb onto the plateau is fairly strenuous. So is the walk down the stream in Grootkloof, which is crossed a total of 21 times. There are some steep sections between crossings and some boulder-hopping is required in places.

From the parking area reserved for hikers, next to the lagoon in the campsite, find the path marked with white shoeprints which runs alongside the Groot River to the bridge on the old National Road. Immediately across the bridge, turn right into the picnic area and follow the path to a forestry track which runs just above the lagoon in the natural forest. Here we saw Knysna Louries and a pair of Blue-mantled Flycatchers in the trees. *Dietes iridioides* (a small blue-and-white flowered iris of evergreen forests) is never floriferous, but some of the many plants along the track grudgingly showed a flower or two. Lesser Doublecollared Sunbirds were taking nectar from erica flowers and nearby, on a damp bank, were massed the small, bright yellow spikes of *Bulbine lagopus*, a plant with succulent-looking narrow leaves which seems (but is not) rather out of place in this environment. A short way beyond the point where the stream which runs down Grootkloof crosses under the track, take the well signposted `Blaauwkrantz' path, which

BELOW LEFT: *On the steep climb from the Groot River, Robberg can be seen on the horizon.*
BELOW: *At the start of the Grootkloof Forest Trail you cross the Groot River; the coastal plateau rises above the bend.*

climbs steeply alongside a telephone line onto the plateau. Where the path clears the trees there are fine views of the Groot River Valley below and along the coast past Nature's Valley to the distant Robberg peninsula.

On the plateau, where the trail joins a track, there is a stretch of attractive fynbos. Further on, where the path leaves the track, it runs beside a dense thicket of black wattle, in which there are signs of previous habitation; this area was once commonage (Covie Commonage). Before the path reaches a grove of Keurboom (*Virgilia divaricata*) which marks the margin of the forest, there are shrubs of *Cyclopia subternata* (Bossiestee), unmistakable in spring when they bear masses of brilliant golden-yellow flowers. On the forest edge, a pair of Knysna Louries were feeding.

In the forest it soon becomes clear why this part of the trail is known as Blackwood Path. There are many of these trees here - so many in places, because the undergrowth is thin and the canopy open, that they form small copses. Some have been felled along the path by forestry staff. In this area, however, there are also some large Kalanders (*Podocarpus falcatus*). A small flock of Redbilled Woodhoopoes noisily made their presence known on this, the first of several occasions on which we saw them, as they (coincidentally) accompanied us all the way down Grootkloof.

Where the Blackwood Path meets a forestry track, the Tsitsikamma Hiking Trail turns right and the Grootkloof Trail turns left; both directions are well marked. Some 40 m down the track the Grootkloof Trail leaves it and turns left, back into the forest, at a pair of yellow footprints on a tree trunk. The return leg of the trail drops along the crest of a ridge, at first gently, then steeply down to the first stream crossing. Over the next rise, on the trunk of a large, dead blackwood on the left of the path, there was an enormous Horse's foot fungus (*Phellinus igniarius*), the largest I have

Arums (Zantedeschia aethiopica) line the banks of the aptly named Black Pool in Grootkloof.

seen, measuring a full half-metre across. Further on, several enormous blackwoods grow next to the path, one giant uncharacteristically multi-stemmed.

The walk down Grootkloof is delightful. You follow the course of the stream, whose dark rock pools provide the perfect backdrop for the arums (*Zantedeschia aethiopica*) flowering on their banks. A host of ferns thrive in the subdued green light beneath the forest canopy. At the bottom of the kloof, next to the path, are excavations in the forest floor - the saw-pits of past woodcutters. If the tide is in, you may have to wade across the stream at one point, to reach the track next to the lagoon. This is where we saw the Redbilled Woodhoopoes for the last time. Turn right on the track, which takes you back to the main road and the campsite.

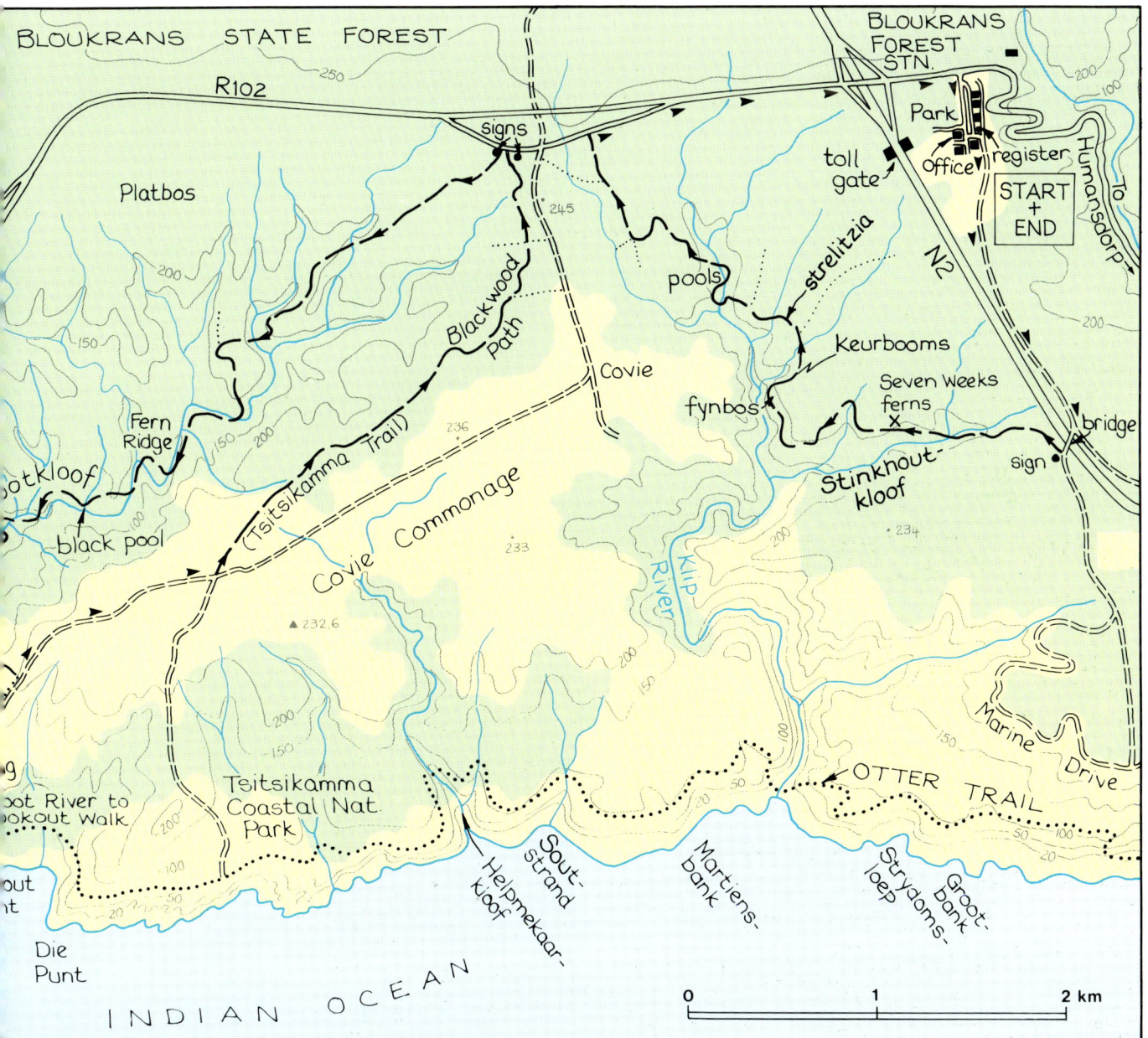

FOREST FUNGI

Fungi provide some of the most colourful sights in the forest. Most common are the bracket fungi, which grow on dead branches and logs, but other types of mushroom also take advantage of the food source that dead wood provides. Fungi form a vital link in the balanced processes of growth and decay which maintain the forest as living whole.

These intriguing organisms are neither animal nor plant. Fungi do not photosynthesize and are either parasitic, in which case they feed on living organisms (athlete's foot and downy mildew are examples), or saprophytic, like the bracket fungi, and live on dead organisms. What manifests as a mushroom or bracket fungus is just one stage - the fruiting body - in the life cycle of that fungus. Beneath the surface of what the fungus grows on (the substrate) is a mass (the mycelium) of thread-like structures (hyphae) which exude enzymes. These enzymes dissolve the substrate to produce chemicals which the hyphae absorb as nutrients for growth. When conditions are right, mycelial strands from different individuals combine to form 'knots' which grow into fruiting bodies. These bodies produce spores, which are minute structures easily dispersed over large distances by wind or water to start new colonies.

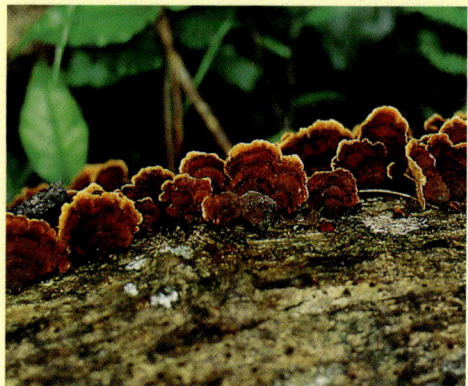

STINKHOUTKLOOF FOREST TRAIL

A fairly easy circular trail which leads through plantations to beautiful natural forest and wooded streams.

Time: 3 hours.

Distance: 8,4 km.

Exertion: Light to moderate.

Controlling authority: Bloukrans State Forest Station.

Permits: None required; register at start.

Maps and information: Sketch map available at register.

How to get there: From Plettenberg Bay, drive east along the N2 and turn left at the toll interchange, to the Bloukrans Forest Station. Take the turn-off to the forest station about 500 m further on, and park where indicated under the oaks.

Start: At the registry point, signposted a short way down the forestry road past the forester's house.

Trail markers: Yellow painted footprints.

End: The parking area.

Best times to walk: Any time.

Precautions: The path in the forest can be slippery when wet.

Features: Magnificent natural forest, streams, and rock pools lined with Tree ferns.

Don't be discouraged by the first part of this trail; it is well worth enduring the noise of high-speed traffic on the N2 national road which dominates the first 2 km of the trail to reach the natural forest, in which the peace is absolute. Stinkhoutkloof is simply splendid.

From the Bloukrans Forest Station, where there is a register to complete next to a sign indicating Stinkhoutkloof (*see* map, page 153), the route initially follows a forestry track alongside the national road, at first past a patch of indigenous forest and then in a plantation. Cross the bridge, signposted `Marine Drive', over the national road. On the other side, the trail leaves the track where there are yellow footprints on a tree trunk and a signboard to Stinkhoutkloof, and drops steadily through pines to a stream in the kloof. Here the path leaves the plantation and enters the first section of natural forest. Tree ferns (*Cyathea capensis*) line the stream where the path crosses it on a small log bridge. On the other side, you pass into the deep shade of tall trees. This is wet forest and, judging by the volume of bushpig droppings, the home of large numbers of these gregarious, nocturnal animals that root in forest litter. Clumps of Seven-

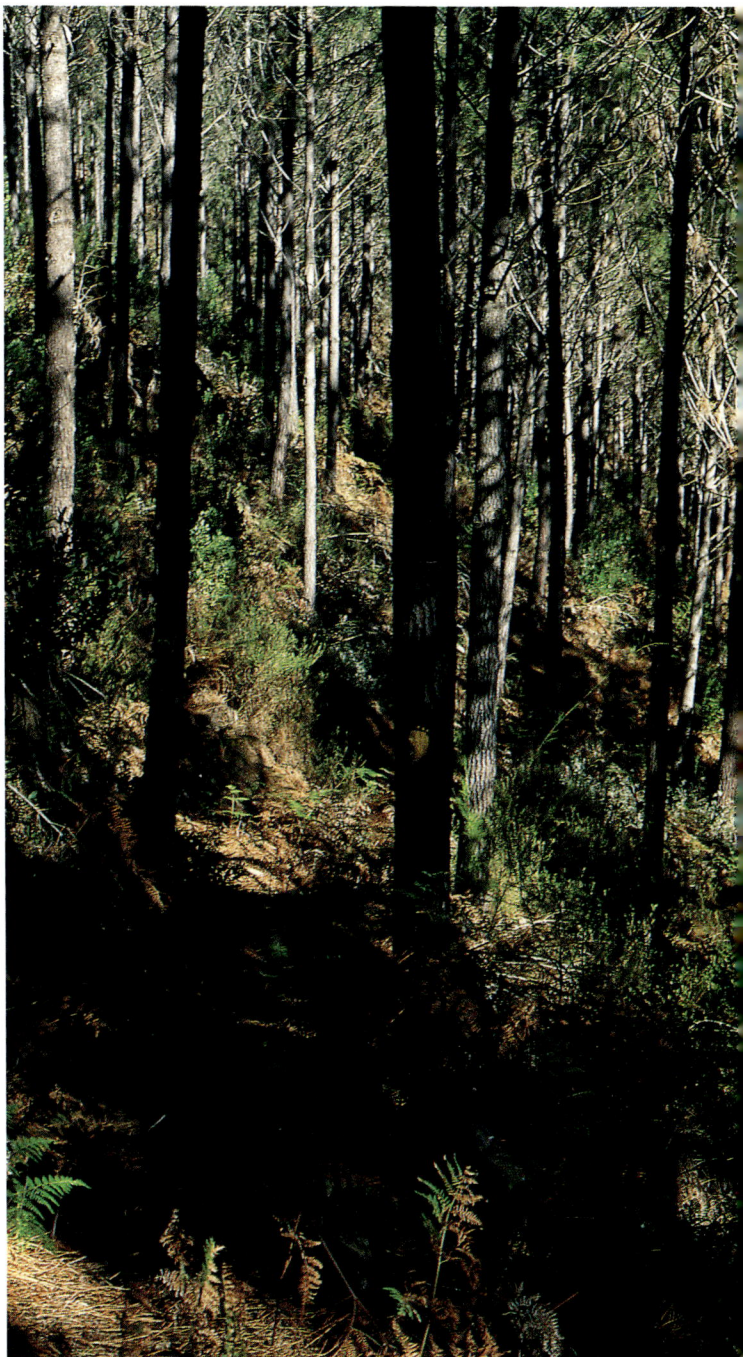

RIGHT: *The path to Stinkhoutkloof leads from a forestry track down through a pine plantation.*

week's fern (*Rumohra adiantiformis*) grow along the path.

In Stinkhoutkloof itself, the trail traverses only a few hundred metres of natural forest before once again reaching pine plantations where there are glimpses (through the indigenous trees below) of the valley of the Klip River and the sea. As the path rounds a bluff with a steep kloof below, you cross a small section of fynbos. Here are plants of *Rhodocoma gigantea* (one of the tallest of the restios, or Cape reeds), with slender flowering stems up to 3 m high and tufts of bright green thread-like leaves at intervals down the lower stem. A grove of Keurboom (*Virgilia divaricata*) marks the fringe of the natural forest and the part of the trail that is, to my mind, by far the most rewarding.

Just within the trees, the path crosses a small stream then climbs up and over a low ridge to a second stream. On the way, there is a single *Strelitzia alba* plant which is clearly fighting a losing battle to reach the light through the forest canopy above. These plants, larger cousins of the well-known Crane flower (*Strelitzia reginae*), can reach 10 m in height and are normally found growing in clumps. They do not typically form a component of the interior of high wet forests and one can only speculate that this plant may have germinated here when the forest canopy was not closed, possibly after logging operations many years ago.

From the second stream, the path climbs over a ridge and drops down to the edge of a third, larger stream. This is an enchanting place of shallow rock pools lined with Tree ferns where the sun, freed by a break in the forest canopy, highlights the golden-green moss on rocks surrounded by placid brown, peaty water. The scene is timeless, probably much the same as it has been for millions of years, and a wonderful counterpoint to man's machines and machinations, which are so intrusive at the beginning of this walk.

The path follows the stream, crossing and re-crossing it at points well marked by the now familiar yellow footprints before climbing into the deep shade of the forest up a steepish slope which brings you, by means of a well-cleared path through the trees, to the old main road. Some of the trees are named, and here you pass a second *Strelitzia alba*. The walk on the old main road (which intersects the national road) back to the forest station makes you long for the peace and beauty of the kloof below.

From the Bloukrans Forest Station, there is a drive (the Marine Drive) on forest tracks to the edge of the plateau overlooking the coast. Below runs the Otter Trail, and there are distant views of Plettenberg Bay. It is well worth the half an hour or so it takes to complete the circuit by car.

ABOVE: *The Knysna dwarf chameleon is restricted to southern Cape wet forests; it can climb high into the canopy and often sleeps in Tree ferns.*
RIGHT: *The Stinkhoutkloof Forest Trail crosses one of the streams that feeds the Klip River; the scene at this crossing is primeval and exceptionally lovely.*

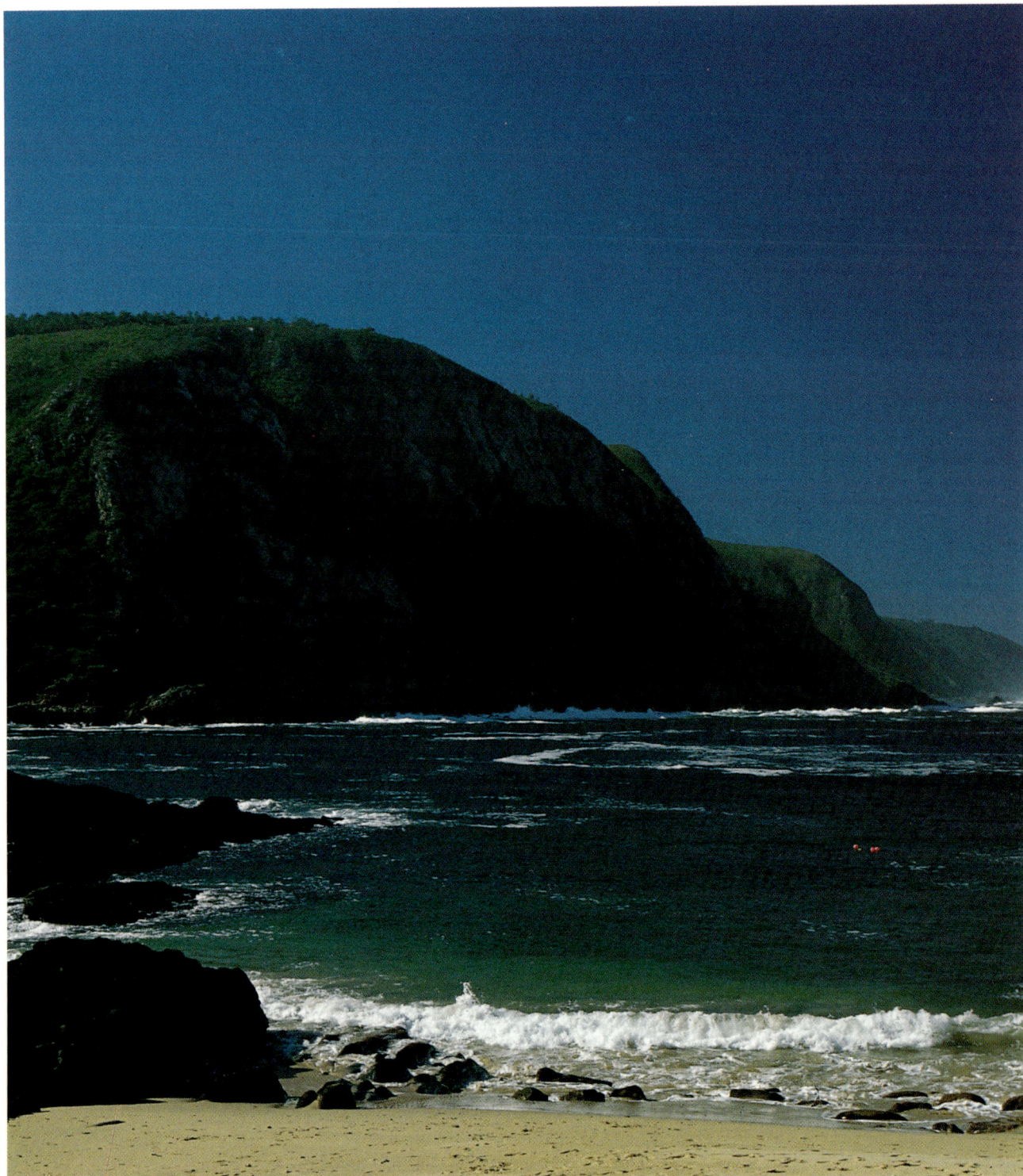

CHAPTER ELEVEN

STORMS RIVER MOUTH TO WITELSBOS

The mouth of the Storms River lies roughly midway along the stretch of coast that forms the Tsitsikamma Coastal National Park. The park extends from the valley of the Groot River (the De Vasselot section) in the west to, coincidentally, the mouth of another Groot River in the east and encompasses the littoral, a substantial portion of the adjoining sea and a narrow strip of the land which rises steeply off the beach to the coastal plateau. The eastern part of the reserve is generally not easily accessible, but along the western half runs the famous Otter Trail (see page 173), which begins from the National Parks Board camp at Storms River Mouth and ends at Nature's Valley.

The precipitous cliffs which dominate the meeting of the Storms River

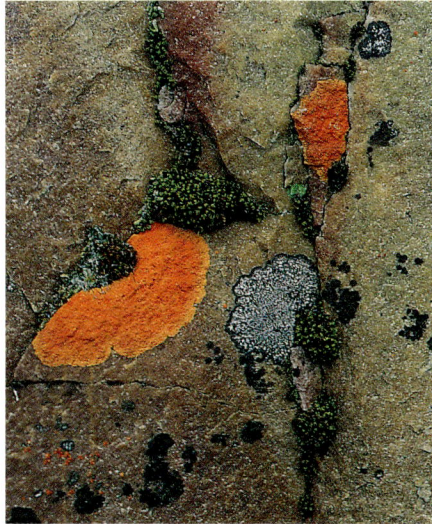

Lichens and moss colour a Table Mountain sandstone rock on Witelskop.

and the sea, and the rocky coastline to either side of the river mouth combine to provide a scenically dramatic setting for the campsite. This is quite an establishment, providing for a large number of day-visitors to the park, as well as campers and visitors who wish to overnight in self-catering accommodation. There are several walks in the park which take advantage of its varied scenery. From the restaurant a boardwalk about 1 km long leads - largely through scrub forest - past a cave containing an interesting exhibit on Strandlopers to the suspension bridge across the river mouth. From this Mouth Trail several paths wind down to rocky bays. Across the suspension bridge is the start of a short but very steep climb to a point on the bluff from which there is a fine view of the river mouth, the camp and the adjoining coast. On the other side of the camp the first 2,5 km or so of the Otter Trail can be walked as far as the Water-

Seen from a small beach below the restaurant, cliffs rise above the Storms River mouth.

fall, a walk which offers an enticing taste (described in this chapter) of the attractions of this renowned and popular 5-day hike. (Only hikers booked on the Trail are permitted beyond the Waterfall.) There is also a lovely walk through the forest on the slopes behind the shore (the Blue Duiker Trail, also described here), with a short cut known as the Loerie Trail.

For those who wish to explore the fascinating world beneath the water, a snorkel trail has been laid out in a protected cove adjacent to the start of the Otter Trail, and there is diving trail off the rocks near the restaurant.

On the N2 highway, some 7 km east of the turn-off to the Storms River Mouth camp in the Tsitsikamma Coastal National Park, and 2 km west of the well-known Paul Sauer Bridge over the Storms River, is the turn-off to a Big Tree. This is the starting-point of a delightful 4,2-km circular route called the Ratel Trail, which runs through indigenous forest and crosses several streams; a short cut provides an alternative 2,6-km route. The trail is administered by the Department of Environment Affairs and Forestry. No permit is needed, but a register must be completed near the start.

Alongside the N2, 18 km east of the Paul Sauer Bridge, lies Witelskop. A steep wedge of Table Mountain sandstone 1 251 m high, this is the most easterly high peak in the Tsitsikamma range. Spread out below Witelskop is the Witelsbos State Forest.

Originally, the coastal terrace between the Tsitsikammas and the sea supported enormous tracts of natural forest, but even in the early years of the 19th century felling of these had begun. Over the next fifty years indiscriminate woodcutting continued virtually unchecked. In 1856 Captain Christopher Harison was appointed the first Conservator of the Tsitsikamma Forests. He set up his headquarters at

Witelsbos. In spite of all his efforts over the next thirty years, the licence system he instituted failed to ensure the conservation of the forests, since a lack of policing allowed illegal felling to continue. The death-knell of the forests was sounded when, in 1882, the famous Thomas Bain completed the construction of the Tsitsikamma road, which made the forests considerably more accessible. Today all that remain are some small patches of indigenous forest, surrounded by plantations of exotic trees, such as blackwood (*Acacia melanoxylon*), which were planted as the natural forests became completely worked out. You will notice that most of the logs stored at the forest station depot are of blackwood.

Between Witelskop and the N2 highway is a remnant patch of natural forest, roughly 5 km by 1 km in extent, through which runs the first leg of a new circular walk - Captain Harison's Trail - described in this chapter. Also in

the Witelsbos State Forest is a longer (24-km) circuit planned as a two-day hiking trail (*see* page 173), the Fourcade Trail, which leads through the plantations to the fynbos on the northern side of Witelskop before returning to the start on the return leg of the shorter trail.

The forest at Witelsbos is uniquely lovely because of the large number of Witels (*Platylophus trifoliatus*) trees growing in it. Despite its small size, this forest is the home of blue duiker, bushbuck, bushpig and forest birds such as the Narina Trogon, Blackheaded Oriole, Knysna Lourie, Redbilled Woodhoopoe and Cape Batis. It is well worth a visit.

ABOVE: *From the top of the cliff on the eastern side of Storms River mouth, you can see the entire camp complex.*
FAR RIGHT: *The waterfall cascades down a series of ledges to a pool just above the sea.*

WATERFALL TRAIL

A short walk from the western end of the Storms River camp along a lovely stretch of coast to the Waterfall and back.

Time: 2 1/2 - 3 hours return.
Distance: 5,3 km.
Exertion: Light.
Controlling authority: National Parks Board - Storms River Mouth.
Permits: None required; a fee is charged to enter the park.
Maps and information: Sketch map and information available at the Information Centre in the camp.
How to get there: On the N2, 9 km west of the Paul Sauer Bridge over the Storms River, take the turn-off signposted `Tsitsikamma National Park'. Drive 9 km to the park entrance. Inside the park, at the bottom of the small pass, turn sharp right towards the most westerly bungalows. Park where indicated on the right, just before these `Oceanettes'.
Start/end: At the end of the road at the indicated start of the Otter Trail.
Trail markers: Yellow painted footprints.
Best times to walk: Any time.
Precautions: The first section of the trail is very slippery when wet. Some easy rock scrambling and boulder-hopping is involved.
Features: The Waterfall, beautiful coastline, interesting rock strata, Guano Cave, birds of the forest fringe and the sea.

This walk (*see* map, overleaf) comprises the first 2,65 km of the Otter Trail and provides a brief taste of the pleasures of that famous five-day, 48-km hike to Nature's Valley. Because it is virtually on the level (unlike other parts of the Otter Trail, which climb steeply up onto and down from the coastal plateau several times) this is not a strenuous walk, but some rock scrambling is required.

Although there is a wealth of interest in the sea life in the rock pools, in the sea birds and the birds of the coastal vegetation and scrub forest, and in the different communities of plants and trees, it is the constant sound, movement and beauty of the sea which makes the most vivid impression. Skietklip (directly translated from Afrikaans, 'shoot stone'), opposite the restaurant at Storms River Mouth, is well known but along this section of the coast there are several other spots where heavy swells breaking onto the rocks provide spectacular displays of spray shooting high into the air. A few metres from the signboard that marks the start of the trail is a map of the underwater snorkel trail which begins in a gully to the left; patently, no fishing is allowed there.

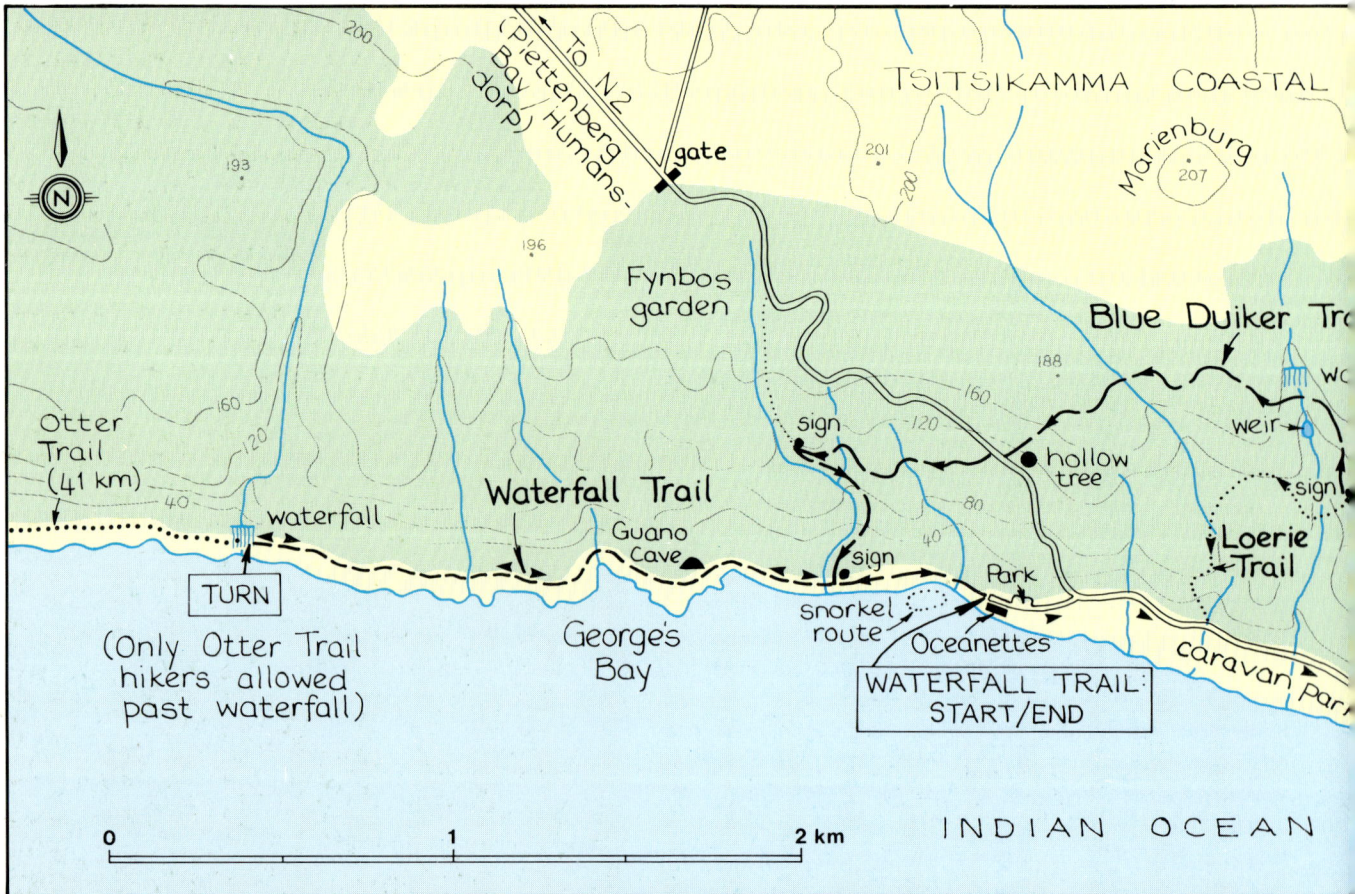

TSITSIKAMMA COASTAL

To N2
(Plettenberg
Bay/Humans-
dorp)

gate

Marienburg

207

Fynbos
garden

Blue Duiker Tr

201

200

188

160

160

120

sign

hollow
tree

weir

WC

Otter
Trail
(41 km)

120

80

sign

Waterfall Trail

waterfall

Guano
Cave

sign

40

**Loerie
Trail**

sign

TURN

Park

(Only Otter Trail
hikers allowed
past waterfall)

George's
Bay

snorkel
route

Oceanettes

caravan Par

**WATERFALL TRAIL
START/END**

0   1   2 km

INDIAN   OCEAN

The first part of the route can be very slippery when wet.

Keep an eye open for birds: I have never walked through the coastal vegetation here without seeing several Greater Doublecollared Sunbirds in the erica bushes (*Erica fourcadei*) next to the path. (Although fairly plentiful here, this species of erica has a small distribution and only occurs along the coast from near Storms River in the east to the dunes of Goukamma in the west.) Other small birds common here are Cape White-eyes, Dusky Flycatchers and Barthroated Apalises. Mingling with the normal sea smells is the aromatic scent of the Everlasting *Helichrysum petiolare*, which forms large, tangled grey mats between patches of scrub forest. In one of these patches is the signposted junction with

LEFT: *A thick sea haze is produced by breakers pounding the coastal rocks.*

BELOW RIGHT: *The fruit of the Kershout (*Pterocelastrus tricuspidatus*) is enjoyed by many species of birds.*

the Blue Duiker Trail on the right. The path keeps largely to the scrub forest edge as it skirts two small bays. The strata in the rocks are striking, particularly in the second of these bays, where the rocks are lined up rigidly parallel to the coast. Trail markers guide you over these rocks and the tumbled boulders beyond, to the opening of Guano Cave. This impressively deep cave, which follows a rock fissure into the mountain, must have sheltered a succession of animals and people down the ages.

On the other side of the cave mouth, there is a steep but easily negotiated climb up the rocks. The path then runs through a bit of scrub forest in which aloes (*Aloe arborescens*) grow amongst tumbled boulders. After passing a vertical rock slab, the path drops to cross the base of a recent rockfall, then climbs back up to its original level. Dassies are common here; fat and unafraid, they bask on the rocks and watch as you pass.

The last section of the route to the waterfall is very well marked over the rocks. In places, it requires some scrambling, which is time-consuming, though nowhere difficult, exposed or demanding. It takes about as long to reach the waterfall from Guano Cave as it does to reach the cave from the start. The waterfall comes into view suddenly and the beauty of this high, graceful series of falls is a surprise. From a large pool surrounded by rocks covered with orange and yellow lichens, the water flows over a ledge straight into the sea. This dramatic sight is a fitting climax to a walk which provides a wealth of spectacular coastal scenery.

The only way back is along the same route. Remember that you are not permitted to walk beyond the waterfall unless you are hiking the Otter Trail.

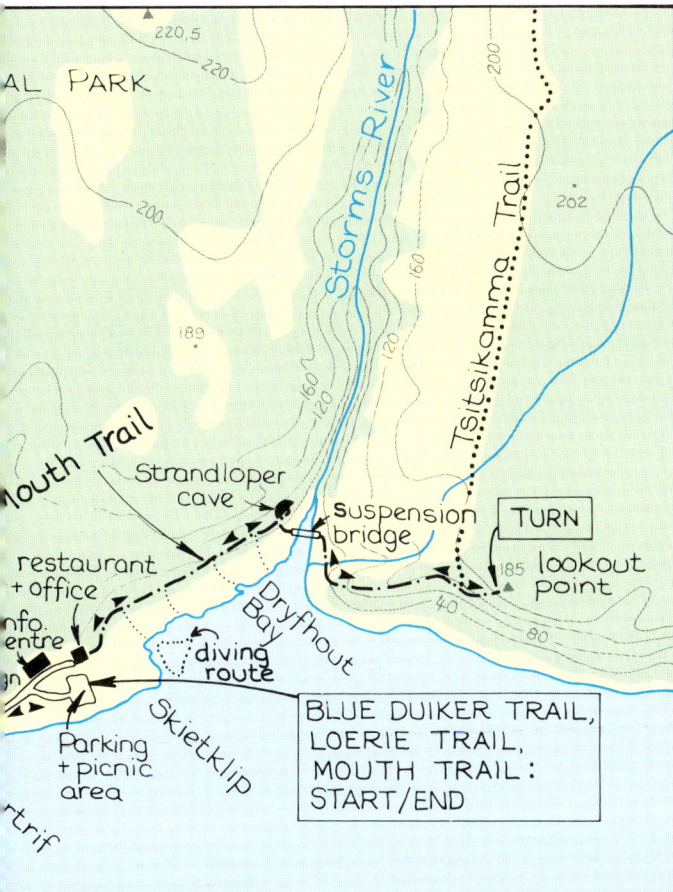

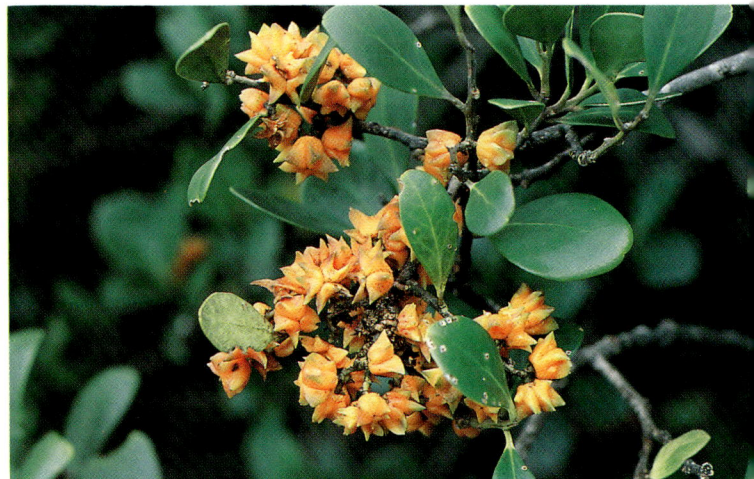

163

BLUE DUIKER AND LOERIE TRAILS

The Blue Duiker route through coastal forest and along the littoral in the Tsitsikamma Coastal National Park has much to offer naturalists of all ages. The Loerie Trail provides a short cut.

Time: 2 ¹/₂ - 3 hours.
Distance: 6 km, including the stretch along the road from the 'oceanettes' back to the restaurant.
Exertion: Light to moderate.
Controlling authority: National Parks Board - Storms River Mouth.
Permits: None required; a fee is charged to enter the park.
Maps and information: Sketch map and information available at the Information Centre in the camp.
How to get there: On the N2, 9 km west of the Paul Sauer Bridge over the Storms River, take the turn-off signposted `Tsitsikamma National Park'. Drive 9 km to the park entrance. Inside the park, turn left at the bottom of the small pass, and drive to the parking area near the restaurant.
Start/end: Signposted 100 m back along the tarred road.
Trail markers: Blue duiker motif on green perspex squares mounted on posts.
Best times to walk: Lovely at any time, but especially rewarding when breeding whales come close inshore between July and October.
Precautions: The stretch shared with the start of the Otter Trail is very slippery when wet.
Features: Observation platform with extensive views of the coast; beautiful coastal forest, especially in the west; forest and forest fringe birds.

Most of the Blue Duiker Trail (*see* map, page 162) runs through the forest which clothes the slopes behind the coastline and the neighbouring part of the plateau. The trail has been laid out with conservation education in mind; many trees and shrubs are numbered and named and there are a series of information boards about several disparate points of interest along the way. The climb from the coastal road is steep but short, and the only other difficult part of the route may be the short section shared with the beginning of the Otter Trail, which is like a skating rink when wet!

A short cut back to the road from the Blue Duiker Trail soon after it enters the forest on the plateau makes a circuit of less than 2 km, called the Loerie Trail.

From the well signposted start to the walk, the path immediately enters scrub forest and zigzags up the slope through shrubs and small trees such as Kershout (*Pterocelastrus tricuspidatus*), Bastard saffronwood (*Cassine peragua*), Cape beech (*Rapanea melanophloeos*) and Num-num (*Carissa*

bispinosa). There are information boards describing the last-mentioned two species on the way.

On the edge of the plateau, the path passes through a short section of coastal fynbos dominated by tall Bietou (*Chrysanthemoides monilifera*), the ubiquitous yellow-flowered member of the daisy family, *Erica fourcadei* (a southern Cape endemic with soft pink tubular flowers) and *Polygala myrtifolia*, which has small, purplish-pink, legume-like flowers. Near the path, a large wooden platform has been built out over the plateau edge to provide spectacular views east and west along this beautiful coastline. In winter, you may see whales in the sea below, and you can read about them on the information board provided; another board discusses the major ocean currents along this coast.

From the look-out point the path makes the transition from coastal fynbos through scrub forest to forest as it swings inland. Shortly after the path enters the trees, it splits. The Loerie Trail (the left-hand branch) drops down to the coastal road over a distance of a few hundred metres. The Blue Duiker Trail is the right-hand branch, which heads deeper into the trees. This is dry forest on poor, shallow soils: the undergrowth is not dense and an old Kalander *Podocarpus falcatus*) growing here - the first of many along the trail - has a massive girth but is peculiarly short. As the path heads westwards the forest becomes moister, the canopy higher and the undergrowth denser. The path drops gently and crosses a stream below a waterfall, an idyllic place to stop, particularly in summer when the sun is high enough in the sky to light up the pool and the falls above. Downstream is a weir which creates a small dam that supplies the camp with fresh water.

As the path heads west, it crosses several small stream beds and passes a number of sizeable Outeniqua yellow-woods. Just before its junction with the tarred road, the path encounters an extraordinary tree. The bole (which is alive) is hollow, and large enough for two or three people to stand in. The gnarled walls of this forest `cave' are reminiscent of illustrations for Tolkien's books. It has clearly delighted many hikers, as the floor of the cavern has been trodden flat.

On the two occasions I walked the Blue Duiker Trail, I saw little bird life on the eastern section but, as soon as I had crossed the tarred road into the forest on the other side, birds were all around. This part of the trail may be less frequented and the surrounding forest is wetter. Here I watched several Knysna Louries feeding in the canopy, while a small flock of Chorister Robins, the most I had ever seen together, flitted in the branches overhead. A pair of Yellowthroated Warblers were busily searching for food in the undergrowth. This warbler is a tiny but beautiful forest bird with a reddish-brown cap and bright yellow chest. A little further along the path I was lucky to spot a Knysna dwarf chameleon on the bright orange under-bark, criss-crossed with termite trails, of a dead *Cassine* tree. The little chameleon was no doubt looking for a tasty insect.

The trail crosses two small stream-beds as it heads westwards through the forest to a T-junction more or less on the level. The path to the right leads up to the Fynbos Garden; the trail proper continues on the left-hand branch. Even in the forest you are never really cut off from the sound of the sea, but this background roar increases in volume as the path descends, fairly steeply in places, to join the coastal path which is the start of the Otter Trail. From this point, it is a short distance to the beginning of the tarred road below the 'oceanettes' which ultimately leads you back to the parking area and the restaurant.

LEFT: *A male Greater Doublecollared Sunbird takes nectar from an Aloe ferox flower.*
BELOW: *The gnarled trunk of the hollow tree which is a landmark on the Blue Duiker Trail.*

165

CAPTAIN HARISON'S TRAIL

A circular route which leads through beautiful natural forest, characterized by a large number of Witels trees, then traverses the slopes of Witelskop.

Time: 3 - 3 1/2 hours.

Distance: 9 km.

Exertion: Light to moderate.

Controlling authority: Witelsbos State Forest Station.

Permits: From the forest station office.

Maps and information: From the forest station office.

How to get there: 11 km east of the Storms River bridge, turn right off the N2 to Witelsbos; 7,5 km on is the Witelsbos

Forest Station. Obtain a permit, drive under the N2, turn left into the depot and park.

Start/end: Behind the big oak.

Trail markers: Yellow painted footprints. There are distance markers at 1-km intervals.

Best times to walk: Any time.

Precautions: None.

Features: Natural forest; streams, ferns and forest birds. There are pretty views from the slopes of Witelskop.

This newly laid out trail is named after Captain Christopher Harison, the first Conservator of Forests of the Tsitsikamma area, who, on his appointment in 1856, made Witelsbos his headquarters. The first 4,5 km of the circuit runs the length of a remnant patch of natural forest at the foot of Witelskop, a sharp wedge of Table Mountain sandstone with steep sides. From the forest the trail climbs some way up the southern flank of Witelskop through pine plantations, then swings back eastwards, more or less following a contour and eventually descends and returns to the start on a forestry road. The return leg shares the same route as the end of the much longer, second trail newly set out here, which is intended as a two-day walk.

Captain Harison's Trail is not strenuous, apart from the short climb up the lower slopes of Witelskop. In my opinion

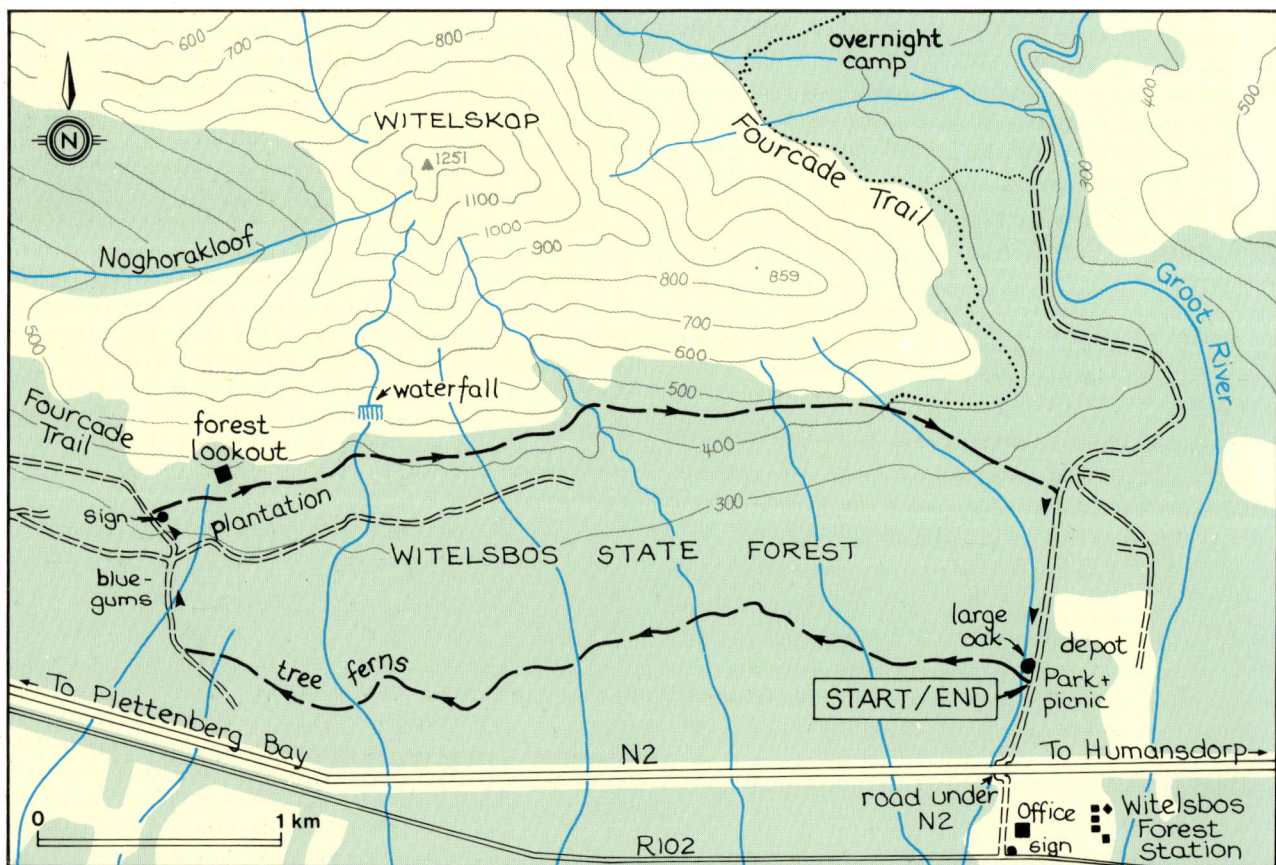

the first part of the walk, through the forest, is by far the more rewarding. Although the second leg provides some pleasant views of the coastal plateau below, it runs through veld which is very badly infested with alien pines, acacias and eucalyptus; in fact, there is little of natural beauty on this part of the trail. Some walkers may prefer to turn back at the far boundary of the natural forest in order to enjoy this environment a second time.

The clearing where you park is shared by a depot where logs, mainly of blackwood (*Acacia melanoxylon*), are stored before being auctioned, and a picnic spot, with benches and tables on the edge of the forest. The forest is alive with the sound of birds, and before setting out I spotted Knysna Louries, Cape Batises and Black Orioles; an African Goshawk was circling overhead. The trail begins from the oak which dominates the clearing. As you walk along the track through the trees, you can soon see how the forest acquired its name. Although there are some fine examples of other indigenous species, including a large Hard pear (*Olinia ventosa*) near the start of the walk, and many Stinkwoods (*Ocotea bullata*), it is the Witels (*Platylophus trifoliatus*) that gives this forest a somewhat different feel from those near Knysna and George. The tree's characteristic pale green leaves, in groups of three, provide much of the canopy of the Witels forest. The tree prefers damp situations, and the number of rivulets you cross on the way through the forest indicates that this is a wet area. Witels trees seldom have single, vertical trunks; instead, they tend to sprawl, and often send up side branches from a leaning main trunk. Along this trail there are some very large, no doubt old, trees which have lost their main trunk but have grown several side branches which are now large enough to be trees in their own right. Another feature of the walk through the forest is the large number of ferns. The streams near the western end of the forest are lined with Tree ferns (*Cyathea capensis*) and are particularly beautiful. A constant accompaniment is the `Willie' call of Sombre Bulbuls; at one spot, the birds became quite frantic when the Goshawk circled overhead. There are obviously plenty of bushpigs around, despite the small size of the forest.

Just beyond the last forest stream lined with Tree ferns, the trail meets a forestry road. Turn right here and you will soon pass some large eucalyptus (bluegum) trees. Continue through the first crossroads (not clearly marked), in a pine plantation, to the clearly marked point on the track where a path leads to the right under the forestry look-out hut along the edge of the plantation. This is the first meeting-point of

ABOVE: *The black bib of this Cape Batis distinguishes it as a male; the female has a brown or chestnut band across the breast.*
OVERLEAF: *A tree fern* (Cyathea capensis) *and mossy rocks along a streamlet are bathed in the green light below the canopy of Witelsbos.*

the path with the two-day Fourcade Trail (*see* page 173).

The slopes of Witelskop above are infested with pines which are smothering the natural fynbos. Further along the path, past a small waterfall, the path traverses areas totally taken over by acacias (*Acacia melanoxylon*), exotic pines and bluegums. This illustrates the problem that invasive alien trees can present when their spread is uncontrolled; the natural balance of the indigenous forest below is in stark contrast. In one section, acacia seedlings grow densely through the thick layer of their seed pods on the ground beside the trail. Finally the path branches; the right-hand fork leads down through a stand of eucalyptus to the gravel forestry road on which you turn right to return to the depot.

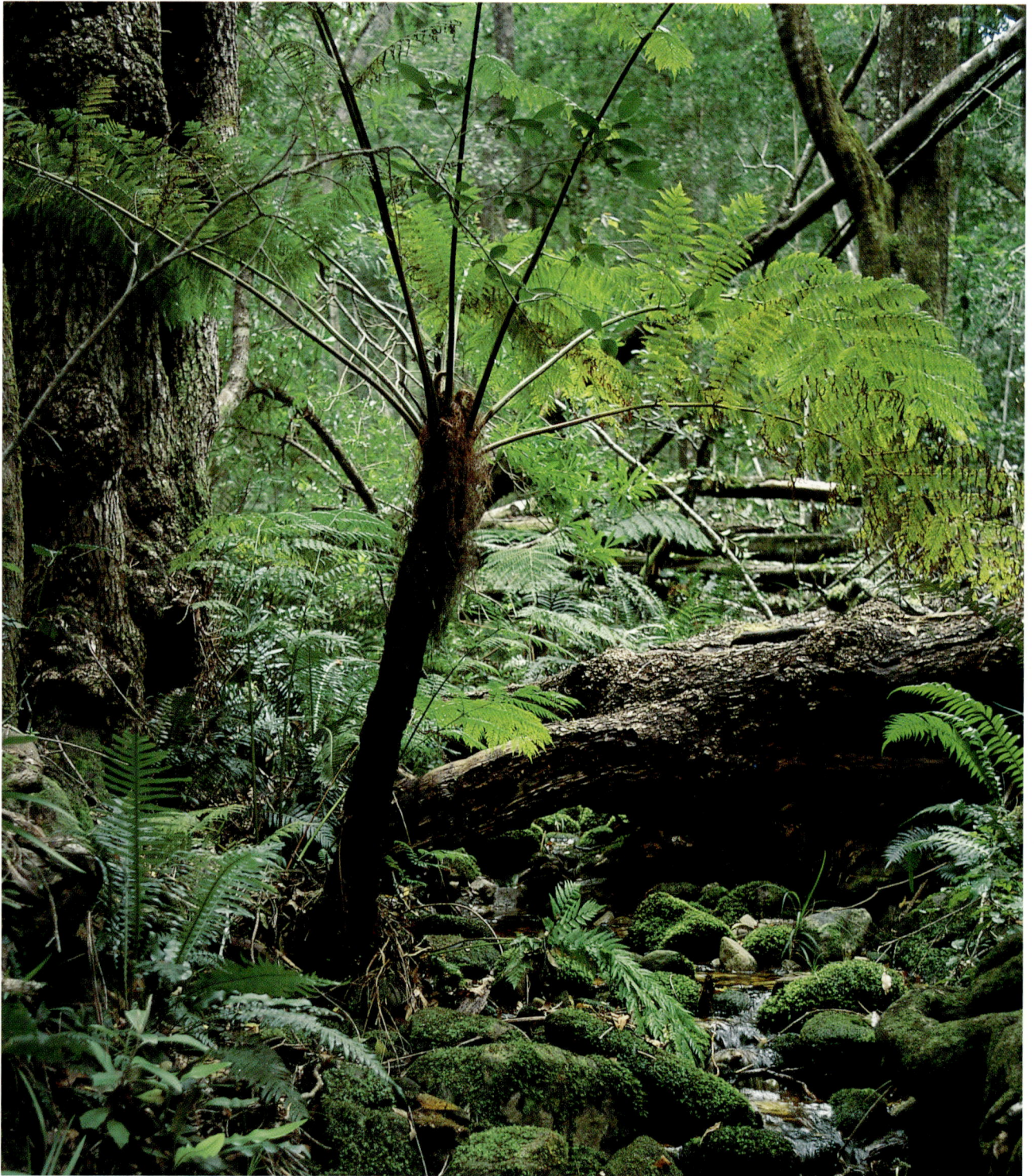

Useful Addresses and Telephone Numbers

Below are the street addresses and telephone numbers of bodies mentioned in the text:

1. Information and Publicity Bureaux

MOSSEL BAY:
Mossel Bay Municipality and Publicity Association
101 Marsh Street
Mossel Bay
Tel: (0444) 91-2215

GEORGE:
Publicity Office
George Municipality
York Street
George
Tel: (0441) 74-4000

OUDTSHOORN:
Oudtshoorn Municipal Publicity Office
Ground Floor, Seppie Greeff Building
Cnr Voortrekker and Baron van Reede streets
Oudtshoorn
Tel: (0443) 22-2221 (office hours);
(0443) 22-2228 (after hours)

KNYSNA:
Publicity Association of Knysna
40 Main Street
Knysna
Tel: (0445) 2-1610

PLETTENBERG BAY:
Plettenberg Bay Tourist and Publicity Bureau
Lookout Centre, Main Street
Plettenberg Bay
Tel: (04457) 3-4065/6

2. Museums

MOSSEL BAY:
Bartolomeu Dias Museum
Market Street
Mossel Bay
Tel: (0444) 91-1067

GEORGE:
George Museum
Old Drostdy, Courtenay Street
George
Tel: (0441) 5343

OUDTSHOORN:
C.P. Nel Museum
Baron van Reede Street
Oudtshoorn
Tel: (0443) 22-7306

KNYSNA:
Knysna Museum
17 Queen Street
Knysna
Tel: (0445) 2-2133 x 234

3. Cape Provincial Administration, Department of Nature and Environmental Conservation Offices

OUTENIQUAS:
Van Kerwelhuis, 117 York Street
George
Tel: (0441) 74-2671

OUTSHOORN:
First Floor
Seppie Greeff Building, Cnr Voortrekker and Baron van Reede streets
Oudtshoorn
Tel: (0443) 29-1739/29-1829

GAMKA MOUNTAIN NATURE RESERVE:
Tel: (04437) 3-3367

GOUKAMMA NATURE RESERVE:
Tel: (0445) 83-0042

PLETTENBERG BAY:
7 Zenon Street
Plettenberg Bay
Tel: (04457) 3-2125/3-2185

4. National Parks Board Camps

Wilderness National Park:
Tel: (0441) 9-1197

Tsitsikamma National Park
DeVasselot section: Tel: (04457) 6700
Storms River Mouth: Tel: (04237) 607

5. Department of Water Affairs and Forestry

Knysna Regional Office
(administers State Forests from Garcia near Riversdale in the west to Diepwalle, Buffelsnek and Harkerville in the east):
Demar Centre, Main Road
Knysna
Tel: (0445) 2-3037

Humansdorp Regional Office
(administers State Forests from Keurbooms River in the west to Longmoor near Port Elizabeth in the east):
D & A Building, Main Street
Humansdorp
Tel: (0423) 5-1180

Two-Day and Longer Hiking Trails

The Garden Route boasts a number of hiking trails which take two or more days to complete. Together they cover most of the region's scenic and natural highlights. Several - such as the Otter, Tsitsikamma and Outeniqua trails - are well established and so well-known and well-loved that bookings to walk them in peak holiday times have to be made a year or more in advance. Others, like the Swartberg Hiking Trail, are unaccountably less frequented. In the last year or two several new trails have been established; some of these are brand-new at the time of writing. The trails are summarized below in the geographical order of the day-walks described in the main text.

Attaquaskloof Hiking Trail

This is a new two-day trail which starts and ends on the Robinson Pass between Mossel Bay and Oudtshoorn. The trail runs through fynbos amid magnificent mountain scenery west of the Robinson Pass; one section follows the old Attaquaskloof Pass. From the overnight hut there is an optional circuit which takes a day to complete, and extends the trail to three days. The Koumashoek Circuit described in the main text provides a sample of this trail's delights.

Bookings and information: Outeniqua's office of Cape Provincial Administration, Department of Nature and Environmental Conservation in George.

Doring River Wilderness Trail

This is another new two-day trail. It leads through a recently proclaimed wilderness area in a valley on the northern side of the Outeniqua Mountains west of the Outeniqua Pass. The trail begins at Waboomskraal and ends at the top of the Robinson Pass. There is an overnight hut below Engelse Peak about halfway. The main attractions of the area are the fynbos, the Doring River and the mountains. This trail links up with the Attaquaskloof Hiking Trail.

Bookings and information: Outeniqua's office of Cape Provincial Administration, Department of Nature and Environmental Conservation in George.

Outeniqua Trail

The long-established Outeniqua Trail runs from Witfontein Forest Station north of George in the west to the Diepwalle Forest Station north of Knysna in the east and passes through the derelict goldmining village of Millwood. The full route takes eight days to walk, but shorter sections (a minimum of two days) can be selected. In the west, the trail is largely on the fynbos-covered slopes of the Outeniquas, where the mountain scenery is breathtaking; in the east, through plantations and natural forest.

Bookings and information: Department of Water Affairs and Forestry office in Knysna.

Swartberg Hiking Trail

On the Swartberg adjoining the Swartberg Pass between Oudtshoorn and Prince Albert there is a network of paths, with an overnight hut at three points, which make up the Swartberg Hiking Trail. The hiker can thus choose from several long or short routes through unspoilt fynbos in one of the most scenically splendid places in southern Africa.

Bookings and information: Cape Provincial Administration, Department of Nature and Environmental Conservation office in Oudtshoorn.

The vividly coloured cliffs of Mons Ruber, an unusual geological formation between Oudtshoorn and De Rust, are the setting for a proposed day-walk which will provide an experience of the Little Karoo. For details contact the Oudtshoorn office of the Cape Provincial Administration's Department of Nature and Environmental Conservation.

Harkerville Coast Hiking Trail

Since its recent establishment, this two-day trail through the natural forests and plantations and along the rugged, scenically spectacular coastline of the Harkerville State Forest between Plettenberg Bay and Knysna is rapidly becoming very popular.

Bookings and information: Department of Water Affairs and Forestry office in Knysna.

Tsitsikamma Hiking Trail

Like the Outeniqua and Swartberg trails, the Tsitsikamma Hiking Trail is a long-established favourite of serious hikers. Beginning near Nature's Valley, it traverses the southern slopes of the Tsitsikamma Mountains to the Storms River, for the most part through fynbos but also through patches of natural forest and plantation. The full four-day trail can be shortened to a minimum of two days by access routes to the three overnight huts en route.

Bookings and information: Department of Water Affairs and Forestry office in Humansdorp.

Otter Trail

The famous Otter Trail is a five-day route along the beautiful coastline of the Tsitsikamma National Park from the Storms River Mouth to the mouth of the Groot River near Nature's Valley. Early booking is absolutely essential and written applications are accepted a year in advance. Only some 5 to 10 per cent of applications to walk the route in holiday seasons are successful.

Bookings and information: National Parks Board offices in Pretoria or Cape Town.

Fourcade Trail

This new two-day walk around Witelskop in the Witelsbos State Forest area east of the Storms River runs mainly through fynbos in a little-known area. There are no overnight facilities on the trail, although there are several suitable sleeping-places with water nearby. The trail is intended to provide a wilderness experience.

Bookings and information: Department of Water Affairs and Forestry office in Humansdorp.

Tierkloof Trail

The management of the Gamka Mountain Nature Reserve west of Oudtshoorn plans to establish rudimentary overnight facilities at the overhang cave on the Tierkloof Trail, which will allow hikers to spend two days exploring this beautiful kloof.

Bookings and information: Cape Provincial Administration, Department of Nature and Environmental Conservation office at the Gamka Mountain Nature Reserve.

LEFT: *Hikers cross one of the many streams which run through the fynbos-covered mountain slopes on the Tsitsikamma Trail.*
RIGHT: *The cliffs surrounding the mouth of the Bloukrans River drop almost vertically into the sea to provide one of the most exciting crossings on the Otter Trail.*

FURTHER READING

Bell-Cross, Graham and Venter, Jansie: *The Passes of the Langeberg and Outeniqua Mountains*, Bartolomeu Dias Museum, Mossel Bay, 1991.

Branch, Margo and George: *The Living Shores of Southern Africa*, Struik, Cape Town, 1981.

Bulpin, T.V.: *Discovering Southern Africa*, T.V. Bulpin Publications, Muizenberg, 1986.

Department of Environment Affairs: `The Swartberg Hiking Trail' (map); (Forestry Branch) `The Outeniqua Hiking Trail' (map), Government Printer, Pretoria, 1988.

Department of Water Affairs and Forestry: `An Introduction to the Tsitsikamma Forests' (pamphlet), Humansdorp, 1991.

Directorate of Forestry: `The Otter Trail and Tsitsikamma Hiking Trail' (map), Government Printer, Pretoria, 1983.

Ginn, P.J., McIlleron, W.G. and Milstein, P. le S. (Comp): *The Complete Book of Southern African Birds*, Struik Winchester, Cape Town, 1989.

Levin, Hilda, Branch, Margo, Rappoport, Simon and Mitchell, Derek: *A Field Guide to the Mushrooms of South Africa*, Struik, Cape Town, 1985.

National Parks Board: `Wetlands' (paper available at the Lakes Conservation Station, Rondevlei).

National Parks Board: `Wilderness Lakes' (pamphlet).

Newman, Kenneth: *Birds of Southern Africa*, Southern Book Publishers, Johannesburg, 1991.

Nimmo, Arthur: *The Knysna Story*, Juta, Cape Town, 1976.

Tapson, Winifred: *Timber and Tides - the Story of Knysna and Plettenberg Bay*, Juta, Cape Town, 1961.

Von Breitenbach, F.: *Southern Cape Forests and Trees*, Government Printer, Pretoria, 1974.

Wallace, J.H., Kok, H.M., Beckley, L.E., Bennett, B., Blaber, S.J.M. and Whitfield, A.K.: `South African Estuaries and their Importance to Fishes' (paper available at the Lakes Conservation Station, Rondevlei).

OTHER LITERATURE CONSULTED

Bond, Pauline and Goldblatt, Peter: `Plants of the Cape Flora - a Descriptive Catalogue', *Journal of South African Botany*, Supplementary Volume 13, 1984.

Burman, Jose: *Trails and Walks in the Southern Cape*, Human & Rousseau, Cape Town, 1980.

Burrows, J.E.: *Southern African Ferns and Fern Allies*, Frandsen, 1990.

Deacon, H.J.: `An Introduction to the Fynbos Region: Time Scales and Palaeoenvironments' in *Fynbos Palaeoecology: A Preliminary Synthesis* (South African National Scientific Programmes Report No 75), CSIR, Pretoria, 1983.

Du Toit, Alex L.: *Geology of South Africa*, Oliver & Boyd, London, 1926.

Hendey, Q.B.: `Cenozoic Geology and Palaeogeography of the Fynbos Region' in *Fynbos Palaeoecology: A Preliminary Synthesis* (South African National Scientific Programmes Report No 75), CSIR, Pretoria, 1983.

Jacobsen, W.B.G.: *The Ferns and Fern Allies of Southern Africa*,

Butterworths, Durban, 1983.

Palgrave, Keith Coates: *Trees of Southern Africa*, Struik, Cape Town, 1977.

Rourke, John: `*Mimetes chrysanthus*', *Veld and Flora*, 74(4), 143-4, 1988.

Smith, C.A.: `Common Names of South African Plants' (Botanical Survey Memoir No 35), Department of Agricultural and Technical Services, Pretoria, 1966.

Storarr, C.D.: `The Phenomenal Dr Fourcade', South African Forestry Journal, No 146, 1988.

Theron, J.N.: `Geological Setting of the Fynbos' in *Fynbos Palaeoecology: A Preliminary Synthesis* (South African National Scientific Programmes Report No 75), CSIR, Pretoria, 1983.

Truswell, J.F.: *The Geological Evolution of South Africa*, Purnell, Cape Town, 1977.

Van der Merwe, C.V.: `Plantekologiese Aspekte en Bestuursprobleme van die Goukammanatuurreservaat', M.Sc. thesis, University of Pretoria, Pretoria, 1976.

INDEX